LET US BE LIKE
THE NATIONS

INTERNATIONAL THEOLOGICAL COMMENTARY

Fredrick Carlson Holmgren and George A. F. Knight
General Editors

Volumes now available

Forthcoming in 1993

LET US BE LIKE THE NATIONS

A Commentary on the Books of
1 and 2 Samuel

GNANA ROBINSON

WM. B. EERDMANS PUBLISHING CO., GRAND RAPIDS
THE HANDSEL PRESS LTD, EDINBURGH

Copyright © 1993 by Wm. B. Eerdmans Publishing Company
All rights reserved

First published 1993 by William B. Eerdmans Publishing Company,
255 Jefferson Ave. S.E., Grand Rapids, Michigan 49503
and
The Handsel Press Limited
58 Frederick St, Edinburgh EH2 1LS

Printed in the United States of America

Library of Congress Cataloging-in-Publication Data

Robinson, Gnana, 1935-
Let us be like the nations: a commentary on the books of 1 and 2 Samuel /
Gnana Robinson.
p.   cm.   — (International theological commentary)
ISBN 0-8028-0608-2 (pbk.)
1. Bible. O.T. Samuel — Commentaries.   I. Title.   II. Series.
BS1325.3.R634   1993
222'.407 — dc20   93-7094
                                                            CIP

Handsel Press ISBN 1 871828 28 7

To
my wife, Florence,
and my children,
Gnana Jeevan and Ratna Ruba

CONTENTS

ABBREVIATIONS

BH	*Biblia Hebraica*
IB	*Interpreter's Bible*
IDB	*Interpreter's Dictionary of the Bible*
KJV	King James Version
LXX	Septuagint
mg	margin
MT	Masoretic Text
RSV	Revised Standard Version
ZAW	*Zeitschrift für die alttestamentliche Wissenschaft*

EDITORS' PREFACE

The Old Testament alive in the Church: this is the goal of the *International Theological Commentary*. Arising out of changing, unsettled times, this Scripture speaks with an authentic voice to our own troubled world. It witnesses to God's ongoing purpose and to his caring presence in the universe without ignoring those experiences of life that cause one to question God's existence and love. This commentary series is written by front-rank scholars who treasure the life of faith.

Addressed to ministers and Christian educators, the *International Theological Commentary* moves beyond the usual critical-historical approach to the Bible and offers a *theological* interpretation of the Hebrew text. Thus, engaging larger textual units of the biblical writings, the authors of these volumes assist the reader in the appreciation of the theology underlying the text as well as its place in the thought of the Hebrew Scriptures. But more, since the Bible is the book of the believing community, its text has acquired ever more meaning through an ongoing interpretation. This growth of interpretation may be found both within the Bible itself and in the continuing scholarship of the Church.

Contributors to the *International Theological Commentary* are Christians — persons who affirm the witness of the New Testament concerning Jesus Christ. For Christians, the Bible is *one* scripture containing the Old and New Testaments. For this reason, a commentary on the Old Testament may not ignore the second part of the canon, namely, the New Testament.

Since its beginning, the Church has recognized a special relationship between the two Testaments. But the precise character of this bond has been difficult to define. Thousands of books and articles have discussed the issue. The diversity of views represented in these publications makes us aware that the Church is not of one mind in expressing the "how" of this relationship. The authors of this commentary share a developing consensus that any serious explanation of the Old Testament's relationship to the New will uphold the integrity of the Old Testament. Even though Christianity is rooted in the soil of the Hebrew Scriptures, the biblical interpreter must take care lest he or she "christianize" these Scriptures.

Authors writing in this commentary will, no doubt, hold varied views concerning *how* the Old Testament relates to the New. No attempt has been made to dictate one viewpoint in this matter. With the whole Church, we are convinced that the relationship between the two Testaments is real and substantial. But we recognize also the diversity of opinions among Christian scholars when they attempt to articulate fully the nature of this relationship.

In addition to the Christian Church, there exists another people for whom the Old Testament is important, namely, the Jewish community. Both Jews and Christians claim the Hebrew Bible as Scripture. Jews believe that the basic teachings of this Scripture point toward, and are developed by, the Talmud, which assumed its present form about 500 C.E. On the other hand, Christians hold that the Old Testament finds its fulfilment in the New Testament. The Hebrew Bible, therefore, belongs to both the Church and the Synagogue.

Recent studies have demonstrated how profoundly early Christianity reflects a Jewish character. This fact is not surprising because the Christian movement arose out of the context of first-century Judaism. Further, Jesus himself was Jewish, as were the first Christians. It is to be expected, therefore, that Jewish and Christian interpretations of the Hebrew Bible will reveal similarities *and* disparities. Such is the case. The authors of the *International Theological Commentary* will refer to the various Jewish traditions that they consider important for an appreciation of the Old Testament text. Such references will enrich our understanding of certain biblical passages and, as an extra gift, offer us insight into the relationship of Judaism to early Christianity.

An important second aspect of the present series is its *inter-*

national character. In the past, Western church leaders were considered to be *the* leaders of the Church — at least by those living in the West! The theology and biblical exegesis done by these scholars dominated the thinking of the Church. Most commentaries were produced in the Western world and reflected the lifestyle, needs, and thoughts of its civilization. But the Christian Church is a worldwide community. People who belong to this universal Church reflect differing thoughts, needs, and lifestyles.

Today the fastest growing churches in the world are to be found, not in the West, but in Africa, Indonesia, South America, Korea, Taiwan, and elsewhere. By the end of this century, Christians in these areas will outnumber those who live in the West. In our age, especially, a commentary on the Bible must transcend the parochialism of Western civilization and be sensitive to issues that are the special problems of persons who live outside of the "Christian" West, issues such as race relations, personal survival and fulfilment, liberation, revolution, famine, tyranny, disease, war, the poor, and religion and state. Inspired of God, the authors of the Old Testament knew what life is like on the edge of existence. They addressed themselves to everyday people who often faced more than everyday problems. Refusing to limit God to the "spiritual," they portrayed God as one who heard and knew the cries of people in pain (see Exod. 3:7-8). The contributors to the *International Theological Commentary* are persons who prize the writings of these biblical authors as a word of life to our world today. They read the Hebrew Scriptures in the twin contexts of ancient Israel and our modern day.

The scholars selected as contributors underscore the international aspect of the series. Representing very different geographical, ideological, and ecclesiastical backgrounds, they come from over seventeen countries. Besides scholars from such traditional countries as England, Scotland, France, Italy, Switzerland, Canada, New Zealand, Australia, South Africa, and the United States, contributors from the following places are included: Israel, Indonesia, India, Thailand, Singapore, Taiwan, and countries of Eastern Europe. Such diversity makes for richness of thought. Christian scholars living in Buddhist, Muslim, or Socialist lands may be able to offer the World Church insights into the biblical message — insights to which the scholarship of the West could be blind.

The proclamation of the biblical message is the focal concern of the *International Theological Commentary*. Generally speaking, the authors of these commentaries value the historical-critical studies of past scholars, but they are convinced that these studies by themselves are not enough. The Bible is more than an object of critical study; it is the revelation of God. In the written Word, God has disclosed himself and his will to humankind. Our authors see themselves as servants of the Word which, when rightly received, brings *shalom* to both the individual and the community.

— George A. F. Knight
— Fredrick Carlson Holmgren

AUTHOR'S PREFACE

Undertaking a serious writing assignment is not an easy task for any person engaged in administrative work in India. The invitation to write this commentary on the books of Samuel came to me as early as 1979, shortly after I took over the principalship of the Tamil Nadu Theological Seminary, Madurai. Though I could do most of the reading during my sabbatical leave in 1982-1983, the final writing of the commentary had to wait until I laid down my principalship and came to Germany. I was invited to teach at the Predigerseminar in Soest, Westfalen, in September 1987, so I had to continue my work on Samuel along with my teaching (in German) at the Predigerseminar; hence, it had to be delayed still further. If, at last, I have been able to complete this work, the credit goes of course to Prof. Dr. George A. F. Knight, whose patience and ongoing encouragement gave me the confidence I needed to continue the work. I owe him a debt of gratitude.

Several friends have helped me in the process of my work. Friends at the Missionsakademie in Hamburg; friends in St. Andrews Theological College, Trinidad; friends of the church in Kurhessen-Waldeck, Germany, with whom I spent one month in 1982; and my colleagues at the Predigerseminar, Soest, have provided me with the facilities I needed for my work and gave me all the encouragement I needed. I thank them all. My former secretary, Mrs. Tanya Figredo, helped me by typing the major part of my final draft of the manuscript, and I thank her for that. Above all, my wife Florence and children, Jeevan and Ratna, have not only been patient with me for giving little time to them, but also have been a source of inspiration for my work in all respects. I dedicate this work to them.

LET US BE LIKE THE NATIONS

This commentary has been written from an Indian perspective, from a Third World context. Certain comments made and questions raised in this work may be read and understood from that perspective.

— GNANA ROBINSON

INTRODUCTION

1. AUTHORSHIP AND COMPOSITION

Critical scholarship has shown us that originally the two books of Samuel and the two books of Kings were a single work and that the fourfold division of the work is a later development.

That Samuel could not have been the author of the books is quite evident from the fact that his death is mentioned in the books in two places (1 Sam. 25:1; 28:3). On the other hand, the fact that Samuel is the leading character in 1 Samuel and that 2 Samuel deals with the fulfilment of his prophetic words to David could have been the reasons why Samuel's name is associated with these books.

It is also obvious that these books do not come from a single hand nor from a particular period. The many repetitions and contradictions found in them indicate that a number of hands have been involved in their composition. These writers could have drawn from sagas and legends on Samuel, Saul, and David along with etiological stories, all of which were already in circulation in oral tradition, and also from certain available written sources such as the Book of Jashar (2 Sam. 1:18). Some special accounts seem to come from particular circles, such as the ark tradition (1 Sam. 4:1b–7:2; 2 Sam. 6), David's accession narrative (1 Sam. 16:14– 2 Sam. 5:12), and David's succession narrative (2 Sam. 9–20).

That editorial hands were at work on the books at different stages becomes evident from references such as "to this day" (1 Sam. 27:6; 30:25; 2 Sam. 18:18) and the editorial comments found in 1 Sam. 9:9 and 2 Sam. 13:18. Since 2 Kings ends with the exile, the final editor could have lived sometime during the exile, that is, during the 6th cent. B.C.

1

Since the history covered in the books of Judges-Kings presents theologically a "Deuteronomic" perspective (namely, that obedience to the laws brings blessings and disobedience brings judgment), it is generally accepted that the whole historical accounts from Judges to Kings come from the hands of Deuteronomic historians. This, however, does not mean that the Deuteronomic historians wrote all the history; they would certainly have used material already available and edited these documents. The Deuteronomic historians who wanted to continue the history of Israel from the period of settlement in the land could well have been responsible for the first draft. This was later edited and re-edited by scholars coming from the Deuteronomistic school, who then placed the whole account within the framework of their own view of history.

The First Commandment of the Decalogue, the prohibition of idols and other images, is central to the Deuteronomistic theology. Thus, all the historical happenings are critically assessed over against this theological basis. According to these theologians, prophets are messengers of the word of God and rejection of the words of the prophets amounts to the rejection of Yahweh (1 Sam. 8:7).

The concluding section of the books of Samuel (2 Sam. 21:1–24:25) is an appendix. It contains different types of material: anecdotes (21:15-22; 23:8-23), a genealogy (23:24-39), two sagas (21:1-14; 24), and two poetic compositions (22; 23:1-7). 2 Sam. 22:2-51 is identical with Ps. 18:2-50.

2. THE CONTEXT

Socioeconomic and Political Context

The importance of the books of Samuel lies in their recording Israel's history during one of its most crucial periods, when the nation was undergoing radical socioeconomic and political changes. Once arrived in Canaan, Israel had been moving from a primarily nomadic, sheep-rearing society into a settled, agrarian society. People were now engaged in settled agricultural activities (cf. 1 Sam. 6:13; 11:5; 12:17; 13:21; 23:1). The consequent private holding of lands with fixed territories and water resources (cisterns, 13:6) and the employment of a market economy (e.g., coins: pims and shekels, 9:8; 13:21; grain measures: e.g., the ephah, 17:17) all contributed to the development of a class society. Thus, Kish the Benjaminite "was a man of wealth" with many servants/slaves (9:1ff.). Nabal of Maon, too, was a rich man, a member of the business community, "whose business was in Carmel" (25:2), and several servants/slaves worked for him.

As private property developed and wealth increased, protection of the same became important (cf. 1 Sam. 25:16). The indigenous inhabitants of the region, with a long history of settled life and infrastructures for both defense and offense, found their neighbors, the Israelites, easily vulnerable. Thus, the Israelites were often raided by their neighbors (cf. 11:1ff.). The book of Judges narrates some of these stories. In the beginning, individual heroes (Judges) rose up to meet the occasion, took up the challenge from these enemies, mobilized the people, and raised an ad hoc army and so defended the people from enemy raids. Since they were not trained in warfare and since they had to depend on the Philistines for their weapons (13:19-22), the Israelites' defense was not adequate. As the threat from enemies became a constant one, the need for a permanent defense force and for an administrative structure was very much felt. Learning from their neighbors, Israel thereupon opted for a monarchic system of government, even though prophetic voice pointed out its pitfalls.

Until taxes were introduced, the royal expenses appear to have been met by gifts brought by ordinary people (1 Sam. 10:27; 16:20) and by the spoils of wars and raids (14:32-33; 15:9).

With the institution of the monarchy, the king became the supreme judge and his word was final (2 Sam. 14:10ff.). His court was constituted after the pattern of the court of oriental kings, with a commander of the army (2:8; 8:16; 20:23), a recorder or scribe (8:16; 20:24), a secretary (8:17; 20:25), ministers (e.g., labor ministers, 20:24), spies (10:3), and priests (8:17; 20:25). As the royal insignia, the king wore a crown and an armlet (1:10).

Israel became a patriarchal society (1 Sam. 3:13; 4:20). Women were now placed in a subordinate position (1 Sam. 25:41; 2 Sam.

3:8ff.). Polygamy was practiced. Slavery was prevalent (1 Sam. 4:9; 17:9).

Social evils such as seeking illegal gains, taking bribes, and perverting justice were common, but came under prophetic condemnation. Justice was understood rather as community loyalty, that is, faithfully adhering to the norms of social relationships laid down by consensus in the community (1 Sam. 24:17; 26:23).

Religious Context

As the Israelites settled down in Palestine, a process of positive syncretism began which continued during the early period of monarchy. The Israelites adapted the Canaanite sacrificial system and festivals and interpreted them in the context of their faith in Yahweh. Old Canaanite shrines were used for Yahweh worship. In this process they certainly met with problems. There were beliefs and practices attached to these shrines which could not be brought into harmony with Yahweh faith. Accordingly these were condemned. The worship of foreign deities such as Dagon (1 Sam. 5:2ff.), Ashtaroth (7:3, 4; 12:10; 31:10), and Baal (7:4; 12:10; 2 Sam. 5:20) was strictly prohibited. Since Baal and Ashtaroth were deities of a fertility cult, the Israelites, who were newly introduced to agriculture, were greatly tempted to worship them.

In the books of Samuel we can still identify some residues of old Canaanite elements which had slipped into the Israelite world of belief without being noticed. Thus, we see that in Samuel certain stones (1 Sam. 6:14, 18; 20:19; 2 Sam. 20:8), trees (1 Sam. 10:3; 14:2; 22:6; 31:13), and high places (1 Sam. 9:12ff.; 10:5; 22:6; 2 Sam. 1:19, 25) receive religious significance. These are, perhaps, elements from the animistic practices of the Canaanites. Some other practices, such as temple prostitution (1 Sam. 2:22ff.) and consulting mediums and wizards (28:3), were openly condemned and banned.

Priesthood, as an institution, was at its initial stage of formation. Sacrificial functions slowly become the exclusive prerogative of the priests. Professional priests like Samuel seem to have traveled around periodically from place to place to offer sacrifices at high places and altars (1 Sam. 9:12; 16:2). Saul, perhaps following the practice found in the nomadic tradition where the heads of families were allowed to offer sacrifice (e.g., Abraham), dared to do so but was promptly condemned by Samuel (13:8-14). We hear of priests resident at some local sanctuaries: Hophni and Phinehas at Shiloh (1:3) and Ahimelech at Nob (21:1ff.). But that the Deuteronomic writers are already anticipating the centralization of worship and the Zadokite priesthood in Jerusalem is evident from 2:35.

Beliefs and Practices

Faith in Yahweh is at the center. However, the Israelites at this stage have not yet reached a truly monotheistic faith; what is prevalent here may be described as monolatry (cf. 1 Sam. 7:3-4). Yahweh is still seen as the God of the Israelites, actually even as a mountain God, whose supremacy on the plains has yet to be proved. The existence of other gods, such as Dagon, Ashtaroth, and Baal, is not denied; they are denounced, however, as inferior to Yahweh (cf. 5:3). Like the other gods, Yahweh, too, has his territorial sovereignty; anyone who moved outside Yahweh's own territory was forced to worship other gods (cf. 26:19; 2 Kgs. 5:17).

In response to God, people make pilgrimages to holy places (1 Sam. 1:3, 21; 2:19), offer sacrifices (1:25; 2:12ff.), make vows and oaths (1:11; 14:24ff.), and offer prayers (7:5, 8-9; 8:6; 12:18-19). Ceasing to pray for the people is a sin on the part of the priest (12:23). Both the priest and the people have to consecrate themselves before offering a sacrifice (16:5).

Circumcision was seen as one of the distinctive marks of Israel's special bond with Yahweh, as against the uncircumcised foreigners like the Philistines (1 Sam. 17:26, 36; 2 Sam. 1:20).

Ritual mourning and weeping was a common practice — mourning at personal tragedies (2 Sam. 13:19), at the death of personal friends, relatives, and national heroes (1:11ff.; 3:31ff.), and over national calamities (1 Sam. 7:2). As a sign of deep grief clothes were rent (2 Sam. 1:11; 3:31ff.; 13:19, 31). The head was not anointed with oil (2 Sam. 14:2), but ashes or dust was put on the head (1 Sam. 4:12; 2 Sam. 13:19). Fasting (2 Sam.

5

1:12) and lying on the ground (12:16; 13:31) were also used. Messengers of sad news arrived in mourning clothes (1 Sam. 4:12; 2 Sam. 14:2).

Divination was practiced. A lot system, know as Urim and Thummim, was used (1 Sam. 14:41; 28:6). What these looked like and how they were used are not known to us. Perhaps, a "head or tails" method was used, in which *urim* meant one thing and *thummim* meant the opposite, as agreed beforehand. It is noted that sometimes no answer was given. In that case, perhaps, nothing fell out of the casting bag or box, or else the dice carried some special sign to indicate "no answer."

Two other objects are mentioned in this connection, the *ephod* and the *ark of God*. What exactly the ephod was like is not clear. In some places it is mentioned as the robe of a priest (1 Sam. 2:28; 14:3; 22:18; 2 Sam. 6:14). Evidently it did not cover much of the body (2 Sam. 6:14, 20). Perhaps it was a kind of loincloth such as the one the Egyptians wore (R. de Vaux, *Ancient Israel*). Probably, again, the dice Urim and Thummim were kept in a pocket or bag attached to this priestly ephod (cf. Prov. 16:33). In some places the ark of God is said to have been used for divination purposes. It was a kind of box having the shape of a coffin today. Saul commanded Ahijah the priest to bring the ark of God, telling him to withdraw his hands from it (1 Sam. 14:18-19). Perhaps the Urim and Thummim were kept inside the ark. Some scholars think that the references to "ephod" above are actually references to the "ark" of God.

Feasts and festivals were also celebrated. New moon was a family festival of great importance (1 Sam. 20:5ff.). Sheep shearing was a day of great feasting (25:8). There is no evidence that the three great annual festivals of the Israelite calendar were strictly celebrated at this time.

The law of *herem*, utter destruction, was practiced (1 Sam. 15:3, 9; 2 Sam. 8:7).

Number symbolism appears to have been popular. "Three" and "seven" seem to have had special significance, as in all oriental religions even today. Both perhaps symbolized fullness or wholesomeness — three men, three kids, three loaves (1 Sam. 10:3), three days (20:5), three arrows (20:20), bowing three times

(20:41), starving for three days (30:12), famine for three years (2 Sam. 21:1); the ark was in the Philistine cities for seven months (1 Sam. 6:1), seventy men were killed in Beth-shemesh (6:19), Saul waits for Samuel for seven days (10:8; 13:8), Jesse's seven sons pass before Samuel (16:10), Saul's seven sons are executed (2 Sam. 21:6), the people of Jabesh-gilead fast for Saul's death for seven days (1 Sam. 31:13).

3. THE MESSAGE

Following the account of "inheriting the land" in the book of Joshua (see E. John Hamlin, *Inheriting the Land: A Commentary on the Book of Joshua.* International Theological Commentary [Grand Rapids: Wm. B. Eerdmans and Edinburgh: Handsel, 1983]), the books of Samuel record Israel's cry for what we today would regard as "conformity to the nations," along with the consequent emergence of a nation under David that was like any other nation in the Middle East. The Deuteronomic writer sees this development as a mistake, even as an act of apostasy. As long as Israel possessed no earthly king, Yahweh ruled the Israelites and Samuel, his prophet, served as the mediator between Yahweh and Israel. Israel's demand for a king is therefore a sin, because it amounts to breaking the First Commandment of the Decalogue. Among Israel's neighbors — e.g., Egypt, Babylon, Canaan — the king was regarded as either a god or a semi-god; consequently he was worshipped by his people. As such, the demand to have a king such as other nations had is seen here as an act of apostasy, as a rejection of Yahweh as king (1 Sam. 8:5-7, 19-20; 10:19; 12:19). That this feeling was widespread in the prophetic tradition is confirmed by Hosea and Ezekiel. According to Hosea, Yahweh gave Israel a king in his anger (Hos. 13:11). Ezekiel sees what followed after inheriting the land as blasphemy and treachery against God (Ezek. 20:27ff.). According to Ezekiel, Yahweh will never again yield to the demand "Let us be like the nations" (Ezek. 20:32); rather, Yahweh himself will be king over Israel (v. 33).

The concept of "nation" is the embodiment of power. The desire to "be like all nations" (i.e., the desire to conform to the ways of those who possess power) is a common tendency found among all peoples. This tendency has never been so strong as it is today, especially among the people of the economically under-developed or developing nations of the world. The superpowers, with their power mechanisms that are supported by advanced technology, industry, dominance in world trade and in the pos-session of destructive weapons, become the models for many developing countries. They want to "catch up" with these powerful nations; they want to conform to the pattern of life of these nations, just as the people of Israel during Samuel's time wanted to do (1 Sam. 8:20). In this sense, then, this account of Israel's kingship is a paradigm for our sinful human desire to conform to world powers at all times.

This was also part of the temptation of Jesus. He was offered all the kingdoms of this world, but rejected the offer outright (Matt. 4:8-10). He also asked his disciples not to conform to the powers of this world. He said to them, "You know that those who are supposed to rule over the Gentiles lord it over them, and their great men exercise authority over them. But it shall not be so among you . . ." (Mark 10:42-43). The powers of this world are oppressive in character; they are exercised to "lord" it over their fellow human beings, to oppress them, to exploit them, and to destory them. This, too, was the danger that Samuel foresaw in the kingship which Israel demanded (1 Sam. 8:11-17).

The Deuteronomic history goes on to say that Yahweh yields to the pressure of the people and gives them a king. Thus, the kingship is seen only as a necessary evil in Israel. Now everything depends upon how Israel gets along in the grips of this new power structure, the kingship. Even with this, if the Israelite king will only listen to Yahweh and exercise his power according to Yahweh's will (1 Sam. 12), there is hope for Israel. For " . . to obey is better than sacrifice" (15:22).

Power structures are necessary evils in society; but how these structures function in society is determinative as to whether they are acceptable to God or not, whether they play a liberative role or an oppressive role in society. When and if these powers are used in the service of God (i.e., in the service of fellow human beings), they can become liberative. But when they are used to boost and secure personal gains, they work against the will of God and become oppressive. God wants to see established liberative power structures, structures which will not domesticate and enslave our fellow humans.

1 SAMUEL

I. THE BIRTH AND CALL
OF A PROPHET
1 Samuel 1:1–4:1a

GOD HEARS THE CRY OF A DISTRESSED WOMAN
(1:1-28)

Hannah stands here as a doubly discriminated against, distressed woman, a typical representative of oppressed women at all times. First, she is discriminated against by a male chauvinistic Israelite society. It treated a woman simply as part of a man's possessions, to be classed along with his other material possessions (cf. Exod. 20:17) and not as his equal, as originally intended by God (Gen. 1:27). Polygamy was the consequence of this discriminative treatment of women, and Hannah was one of its victims. She was one of the two wives of Elkanah, and she suffered under this condition. Second, the fact that she had not produced any children, especially male children, became another social stigma upon her. She was discriminated against still further on account of this biological fact of life, though no fault of her own. Elkanah treated her with partiality and discriminated against her when it came to sharing the portions from the sacrifices, over against Peninnah and her children. Hannah suffered utter humiliation under this double discrimination and was troubled sorely.

It is the greatness of biblical revelation that we meet here with a God who responds to the cries of those who suffer discrimination and humiliation. This assurance has been the hope of all suffering people at all times.

The Cry of Hannah (1:1-20)

The location of Ramathaim-zophim, the native place of Elkanah,

13

is not certain. That it is another name for Ramah, the birthplace of Samuel, is clear from other references (1 Sam. 1:19; 2:11; 7:17; 8:4; 15:34; 19:18ff.; 25:1). Ramathaim is a dual form found only here, and it may mean "double hill." Four localities have been identified with the Ramah of Elkanah and Samuel — Beit-rima, 21 km. (13 mi.) NE of Lydda or 19 km. (12 mi.) NW of Bethel; Ram Allah, 14 km. (9 mi.) N of Jerusalem on the western slopes of Mt. Ephraim; er-Ram, 8 km. (5 mi.) N of Jerusalem; and Nebi Samwil, about 8 km. (5 mi.) NW of Jerusalem. The first of these is closer to the Philistine territory, and the last two are in Benjamin. Judg. 4:5 speaks of Ramah of Ephraim, and 19:13 mentions Ramah of Benjamin. The Benjaminite Ramah is what is today known as er-Ram. According to some scholars, this is Samuel's home, wrongly ascribed in Judg. 4:5 to the hill country of Ephraim (H. W. Hertzberg, *I and II Samuel*). Zophim distinguishes Elkanah's Ramah from other towns of the same name. Zuph is mentioned in 1 Sam. 9:5 as the district in which Saul finds Samuel's home, and it is possible that both Zuph and Zophim are connected with Elkanah's ancestor Zophai (1 Chr. 6:26). Elkanah is presented here as an Ephraimite from the hill country of Ephraim. In 1 Chr. 6:16ff. Samuel is listed as a member of the Levite line, which perhaps is not historically correct.

The name "Hannah" means "grace," and "Peninnah" means "woman with rich hair." The name Peninnah occurs only here (1 Sam. 1:2, 4). Barrenness for women in Eastern countries is seen as a great misfortune even today.

Elkanah and his family made annual pilgrimage to the temple at Shiloh (1:3), the modern Seilun, about 16 km. (10 mi.) N of Bethel. Joshua had set up the tabernacle there long before (Josh. 18:1), so that the ark of God was to be found there (1 Sam. 3:3). One can still notice at this ancient site a 122 by 21 m. (400 by 70 ft.) platform roughly hewn out of the rocky hillside, which was most likely the site of the sanctuary of Elkanah's time. The festival here in question is probably the autumn festival at the end of the year. The three annual festivals seem not yet to have become obligatory (cf. Exod. 34:23). "LORD of hosts" (1 Sam. 1:3) is a shortened form of "Yahweh, the God of hosts" (Hos. 12:5; Amos

5:27). In some places "hosts" means the "armies of Israel" (1 Sam. 17:45; cf. Exod. 7:4; 12:17). In other places heavenly armies are meant, as indicated in 2 Kgs. 6:17 (1 Sam. 4:4; 15:2; 2 Sam. 5:10; 6:2). In ancient mythological thinking, God was considered to have heavenly armies. That is how this expression is employed in the idea of "the holy war," where it is Yahweh who fights the war (Num. 21:14) and the army of Israel plays practically no significant part.

Hophni and Phinehas, sons of Eli, were the officiating priests in Shiloh. Eli was perhaps already retired from active service, but as the head of the priestly family he was still available in the temple to pronounce oracles to the devotees who came to worship.

It is interesting to note how structural or systemic oppression works in society (1 Sam. 1:5). Because of the social stigma of barrenness, Elkanah was not able to give full expression of his love to his wife — "although he loved Hannah." The same principle is at work even today in societies ridden with color, caste, sex, and class discrimination. Very few have the courage to break through systemic oppressions and to act freely in obedience to God's will. In India, for example, we often hear of dowry deaths, where many young married women are forced to burn themselves to death. In this case, young husbands, in spite of their love for their beautiful young wives, succumb to pressure from the parents and relatives and join in inflicting torture on their wives so as to extract more money from their parents.

Peninnah took pleasure in inflicting more pain on Hannah (v. 6), a tendency which we find in all ego-centered persons who do not want to share their joy and happiness with others. In the absence of any human support — not even from her husband, who was supposed to be her own flesh (Gen. 2:24) — Hannah felt abandoned and so was bitterly distressed (1 Sam. 1:7). Elkanah tried to console his wife, but with only empty words, in an attempt to justify his unjust discrimination. Again, such is typical of male exploitation (v. 8). He told her that he was of more value to her than ten sons. Women in oriental societies are still brainwashed by such slogans. In Tamil Nadu in South India, for example, there is a popular saying among women: if a man is married to a woman, then he is her husband, even if he proves himself to be a stone or a vegetable. With this kind of mental framework, women in India may have to bear all kinds of humiliations, including even physical torture from their husbands.

Elkanah's empty words of consolation did not help Hannah in any way. Words without corresponding actions have no value. Hannah seeks her refuge in the LORD (vv. 9-11; cf. Ps. 46:1). She pours out her heart before God. Eli sits "on the seat beside the doorpost of the temple of the LORD" (1 Sam. 1:9; cf. 4:13). Perhaps this was his special place from where he received oracles from God and pronounced them to the people. The eastern door of the temple as well as the post or pillar (2 Kgs. 11:14; 23:3) seems to have had special significance. It was the door through which Yahweh entered and took his seat (cf. Ezek. 43:7-9; 44:1; 46:2ff.). Eli, as the priest of God, sat by it and spoke on behalf of God.

Prayer is the means we have of opening ourselves to God. Hannah, through prayer, gives vent to her intense distress and pain (1 Sam. 1:11). In her prayer, she vows that if God would but grant her a son she would "give him to the LORD." Faith in most religions is seen as a reciprocal relationship where the worshipper promises to do something or other or give God something, and God in return grants the prayer of the worshipper. We seldom find devotion to God which does not expect personal gains. This kind of vow-making is very common both among Christians and non-Christians in the East.

It is worth noting that Hannah, instead of praying for a child, prays particularly for a son. Even her prayer is conditioned by the society in which she lived. Here again she is the typical representative of many Asian women today, who much prefer to bear male children. In a clinic in Bombay, 8,000 abortions were performed in one year, out of which 7,999 were identified to be female fetuses. We are also reminded here of the shocking stories of the killing of female children in China, where, because of the government's "one child policy," parents kill their female babies to allow them to continue trying for a male child! Discrimination against women seems still to be deeply rooted in the psyche of many human communities.

The writer of 1 Samuel does not raise the question whether

Hannah can make such a vow without the consent of her husband. Again, he would never have thought of Elkanah as stemming from Levi's line, for in that case the vow would have been superfluous. He also seems to be unaware of the law regarding the firstborn, according to which every male that opens the womb already belongs to Yahweh (Exod. 13:2; 22:29). "No razor shall come upon his head" is a Nazirite vow (Num. 6:5; Judg. 13:4-5; Amos 2:11).

The intensity of Hannah's emotional distress is indicated by the fact that her thoughts were internalized and her mind was fixed on God, so that her lips moved without sound (1 Sam. 1:12-14). Eli mistook this for drunkenness and admonished her to abstain from wine. That excess in wine was a common condition in religious feasts is indicated by the readiness with which Eli's suspicion was raised. Hannah denied the charge and explained that she was only speaking to God out of her "anxiety and vexation" (vv. 15-16). "Base woman" (literally, "daughter of Belial") means "worthless woman."

Eli pronounced the oracle, without knowing what exactly Hannah's prayer was (v. 17). Whatever prayer she made would be granted. This "peace" oracle from the priest was the assurance Hannah needed that God would grant her prayer; and so this faith relieved her from her anxiety and made her happy (v. 18). We are here reminded of the words of 1 Pet. 5:7, "Cast all your anxieties on him, for he cares about you." 1 Samuel 1:19-20 speaks of the fulfilment of the priest's peace oracle. Hannah conceives and bears a son and calls his name Samuel, saying "I have asked him of the LORD." However, this explanation seems to suit the name Saul better than Samuel (cf. 9:2).

Hannah Fulfils Her Vow (1:21-28)

Elkanah and family went once more to offer the LORD "the yearly sacrifice, and to pay his vow" (1:21). To which place is not mentioned here, probably to Shiloh. Nor is it mentioned what Elkanah's vow was. Hannah, in view of her vow to bring Samuel to the temple after weaning him, excused herself from joining the pilgrimage on this occasion. (Children in the Orient are fed by their mother's milk up to the age of two or three years. Weaning was celebrated in ancient times as an important feast; cf. Gen. 21:8.) Hannah, after weaning Samuel, took him to Shiloh with the things necessary for sacrifice (1 Sam. 1:24). The "three-year-old bull" (Hebrew "three bulls") probably corresponds to the age of Samuel. It is not said whether Elkanah also went with her, but the plural "they" in vv. 25 and 28 (in the latter the Hebrew reads "he") and in 2:11, where Elkanah alone is mentioned, indicates that he did accompany Hannah. However, the focus here is not on Elkanah, but on Hannah.

Hannah's dedication of Samuel to the service of God has inspired many mothers all over the world to dedicate one of their children to the service of God. This trend is becoming weaker today, because of the new generation of children who insist on exercising their own freedom in deciding their future.

GOD OF THE POOR AND THE NEEDY (2:1-10)

This is a thanksgiving psalm which comes from a later period, but here it is ascribed to Hannah. It has no reference to Hannah's special situation. The reference to "the barren" in 2:5 is only an example of God's sovereign dealings. Perhaps this reference made the author feel that this psalm was appropriate for this occasion. The reference to the king in v. 10 points to its late origin. The content of the psalm is similar to the content of the Magnificat in Luke 1:46-55. Both speak about the uplift of "the feeble" (1 Sam. 2:4), "the hungry" (v. 5), "the poor" and "the needy" (v. 8), and the bringing down of the proud and the arrogant (v. 3), the mighty and the affluent (vv. 4-5), as well as the wicked (v. 9).

"Rock" in v. 2 is a figure applied to God's eternity and reliability (cf. Deut. 32:4; 2 Sam. 22:3). In 1 Sam. 2:6, death and the grave (Sheol) are used figuratively for indicating the depth of misfortune and peril humankind can experience (cf. Ps. 86:13), and resurrection ("brings to life") is the word used for God's deliverance from such perils. It has no reference to resurrection in the NT sense. Sheol is believed to be that place in the depths of the earth to which the dead descend and remain forever. Those who are sick or otherwise suffer are believed to be slowly descending to Sheol already. So when they recover from their suffering, it is said that God has delivered them out of Sheol.

1 Samuel 2:8a is almost identical with Ps. 113:7-8. 1 Samuel 2:8b recalls the ancient cosmogony, according to which the world was conceived as being flat and resting on primordial pillars (Job 9:6; 38:4ff.). Yahweh is conceived of as a God of nature, as a God of thunder and lightning (1 Sam. 2:10; 7:10).

At the end of the Psalm is an intercessory prayer for the king, the anointed one. The king in Israel was regarded as the servant of Yahweh who was to defend the rights of the poor and needy. Such intercessory prayers are also found in other Psalms (e.g., Ps. 61:6-7; 63:11).

ELI AND HIS HOUSE (2:12-36)

The Evil of Institutional Religion (2:12-17)

The author explains in detail how the religion of Israel was distorted by the hierarchy, the priesthood, in the absence of judges or kings. The priesthood, which had only a mediatory role, had become an end in itself. The priests, with "no regard for the LORD" (1 Sam. 2:12), had made religion a means to further their own interests, to meet their own avaricious ends (cf. v. 29).

The sons of Eli are described here as worthless men, "sons of Belial" (cf. 1:16). What they did as a regular practice is indicated by the reference to "the custom of the priests" (2:13). That the priest occupied a socially higher status is evident from the fact that he had at his disposal "servants." According to Lev. 7:34, the priest's rightful share of an animal sacrifice was the breast and the right thigh; but according to Deut. 18:3, the priest should get "the shoulder and the two cheeks and the stomach." Eli's sons were not content with their due shares. When one wields authority and possesses power, the temptation is always to acquire more than what is legally due.

"The three-pronged fork" (1 Sam. 2:13) is a common temple instrument, found in Hindu temples even today. Burning the "fat" is required by the law (vv. 15, 16; Exod. 23:18; 29:13). "Sin" (*hattah* or *hattath*), according to Hebrew etymology means

19

"missing the mark" or "missing the goal." Here, the sons of Eli missed the goal of serving the LORD and guiding people to him; and that was the great sin "in the sight of the LORD" (1 Sam. 2:17).

Reciprocity in Religion (2:18-21)

Eli's assurance to Elkanah that the LORD would give him children through Hannah in return "for the loan which she lent to the LORD" (v. 20) is typical of popular piety in all religions (cf. v. 30b). The NT, however, points to a reward — free devotion to God. Love *(agape)* is its own reward; it does not expect anything in return.

As a regular practice, Elkanah and Hannah visited Samuel in Shiloh, and each time Hannah used to bring him a robe, probably "the linen ephod" (v. 18; see Introduction).

Unforgivable Sin (2:22-25)

The sin of Eli's sons is actually sin against God and, therefore, unforgivable (v. 25). Here we are reminded of Jesus' words regarding the sin against the Holy Spirit (Mark 3:29), which is also not forgivable. God as an interested party cannot of course be the mediator in such a case (cf. Job 9:32-33). The implied meaning seems to be that God is the source of forgiveness; so if one rejects God, then there is no possibility for that person to avail himself of forgiveness from another source (cf. 1 Sam. 3:14).

It is possible that vv. 22-25 come from a different hand. Here Eli exercises his responsibility as father in warning his children against their evil practices in the temple. But in v. 29 and 3:13 Eli is charged for not restraining his sons, seeming to contradict this section. Eli's children lying with women at the entrance of the tent of meeting is also new here; it is not mentioned among the evils listed earlier in vv. 12-17. Temple prostitution was common among the Canaanites, and it was condemned in Israel (1 Kgs. 14:24; 15:12; 22:46).

Eli's sons would not listen to the voice of their father (1 Sam. 2:25), and that meant their self-destruction. The author comments, "for it was the will of the LORD to slay them." According to the OT, nothing happens outside the sovereign purpose of God; as such, even what happens as the result of one's own sin is seen to be happening by God's will (cf. Exod. 9:12; 10:20, 27; 2 Sam. 24:1; Isa. 6:9-10).

Samuel Grows in Favor with the LORD (2:26)

The author contrasts the gradual crumbling of an old order, the priesthood of Eli's house, with the gradual growth of a new order in the prophet-priest-judge Samuel. After every section dealing with the gradual deterioration of Eli's priesthood, there is a reference to Samuel's "growth in the LORD" (cf. 1 Sam. 2:11, 21; 3:1). Pulling down an unjust structure and building up a new just structure are aspects of God's dealing with humankind (cf. Jer. 1:10). Construction of a just order is not possible without the destruction of the unjust order. There is no compromise between righteousness and iniquity; light and darkness have nothing in common (2 Cor. 6:14; Eph. 5:8-11).

Judgment on Eli's House (2:27-36)

Eli was chosen by God to be his priest, to serve as a mediator between God and his people; but in this calling Eli and his house failed. Consequently words of judgment came upon them. Election, according to the OT, is not for privilege but for responsibility. Failure to fulfil one's responsibility makes one doubly accountable to God (cf. Amos 3:2).

"A man of God" in 1 Sam. 2:27 probably refers to a prophet. It is twice used for Moses (Deut. 33:1; Josh. 14:6). In Judges "the man of God" is said to be the "angel of God" (Judg. 13:6, 8, 9). Here the whole account aims at the replacement of the priestly order whose origin goes back to the time of the Exodus (1 Sam. 2:27). Samuel appears to be the natural successor; subsequently, however, other members of Eli's house have also been functioning in different locations — Ahijah (14:3) and Abiathar (22:20). Eventually Abiathar was exiled, and thus Eli's line came to an end. Zadok then became the head of the priestly order (1 Kgs. 1–2).

"House of your father" (1 Sam. 2:27, 30) is probably a reference to Levi, to the Aaronite line in particular. A promise by God cannot stand unless there is corresponding obedience (v. 30), because God deals with humans who possess free will. That God's dealings correspond to human response (v. 30b; cf. vv. 18-21) is part of popular piety in all religions. But that God's love and grace outweigh human response is the truth of the revelation in Christ, which has its forebodings in the OT as well (Jer. 31:31-34; Hos. 11:8-9): " . . . while we were yet sinners Christ died for us" (Rom. 5:8).

Eli's posterity will be cut off (1 Sam. 2:31-34). In the absence of a belief in resurrection, the early Israelites seem to have believed in some kind of an ongoing existence (remembrance) through their posterity, through male progeny. That is the main reason why the Israelites were keen on having male offspring and why they saw the need for the levirate marriage system, which covered the case of a man dying without issue. To have one's posterity cut off was considered to be a great curse and a terrible misfortune (cf. Exod. 17:14; Deut. 25:19; Ps. 34:16; Jer. 11:19). To die in old age was a sign of God's blessings in Israel (cf. Gen. 15:15; 25:8), but to die prematurely was considered to be a curse. All the young men of Eli's house are to fall by the sword (1 Sam. 2:33). Verse 35 anticipates the Davidic kingship and the Zadokite priesthood in Jerusalem. "Before my anointed" is a reference to the king. Verse 36 anticipates that some of the priests who still survive from Eli's line will play a subordinate role in the new order. Perhaps the writer has in mind the conditions that prevailed after the centralization of worship in Jerusalem, when the priests of the local sanctuaries lost their jobs and sought subordinate positions in the Jerusalem temple (2 Kgs. 23:5, 9; 2 Chr. 35:2ff.).

SAMUEL'S CALL (3:1–4:1a)

This account of Samuel's call is similar to the other call accounts in the OT — the calls of Moses, Gideon, Isaiah, and Jeremiah. A theophany of some sort is part of all these accounts.

Josephus (*Antiquities* v.10.4) preserves a Jewish tradition which says that Samuel had just completed his twelfth year when the word of God came to him. In other words, he had attained his religious maturity. We are here reminded of Jesus' visit to the temple when he was twelve years old and his discussion with the teachers of Scripture there (Luke 2:42, 46).

Eli, being blind, "was lying down in his own place," probably at the doorpost (cf. 1 Sam. 1:9). "The lamp of God had not yet gone out" (3:3; cf. 2 Chr. 13:11). That means it was the morning hours, but it was still dark and therefore the lamp had not yet been put out. Samuel was sleeping near the ark, which was believed to be the abode of God (1 Sam. 4:5-7). On the top of the ark were two images of cherubim (Exod. 25:18); Yahweh was believed to be enthroned on the cherubim (cf. 1 Sam. 4:4; 2 Sam. 6:2). Thus Samuel was in a fitting place to receive the revelation of God (cf. Gen. 28:11-18; Isa. 6). The fact that Samuel could not identify the source of the voice points to the fact that there was nothing visual; he could only hear the voice.

In this account, we come across three characters: God, represented through his word, the *dabar;* Eli the priest, the mediator or guide; and Samuel, the receiver. The main character here is neither Eli nor Samuel, but the word of God. In this chapter, the Hebrew root *dbr* occurs fifteen times, both in its nominative and predicative forms. We shall therefore start our inquiry with *dabar,* the word of God.

Dabar, the Word of God

The chapter begins with the words, "Now the boy Samuel. . . . And the word of the LORD was rare in those days; there was no frequent vision" (1 Sam. 3:1). Thereby, the writer points out to the reader the subject matter with which he is going to deal in this chapter. He is going to tell us about the revelation of the word of God to Samuel. Later, at v. 12, Yahweh says to Samuel, "On that day I will fulfil against Eli all that I have spoken concerning his house, from beginning to end." But according to 2:30, Yahweh has earlier promised to Eli, "your house and the house of your father should go in and out before me for ever." This promise of God is no longer honored; the house of Eli is now to be removed. At this point, then, one may ask, how is this possible? How can the word of God get lost, without its being fulfilled (cf.

23

Isa. 55:11)? Thus, we must seek to get a clear understanding of the meaning and use of the Hebrew word *dabar.* We identify three senses in which this word is used, and all these three uses are found in this chapter.

1. *Dabar* indicates the content of the word (i.e., its purpose), and so here the revelation of God's will: "And the word of the LORD was rare in those days." Here, the word of the LORD clearly refers to the revealed will of God (cf. 1 Sam. 3:21). This is the content of the word of God, which remains the same for all times, since it never changes.

2. It represents the word of the LORD as the medium of the communication of the will of God. In this sense, the word changes from time to time, from generation to generation, from place to place. The phrase "in those days" in v. 1 thus points to a new situation. The context of the word has now changed, and so also has the need for the will of God to be communicated differently. What came earlier to Eli as an oracle of salvation comes to him now as an oracle of doom.

Many pious Christians ask today whether the *context* influences or changes the word of God. The answer must be that it does not change the *content* of the word of God, namely, the ultimate purpose of God. The ultimate purpose of God is always the salvation of his people. God wants to give all people "abundant life" (John 10:10). It is not his purpose that any one in humanity — black, white, or colored, male or female, rich or poor — should be lost (2 Pet. 3:9). All that God does, whether in judgment or in blessing, is towards this ultimate purpose of salvation for humanity, and this ultimate purpose never changes. However, the word, as the medium of communication of this eternal message of God, may be influenced and changed by its context. Thus Eli was only an instrument in the hand of God towards the fulfilment of the ultimate purpose of the salvation of his people. The earlier word came to him as an oracle of salvation. But the house of Eli had failed in its role; instead of mediating God's salvation to his people, it had itself become a hindrance to the people. Therefore, in the larger interest of the welfare of the people, and for the sake of God's original purpose, Eli's house has now to be removed. The earlier oracle of salvation now becomes the oracle of doom to the house of Eli.

3. *Dabar* also means the concretization or realization of the will of God. In 1 Sam. 3:11 we read, "Behold, I am about to do a thing in Israel. . . ." Here, the word used for "a thing" is *dabar.* The word, as the work of God, also changes from situation to situation.

The NT claims that Jesus Christ is the true Dabar, the Logos, in all these three senses at once (cf. John 1).

The word of God comes to Samuel with such an urgency that one expects something very important in the communication of it. But what is communicated to Samuel is with regard to the judgment on the house of Eli. Perhaps we find an important message here. God has called Samuel to do something new in Israel, something different from what the house of Eli has done. The house of Eli, instead of guiding people to Yahweh, had become a hindrance. Consequently it must be removed before God could work through Samuel. Removal of oppressive structures precedes the creation of liberative structures (cf. Jer. 1:10).

Eli, the Guide

Eli symbolizes institutional religion. The judgment against Eli is not a judgment against an individual person or family, but against a structure. It is against the priestly religion as a whole, which had failed in guiding people to God (cf. 1 Sam. 2:28ff.). The task of the priesthood is to guide people to God and to help them to abide in an active relation to God, to listen to God and to handle matters according to his will. In this task Eli and his priestly religion had failed. Instead of leading people to God, they were leading the people to themselves, to listen to their own words and to act accordingly (cf. 2:12-17).

The young man Samuel had no problem in hearing. He heard the voice very clearly, but he did not know from where the voice came. Instead of running to God, Samuel ran to Eli. Eli the priest was perhaps convinced at this time that God would speak only through him. He was the one to receive any oracle from God and to communicate it to the people. He could not at first believe that God could also reveal his will to other people. Therefore, he rejected Samuel's claim to have heard a call and tried to silence him and make him sleep. It took some time for him (three is a symbolic number indicating fullness) before he realized that it could be that Yahweh was calling Samuel. Only then did he give proper instructions to Samuel as to how he should receive the call.

In the house of Eli we see today the institutional Church. The task of the Church as "a kingdom of priests" (cf. Exod. 19:6) is to guide people to God and to help them to listen to God's voice and to obey it. But the Church, from what we see today, seems to draw people to itself to listen to its voice. Because it is very much conditioned by its own traditions, theologies, and activities, the Church is not able to listen to new voices. Like Eli, it tries to silence and suppress new voices, new initiatives and impulses coming from people — especially from people in the Third World — because it believes that outside of itself there can be no revelation of God's will. But as in the case of Samuel, God speaks to people whom the official Church may never think of, at different times and in different places. It is time that the institutional Church, as Eli, should take note of this reality and act — before it is too late.

Samuel, the Receiver

Samuel, for the first time, learns from Eli how he should respond to God: "Speak, LORD, for thy servant/slave hears" (1 Sam. 3:9). This is no magical formula, but an expression of adequate human response to God. The Hebrew word used here is 'ebed, a noun which is translated both as "servant" and "slave." 'Ebed, the slave, is one who submits his personal will to the will of his master. That condition is reached when one can sincerely say, "Thy kingdom come, thy will be done on earth as in heaven" — when one can say with Paul, "I have been crucified with Christ; it is no longer I who live, but Christ who lives in me . . ." (Gal. 2:20). This, then, is the condition in which one can receive God's word. When self-seeking personal will stops, then the saving will of God can begin to work in and through the human mind. This is what happened in Samuel.

Eli is anxious to know what God told Samuel, and Samuel shares everything with him. Eli accepts God's will and submits himself to it (1 Sam. 3:16-18). With that Eli's role comes to an

26

end, though we do meet him again in 4:12-18. Moreover, the account of Samuel's ministry begins, "The LORD was with him and let none of his words fall to the ground" (3:19). All people from Dan to Beer-sheba (i.e., from the whole land, from north to south) came to know him as a prophet (v. 20). "The LORD revealed himself to Samuel at Shiloh by the word of the LORD" (v. 21), "and the word of Samuel came to all Israel" (4:1a). It is important that people who speak in the name of God first receive that word from God.

II. THE STORY OF
THE ARK OF GOD

1 Samuel 4:1b–7:2

Symbol and Reality in Faith

Samuel is never mentioned in this section. Hence, it is believed that this ark account comes from an earlier tradition. The interchange of the names "the ark of the covenant of the LORD" (1 Sam. 4:3b, 4, 5), "the ark of the LORD" (4:6; 6:8), "the ark of the God of Israel" (5:7, 8, 10, 11), and "the ark of God" (4:11; eight times between 4:13–5:2; twice in 5:10) further indicates that more than one hand is involved in the composition of this section. The flow of the account of the capture of the ark is interrupted in 4:1; it is picked up again in 5:1. 1 Samuel 4:12-22 deals with the news of the capture of the ark being brought to Eli and the people in Shiloh and its impact on Eli's house. It is possible that these verses come from a different hand. Since these various sources all refer to the same historical incident, the historicity of that incident is thereby enhanced.

The fact that the destiny of the house of Eli is closely tied up with the ark indicates that this narrative in its present form should have come from the time of David, when the Zadokite priesthood of Eli's lineage was still in active service. That also explains the positive attitude to the house of Eli here, as different from what is said in chs. 2 and 3. This means that the Eli account here is independent of the account in chs. 2 and 3.

ISRAEL'S DEFEAT BEFORE THE PHILISTINES:
THE QUESTION OF THEODICY (4:1b-3a)

The Philistines (4:1b) were a non-Semitic (14:6; 17:36) sea-people. The reference to "Pelethites" in 2 Sam. 8:18 is considered to be a variant of "Philistine" (Peter R. Ackroyd, *The Second Book of Samuel,* 47). The Philistines were survivors, it seems, of an Aegean people which had established an advanced civilization in Crete, Asia Minor, and the Greek mainland. Pressed by more barbaric tribes from the north, they had migrated southward and established themselves in the Shephelah, the coastal plain of Canaan, early in the 12th cent. B.C. (Solomon Goldman, *Samuel,* 21). Their association with Caphtor, probably another name for Crete, is attested in the OT (cf. Deut. 2:23; Jer. 47:4; Amos 9:7). By their discovery of the use of iron weapons, the Philistines superseded the use of bronze hitherto current in the region. The records of Ramses III of Egypt tell of a clash around 1200 with such a people who controlled much of Palestine. We are told that during Samuel's lifetime there was a Philistine presence in Geba (1 Sam. 13:3), Gibeah (14:1, 6, 15) and Beth-shan (31:10-11). They were considered to be oppressors since the time of Samson and seem to have occupied the great maritime plain from Joppa southwards to the border of Egypt, a confederacy of five cities, each with a chief administrator (in some places called a king) bearing the title *seren,* "lord" (5:11; 6:18).

The name Philistia, in its Latin form *Palestina,* was used by the Romans to describe the whole province in the 2nd cent. A.D. This term came to be used for the land.

The Israelites encamped at Ebenezer, and the Philistines at Aphek. 1 Samuel 7:12 etiologically explains the origin of the name Ebenezer, which means "stone of help." It seems to be located between Mizpah and Jeshanah. Aphek is probably the same place as the one mentioned in Josh. 12:18; see also 1 Sam. 29:1. It has not yet been identified. Probably it was somewhere in the plain of Sharon.

The Philistine superiority in weapons (cf. 13:5; 2 Sam. 1:6) and warfare could have been the reason for their success. Israel was defeated. Because the Israelites considered this to be a holy war, a war in which Yahweh fought on their behalf against their enemies, they ascribed their defeat to Yahweh and asked, "Why has the LORD put us to rout today before the Philistines?" (1 Sam. 4:3). This is a question of theodicy, a question raised by many even today, by people who fail to see that mankind in their freedom can fall away from doing the will of God. In the archetypal Cain-Abel account in Genesis, for example, we are presented with the issue of who was responsible for the death of Abel.

The Israelites raised the proper question but found the wrong answer. Instead of trying to find the causes of defeat among themselves, they hurried to find external means of activating God. They decided to "bring the ark of the covenant of the LORD" from Shiloh and thus activate the LORD to go with them into the battle and so save them from their enemy.

THE ARK AND THE LORD:
THE SYMBOL AND THE REALITY (4:3b-22)

The ark was just a symbol which, as the "seat" of Yahweh, indicated the presence of Yahweh in the midst of his people, Israel. But the Israelites wrongly identified the symbol with the reality itself and thus mistook the material presence of the ark for the real presence of Yahweh. They believed that the ark would activate the power of Yahweh in a magical way against the enemy, the Philistines, while revealing no relationship to their covenant bond with Yahweh. This story of the ark thus shows the fallacy of blindly identifying a symbol with the reality behind it.

Yahweh is not just an objective power which can be manipulated and used through technical or magical means. Yahweh is a God who stands in a covenant relationship with Israel. With or without symbols, what is of primary importance for Yahweh is Israel's loyalty to him. Symbols, such as the ark, are of course of value; the ark reminded Israel of its covenant relationship. But when this relationship fails, such symbols lose their value; they have no inherent power outside that living relationship with God. This is also true of all the symbols, including the sacraments, baptism and the eucharist, which are used in the Christian Church.

Similar efforts are also made today in churches worldwide where people feel the absence of the living God in their midst, because "the power of . . . enemies" seems to have gained the upper hand. In such situations the elders and leaders of the churches, instead of looking for the reason for the absence of God in their midst, and instead of trying to rectify their broken and strained relationship with God, seek to rectify the situation through some external means such as consultations, conferences, seminars, and the like. To be sure, these are all useful and important activities, but basic to all else is our relation to God. The God whom we worship is the God who desires "*hesed* (covenant love) and not sacrifice" (Hos. 6:6).

4:4 The Israelites believed that Yahweh as king over Israel was "enthroned on the cherubim," which were situated over the ark. Belief in the kingship of Yahweh appears to be very ancient in Israel; possibly it comes from Israel's nomadic period. This belief runs through the whole OT, continuing on into the NT in the preaching of the kingdom of God. It stands as a warning and judgment against all worldly governments, which try to rule over, exploit, and oppress humanity instead of serving them (cf. Mark 10:42-45). On "the LORD of hosts" see above on 1 Sam. 1:3.

Hophni and Phinehas, the sons of Eli the priest, were the custodians of the ark. Probably they carried the ark when it had to be moved. The ark was holy; non-Levites could not touch it, as we shall see below (cf. 6:19, 20; 2 Sam. 6:6-7).

4:5 As the ark came into the Israelite camp, "all Israel gave a mighty shout." This appears to be a ritual shout to indicate that Yahweh was assuming his kingship and was rising up against his enemy from his position of residing on the ark. It is a war cry such as that in Num. 10:35-36: "Arise, O LORD, and let thy enemies be scattered; and let them that hate thee flee before thee . . ." (see also Josh. 6:5, 20; Ps. 95:1-5). Such a shout also seems to have become part of the later ritual at the king's enthronement in Israel (cf. 2 Kgs. 11:12-14).

4:6-8 The shouting in the Israelite camp had its expected result in drawing the attention of the Philistines and creating panic among them. The fear that fell upon the Philistines is an element of the holy war concept in Israel (cf. 1 Sam. 5:11; 7:10; 11:7;

14:15, 20; also Exod. 23:27; Deut. 7:21). The author puts in the mouth of the enemies an acknowledgement of Yahweh's glory, a literary strategy to assert Yahweh's reputation among the nations. This is attested to by other OT writers as well (cf. Exod. 9:27; Josh. 2:9-11; 5:1; 1 Kgs. 20:23; 2 Kgs. 5:15).

The Philistines refer to the Israelites here as "Hebrews" (1 Sam. 4:6), a term normally used of the Israelites by foreigners and by the Israelites themselves while speaking to foreigners (cf. Exod. 2:6-7, 13; 3:18; 5:3). The origin and meaning of this term are not very clear; there are differing views among OT scholars. Some think that the term was probably derived from the name Eber, one of the ancestors of the Israelites (Gen. 10:21, 25). Another popular explanation is that the Israelites were so called because they came from "beyond the river (Euphrates)" (*be'eber hannahar;* Josh. 24:2). Most scholars try to find a socio-logical explanation and think that the term is derived from *Hab/piru,* designating a group of people somewhat discriminated against in the society, probably those "who forfeited their freedom by a semi-voluntary slavery" (cf. 1 Sam. 14:21; Roland de Vaux, *Ancient Israel,* 83).

The Exodus from Egypt played an important role in Israel's faith; the author assumes that this was known also to Israel's enemies (4:8). The name Yahweh is not put into the mouth of the enemy; they refer to him by the generic term god/gods *(elohim).*

4:9-11   Instead of making the Philistines flee, however, the panic challenged them to pool their resources and to fight with determination. The fear of becoming "slaves" in the hands of enemies, the worst thing that could ever happen to a warrior, roused their survival instinct and made the Philistines fight with determination. As a result Israel was defeated, the ark was captured, and Hophni and Phinehas were slain.

That God cannot be manipulated through external means becomes evident here.

4:12-22   A Benjaminite brings the tragic news of Israel's defeat to the people in Shiloh and to Eli. The news of the capture of the ark causes the immediate death of Eli, "for his heart trembled for the ark of God" (4:13). Eli is presented here not only as the priest but also, for the first time, as the judge who "judged Israel forty years" (v. 18). Perhaps, the author here prepares the ground for presenting Samuel as the judge in Israel (cf. 7:15ff.).

On hearing the shocking news of the capture of the ark and the death of her husband and father-in-law, Eli's daughter-in-law, Phinehas' wife, who was in full pregnancy, was overcome by "pains" and delivered of a son, whom she named before dying as Ichabod. This means literally "no glory." This name was supposed to indicate that "the glory has departed from Israel" (4:21). It was Yahweh who was the "Glory of Israel" (15:29). Because Yahweh was identified with the ark, its capture meant for the Israelites the departure of Yahweh from their midst (4:22). Yahweh's departure meant disaster for the people of Israel (cf. Ezek. 10:18ff.; 11:23).

Rending one's clothes and putting earth upon one's head was a sign of mourning (1 Sam. 4:12; see Introduction). A person bringing sad news to the people was expected to come in mourning clothes (cf. 2 Sam. 1:2; 15:32). On hearing the sad news, "all the city cried out" (1 Sam. 4:13), which perhaps refers to the national mourning.

The women greeted Eli's daughter-in-law about the time of her death with the words "fear not, for you have borne a son" (v. 20). In these words one may hear again the voice of Israel's male chauvinistic society, which preferred the birth of males to females (see above on 1:1ff.). These words seem to imply that because she had given birth to a son she could now die in peace, for she had achieved the purpose of her life. Bearing a male heir to the husband was regarded as the primary role of woman in Israelite society. This was obviously the intention of the institution of levirate marriage (cf. Gen. 38:1ff.).

Naming children with symbolic meanings which have national, as well as cultic, significance was a practice known in Israel (cf. Hos. 1:3-9). Naming the child in Israelite society was normally the prerogative of the father (cf. 2 Sam. 12:24); in later days, however, the woman also seemed to have had a say in the matter (cf. Luke 1:59-63). Here Phinehas' wife named her child during a crisis when the father was no more and she herself was about to die.

The Ark among the Philistines (5:1–6:1)

The captured ark was brought from Ebenezer first to the Philistine city Ashdod and was kept there before the Philistine god Dagon. In so doing the Philistines, just as the Israelites, committed the mistake of taking the symbol for the reality. They thought that by placing the ark before Dagon they could humiliate the God of the Israelites and assert Dagon's superiority over him. Yahweh, who looks at the hearts of men and women, frustrated the Philistines' intentions by creating panic among the people and by causing many deaths through plagues such as tumors (1 Sam. 5:6, 11-12) and mice (cf. 6:4-5, 18). The ark therefore was moved from one city to another, in fact to all the five cities of the Philistines (cf. 6:17-18), in the hope that such human adjustments would avert the plagues. But wherever the ark went, "there was a deathly panic throughout the whole city" (5:11).

5:1-5 The city Ashdod lay midway between Joppa and Gaza. A village in that region still bears the name Eshdud today. The temple of Dagon, said to have existed there, seems to have continued until the time of the Maccabees (1 Macc. 10:83-84; 11:4). According to Judg. 16:23, there was another shrine of Dagon in Gaza. The nature and attributes of Dagon are not fully known to us. It is possible to relate this name to two Hebrew words — *dg* ("fish") and *dgn* ("corn"). Since the Philistines were originally a sea-people, it is possible that the name is derived from the root *dg*. Jewish traditions (Isaaki and Kimchi) support this derivation. The worship in Syria of a fish-god with the head and hands of a man and the body of a fish is well attested. On the other hand, deriving the name from *dgn* would make Dagon a fertility god, "the god of the corn." He would be at home in the five grain-growing cities of the plains of the Shephelah. Some scholars prefer this derivation (H. W. Hertzberg, 37; Ackroyd, 54-55).

Yahweh proves to the Philistines to be more than the symbol of Yahweh's presence, the ark, and that the capture of the ark does not mean Dagon's supremacy over him. This was symbolically indicated by the fact that the image of Dagon fell down before the ark and that its head and hands were cut off and were lying on the threshold of the temple. The author of 1 Sam. 5:5 gives the reader an etiological explanation to the Philistine cultic practice of not treading on the "threshold of Dagon in Ashdod." Because the broken hands and head of Dagon lay on the threshold, according to Philistine belief, the threshold itself became holy in a special way. Consequently it should not be trodden upon. With no head and no hands, only the "trunk" remained. This word "trunk" is not found in the Hebrew; it is supplied from the Targum and other ancient versions. The medieval Jewish exegete David Kimchi, who takes Dagon as a fish-god — as half-fish and half-human — notes that only the Dagon part (i.e., the fish part) was left of him (Goldman, 5). In Zeph. 1:9, "leaping over the threshold" is paralleled by "Fish Gate" in the next verse; it is not clear whether this has any reference to the Dagon worship. Such ritual jumping over the threshold of temples was widely practiced in ancient times. The phrase "to this day" (1 Sam. 5:5) indicates that the author of this account lived at a later period, and that this ancient practicce of leaping over the threshold was still continuing during that time.

5:6-12 The description of plagues among the Philistines reminds us of the plagues of Egypt (Exod. 7–11). The "tumors" here are similar to the boils in Egypt (Exod. 9:8ff.). Just as the Israelites were allowed to go out of Egypt as a result of the plagues, the ark of God was allowed to return to its place as the result of the plagues here (cf. Exod. 6:5, 6). In both accounts, the plagues cause great panic among the people (1 Sam. 5:12; cf. Exod. 14:24). Perhaps both stories go back to a multifaceted literary development of the plague motif in Israel, which people used on various suitable occasions (Fritz Stolz, *Das erste und zweite Buch Samuel,* 47). The Hebrew word used here for tumors *('epholim)* is used elsewhere only in Deut. 28:27, where it refers to the boils in Egypt. Perhaps both refer to the same plague.

Through the panic caused by the plagues, Yahweh's supremacy over Dagon and his people was asserted (1 Sam. 5:7). The "lords of the Philistines" came together for consultation (v. 8). They first thought that some territorical adjustment might help to avert the plagues. So the ark was first sent to Gath and then to Ekron (v. 10). 1 Samuel 6:17, however, implies that the ark was sent to all five cities of the Philistines and that wherever it went the people were affected by the plagues.

Gath (5:8) cannot be identified with certainty now. Modern Tel es-Safi, about 19 km. (12 mi.) E of Ashdod, has been suggested as a possibility. Ekron (v. 10) was the most northerly of the Philistine cities but the nearest one to the land of Israel. Because the destruction caused by the ark was already known to the people of Ekron, they were terrified when the ark was sent to them. They saw the presence of the ark in their midst as a means of their sure destruction (v. 11), so "the cry of the city went up to heaven" (v. 12). "Going up to heaven" is an idiomatic expression for prayers reaching to God. The author seeks to make clear that evils caused by human disobedience to God cannot be rectified by mere human maneuvers such as shifting the ark from place to place or, in the case of the Israelites, by carrying the ark in the army camp. Rather, such evils can be rectified only by real repentance and reconciliation with God (cf. 7:3ff.). When the Philistines saw that all their maneuvers had failed, they cried out to Israel's God, and, as the writer says, their cry "went up to heaven." The story that follows implies that God answered their cry.

The question is often raised whether prayers offered by people of other faiths ever reach the God of the Bible. This passage perhaps points to those in such non-Christian contexts, that all genuine cries of repentance and prayers reach the only God, the Father of Jesus Christ (cf. John 9:31). Here we recall what Peter said after his meeting with the heathen Cornelius.

> Truly I perceive that God shows no partiality, but in every nation any one who fears him and does what is right is acceptable to him. (Acts 10:34-35)

In Hinduism, the Bhagavad Gita also speaks to the same effect, where Krishna says,

> Even those who worship other gods, if they worship truly in full faith, they do really worship me, even though they do not worship according to the prescriptions. (Gita IX 23, 17)

We are told that the ark was in the country of the Philistines "seven months" (1 Sam. 6:1). Seven is a mystical number widely used in all the oriental religions and extensively used in the OT (Gnana Robinson, *The Origin and Development of the OT Sabbath*, 109ff.). The number indicates "wholeness" or "completeness," and in the OT often refers to complete periods of chastisement and purification (cf. Lev. 26:21, 24, 28; Dan. 9:1-2). Perhaps the author sees the seven months when the ark was in Philistine country as a period of complete chastisement for the Philistines. In seven months, the Philistines received punishment in full for all their iniquities. Relief comes when the punishment for sin is over (cf. Isa. 40:2).

THE RETURN OF THE ARK TO THE ISRAELITES (6:2–7:2)

The Philistine lords took the counsel of "the priests and diviners" to find out what to do to avert the plagues. Following their advice, the Philistines returned the ark to Israel and the plagues were stopped.

Here again, one might ask, how is it possible that God's will was revealed to Philistine priests and diviners? Can we not say that God at no time left any people without a witness for him, including the Philistines (cf. Amos 9:7)? Many Christians today find it difficult to believe that God works among non-Christians and reveals his will to them in different ways. Several texts in the Bible, such as this one, point in that direction (cf. Jonah 4:10, 11; Isa. 44:28; 45:1; 2 Chr. 36:22-23; Ezra 1:1ff.).

In 1 Sam. 6, it is the plague of mice that "ravage the land" (v. 5), rather than the tumor mentioned in 5:6ff., that is implied. It is possible that originally two versions of the ark account, with the plague of tumors in one and the plague of mice in the other, were circulating and were later combined.

6:2-9 This section deals with the counsel of the priests and diviners who remind us of the "magicians" of the Exodus plague account. But their role seems to be different here. Here, the priests and diviners persuade the people to repentance. (Diviners were later forbidden in Israel; 28:3, "medium.") The priests and diviners assume that the plagues were due to the anger of Yahweh and advise their people to return the ark with "a guilt offering" (6:3). The word used here is *asham* (Lev. 5:14ff.). Outside the Priestly writings (P) the word occurs only here and in 2 Kgs. 12:16. It denotes primarily compensation or reparation for the infringement of the rights of another or for the misappropriation of one's property. Here the Philistines have misappropriated Yahweh's ark; that is their sin.

The remedy prescribed in 1 Sam. 6:4-5 comes from the background of imitative magic known in all primitive religions (cf. Num. 21:4ff.; 2 Kgs. 6:5-6). The guilt offering consisted of five golden tumors and five golden mice, one each for every Philistine city ruled by one of the "lords"; the five cities are Ashdod, Gaza, Ashkelon, Gath, and Ekron (1 Sam. 6:17).

Remnants of such imitative magical acts of healing are to be found in all popular religions. There are many Hindu temples in India where worshippers offer to their gods images of human organs such as hand, leg, or head, and sometimes even images of babies, in gold, silver, wood, or clay, along with their prayers for healing or with prayers in fulfilment of prior vows in connection with healing. Such practices are not totally absent in Christianity. In South India, in Tamil Nadu, is a Roman Catholic church dedicated to Mary (called in Tamil *Velankanni*) where images of bodily organs are offered in gold or silver. I have come across remnants of such practices in Europe as well.

The purpose of the offerings here is to avert Yahweh's anger from the people: "perhaps he will lighten his hand from off you and your gods and your land" (v. 5b). The people are here asked to "give glory to the God of Israel." Again, the same question is before us today: can the name of God, the Father of Jesus Christ, be glorified in the midst of foreigners? Can these foreigners and unbelievers really bring glory to God?

The author sees what is happening to the Philistines here as an exact parallel to what happened to the Egyptians at the time of the Exodus, and warns the Philistines not to commit the mistake of the Egyptians in "hardening their hearts" (v. 6). In this sense, the example of the Egyptians stands as a perennial warning to all oppressive powers in history.

The Israelite idea of the "holiness of God" (cf. v. 20) is behind the whole prescription that follows v. 7. The Hebrew verb *q-d-sh* means "to set apart"; it refers to setting apart things or persons for the use or service of God, and is employed for cultic purposes. Persons or things thus set apart are forbidden for profane (or common) use; they become taboo (holy) for other people (cf. 24:6; 26:11). Anyone coming into direct contact with such a forbidden thing or person is in great danger. That this early conception of holiness in Israel lacked ethical content is evident from what happened to the people of Beth-shemesh for inadvertently looking into the ark (6:19) and to Uzzah who, with good intentions, touched the ark to save it from falling down and being smashed (2 Sam. 6:7).

Thus, the animals or objects that are to be presented as guilt offerings should be those which have not hitherto been taken for any common use. Accordingly, the Philistines are required to prepare "a new cart and two milch cows upon which there has never come a yoke" (cf. Num. 19:2; Deut. 21:3). When the ark is placed in the cart, the cart and the cows come into contact with the ark and thus become "holy" too; therefore they cannot be used for any other purpose. That is why the cows and the wood of the cart were later offered as burnt offerings to Yahweh (1 Sam. 6:14). This should also explain why the Philistines had problems when the ark entered their cities.

The purpose of taking the calves "home, away from them" (v. 7) was to find out whether the cows were moved by their natural motherly instinct of following their own calves or whether they were animated by the spirit of Yahweh. Similar beliefs are common among popular religions such as Hinduism. In Indian villages cows, bulls, or goats dedicated to temples are regarded as holy, and people refrain from doing them any harm. It is believed that these are animated by the spirit of the deities worshipped in their respective temples.

The priests and diviners are not 100 percent sure if the plagues were caused by the spirit of the God of Israel. They use this trial-and-error method to determine whether the plagues were actually caused by the God of Israel or whether they happened by chance. If the cows were moved by their natural instinct and returned to their calves, then it was evident that the plagues happened by chance; but if the cows moved against their natural instinct and went towards Israel to Beth-shemesh (v. 9), then it was a clear indication that they were animated by the spirit of Yahweh and that Yahweh was the cause of the plagues. Beth-shemesh means "house/temple of the sun." Modern 'Ain Shems, which means "fountain of the sun," lies at the mouth of Wadi es-Sarar, the ancient valley of Sorek (Judg. 16:4). According to Josh. 15:10, Beth-shemesh belonged to Judah as a border city, and according to 21:16 it contained the pasture land assigned to the descendants of Aaron by Judah; but according to Judg. 1:33, this was part of the area not yet conquered by Israel. Perhaps Beth-shemesh was a Philistine settlement until the Philistines were defeated by David, as indicated by archaeological evidence lying closer to the border of Judah. When the Ephraimites were defeated by the Philistines, it is possible that the ark was brought to Beth-shemesh, the border town, and there it received some cultic treatment. Due to some unfortunate events happening in Beth-shemesh, for which the ark was considered to be the cause, the ark was sent to Kiriath-jearim, a Canaanite city (1 Sam. 6:21).

Jan Dus sees here an old Israelite practice where every seventh year a new home was found for the ark. A new cart with new cows separated from their calves would carry the ark, and the place where the cows stopped would be the correct place for the ark to remain for the next seven years ("Noch zum Brauch der 'Ladewanderung,'" *VT* 13 [1963]: 126-132; "Der Brauch der Ladewanderung im alten Israel," *ThZ* 17 [1961]: 1-16).

6:10–7:2 The Philistine lords did according to the advice of the priests and diviners (1 Sam. 6:10-12). The experiment proved good; "the cows went straight in the direction of Beth-shemesh," and the lords followed the cart "as far as the border of Beth-shemesh." It was the season of the "wheat harvest" (v. 13). Wheat harvest is the time of the *massot* festival, when probably the spring new year began (Robinson, *Sabbath,* 135). Perhaps some cultic event was taking place when this happened.

The cart stopped in "the field of Joshua of Beth-shemesh" (v. 14). We know nothing about the identity of this person. The reason why the cows stopped at this place is indicated by the fact that there was "a great stone." This probably was a cultic center, and the stone was the altar. Because Canaan was an agricultural land formerly under the influence of the fertility deity Baal, there could have been many such cultic centers, simple in form, in the fields and most often near threshing floors. Such threshing floors with cultic significance are found in 2 Sam. 6:6; 24:16. In the reference to the great stone, therefore, we meet with remnants of early animistic beliefs. (In India, such fertility centers can be seen in agricultural fields wherever we go.) Because the cart and the cows were holy to Yahweh, they were offered as a "burnt offering," evidently upon the great stone. In a burnt offering, everything is offered to God; nothing is left for the use of the priests or the devotees.

1 Samuel 6:15 repeats what is already said in v. 14 and interrupts the narrative. It seems to be a postexilic addition by a redactor who apparently wanted to show that the holy ark was not touched by ordinary people, but by the sanctified Levites. According to the editor, because the Levites were sanctified people, they alone could touch the sacred ark and the box which contained the guilt offerings. They took up the ark and the box and set them down, not on any common place but on the "great stone," which as a cultic stone was obviously holy.

The Philistine lords were satisfied to see that the ark had reached its proper destination and thus completed the reparation of their guilt. They then returned to Ekron, their next halting place (v. 16).

Verses 17-18 seem to be another late addition, which tries to explain why five golden tumors and five gold mice were sent, whereas only three cities are mentioned in the preceding account (Ashdod, Gath, and Ekron). Gaza and Ashkelon are added here. In v. 18b, the redactor draws the reader's attention to "the great stone" which in his time was still situated "in the field of Joshua of Beth-shemesh."

Because some people of Beth-shemesh looked into the ark of the LORD, it is said that Yahweh "slew seventy men of them." The Hebrew text reads "of the people seventy men, fifty thousand men." "Fifty thousand men" is an exaggeration, and it is probably a gloss. This section stands in contrast to the preceding section,

41

which speaks of the good-natured people of Beth-shemesh who rejoiced at the coming of the ark (vv. 13-14). The text which lies behind the LXX tries to give a reason for the death of the Beth-shemites: "Now the sons of Jeconiah rejoiced not with the men of Beth-shemesh when they beheld (with joy) the ark of Yahweh, and he slew them seventy men." It is possible that the Beth-shemites suffered because of some deadly disease causing the death of many and this was ascribed to the presence of the ark. About this there were perhaps two traditions. According to one, seventy men were killed, and according to the other the whole village of fifty thousand men were killed. Verse 20 is a typical lamentation. The reference to "this holy God" is the key to understanding this whole account regarding the ark.

Why the Beth-shemites sent messengers to the inhabitants of Kiriath-jearim and why the people of Kiriath-jearim immediately responded and felt obliged to receive the ark and lodge it in their city on a permanent basis are not clear (6:21–7:2). Perhaps there were cultic reasons to which we have no access. The author apparently wants to show that Kiriath-jearim was the destination to which the ark was moving under the animation of the spirit of Yahweh, and that until it reached its destination it could not rest. It apparently was a punishment for Israel that the ark went to a non-Israelite city, which is why "all the house of Israel lamented after the LORD" (7:2).

Kiriath-jearim means "the city of thickets," usually identified as Tell el-'Azhar, 14 km. (9 mi.) W of Jerusalem and about the same distance NE of Beth-shemesh. It was a Canaanite city, one of the four cities which formed the Gibeonite league (Josh. 9:17). This was also known as Baalah (Josh. 15:9) or Baale-judah (2 Sam. 6:2). We meet the ark again in 2 Sam. 6:1ff.

The people of Kiriath-jearim sanctified Eleazer, the son of Abinadab, to be in charge of the ark of the LORD. "The hill" on which the house of Abinadab was located was probably a cultic place (cf. 2 Sam. 6:3). This account probably comes from an author who was a supporter of the Zadokite priesthood (cf. 1 Chr. 24:3) and hence wanted to introduce Zadok as the son of Eleazer, coming from the ark-priesthood immediately succeeding the Eli-priesthood.

III. SAMUEL AS JUDGE

1 Samuel 7:3-17

Repentance Brings Reconciliation

We have here an independent tradition which presents Samuel as a judge in the line of the charismatic saviors found in the book of Judges. This tradition has no literary connection to 1 Sam. 1–3 and to what follows in ch. 8. 1 Samuel 7:15 says that "Samuel judged Israel all the days of his life," and this is confusing in view of the account in ch. 8. According to ch. 8, Samuel's sons were judges even during Samuel's lifetime, and it was their misconduct which was the immediate cause for people's demand for a king. Also, 7:3-17 implies that the Philistine menace was once and for all removed from Israel (v. 13), which contradicts the reality of the Philistine threat during the reign of Saul. This section also does not know the ark tradition; there is no reference to it, though the account of the war offers many opportunities for its mention.

The account here stands in the deuteronomistic tradition of the book of Judges. The sin-punishment-salvation scheme of history found in the book of Judges (Judg. 2:11ff.; 4:1ff.; 10:6ff.) is also found here.

1 Samuel 7:3-4 and 13-14 come from redactors. The redactor of vv. 3-4 is responsible for placing this section in its present context. He presumes that the reason for Israel's defeat before the Philistines (4:1b–7:2) was the fact that Israel had gone away from Yahweh in following "the foreign gods and the Ashtaroth," "the Baals and the Ashtaroth," a fact which was not mentioned earlier. According to the redactor, repentance and return was the only way open to Israel to become reconciled to God and to obtain

43

God's favor. The redactor of 7:13-14 assumes that at that time Israel was at peace with the Philistines and Amorites.

Call to Turn Away from the Gods of Fertility (7:3-4)

Samuel calls the people to repentance, to "return to the LORD with all your heart." Repentance is primarily a matter of the heart — "direct your heart to the LORD." It is not a matter of human maneuvers such as the Israelites had earlier tried (cf. 4:2ff.). Directing one's heart to God naturally implies turning away from false gods — "foreign gods." So Israel was asked to "put away the Baals and the Ashtaroth."

The Baals and the Ashtaroth were the Canaanite fertility deities representing the male and the female principles of forces that cause fertility. Baal was the male principle, the supreme god in the Canaanite pantheon; he was primarily an agricultural deity. Baal means "lord," "owner," and "husband," all describing his relationship to the land. Each territory had its own Baal, and thus Baal had many names — e.g., Baal-peor (Num. 25:3, 5), Baal-berith in Shechem (Judg. 8:33; 9:4) — and therefore he is often referred to in the plural as Baals. Ashtaroth was the female fertility deity and was considered to be Baal's consort. Worship of such fertility deities stood in sharp contrast to the worship of Yahweh. Yahweh is not to be identified with creation, because the whole universe is Yahweh's creation.

The nomadic Israelites who learned agriculture from the native Canaanites were tempted to ascribe agricultural fertility to Baal and Ashtaroth (cf. Hos. 2:5, 8) and to worship Yahweh with the cultic rituals of Baal (cf. Hos. 4:12-14; Amos 4:4-5; 5:5). The prophets of the OT had to warn the Israelites against such negative syncretism. The Israelites listened to Samuel's call for repentance and "put away the Baals and the Ashtaroth, and they served the LORD only" (1 Sam. 7:4).

People in the 20th cent. A.D., entering into the 21st, are no longer tempted to worship these fertility gods, Baal and Ashtaroth. But these "fertility" gods are today replaced by the gods of "consumerism," the Mammons (like the Baals, the Mammons are also localized), the gods of power, wealth, and consumer goods. Repentance in today's context would then mean putting away these Mammons, the gods of consumerism, and in serving only the LORD.

Samuel's Prayer (7:5-6)

Mizpah was the center of Samuel's administration. Samuel gathered all Israel at Mizpah and there fasted and prayed for the people. The people repented and confessed their sin.

There is no indication that Mizpah was at any time the center of an Israelite amphictyony. When Gibeah revolted, the Israelites gathered at Mizpah (Judg. 20:1, 3; 21:1, 5, 8). The city belonged in Benjaminite territory, and a sanctuary was there (Judg. 20:1ff.). One tradition connects Samuel with Mizpah (cf. Judg. 10:17), while another tradition connects him with Ramah (cf. 1 Sam. 1:1ff.; 7:17). For the writer of this account, Mizpah was the center of activities for the Israelites. This was in fact the case after the fall of Jerusalem until the beginning of the 6th cent. (2 Kgs. 25:23). Therefore some scholars think that this author could have come from a later period (Fritz Stolz, *Das erste und zweite Buch Samuel*, 54). Mizpah is modern Nebi Samwil, 8 km. (5 mi.) N of Jerusalem.

As a ritual act the people "drew water and poured it out before the LORD" (1 Sam. 7:6). This was not a common act of sacrifice in Israel. The only other place where a similar instance occurs is 2 Sam. 23:16-17, where David pours out to the LORD the water which his men drew from the well of Bethlehem before capturing that city. Perhaps that was a ritual act to claim David's right over Bethlehem. The fact that the Philistines saw in Israel's gathering at Mizpah a political act and decided to attack perhaps suggests that Mizpah was under Philistine occupation. Thus the Israelite gathering there and the Israelites' performance of this "water-pouring ritual" were meant to assert Israel's claim over the land. The fact that Samuel judged Israel from Mizpah was again meant to stress Israel's sovereignty over Mizpah.

Praying for the people was one of the important functions of a prophet; ceasing to pray was a sin (1 Sam. 12:23). Samuel was known in Israelite tradition as a man of prayer (8:6; 12:19, 23;

Jer. 15:1). Fasting accompanied prayers; it was believed that it added to the efficacy of prayers (cf. Mark 9:29 mg; Matt. 17:21).

Prayer is the human act of directing one's heart/mind to God and of bringing one's will into harmony with God's will, with the intention of ensuring that the will of God is done on earth in all spheres of one's life. This is what Our LORD meant when he taught his disciples to pray, saying, "Thy will be done, on earth as it is in heaven" (Matt. 6:10). Through prayer heaven and earth are brought into harmony. In intercessory prayers, the one who prays stands in solidarity with those for whom he prays and brings their needs and concerns before God. Here, Samuel stands in solidarity with his people and prays on their behalf. Likewise the Church is called upon to identify itself with suffering people and to pray to God on their behalf. This is therefore the task also of every member of the Church.

The Lord Routs the Philistines (7:8-11)

Israel's repentance brings reconciliation with the LORD. The LORD responds to the cry of the people through Samuel's intercession.

Samuel's role as intercessor is stressed once again (1 Sam. 7:8). His prayers were accompanied by an animal sacrifice. A "sucking lamb" was offered "as a whole burnt offering" (v. 9). This probably was part of the ceremony of expiation following the confession (cf. Lev. 22:18); it was not to be identified with the sacrifice offered before the beginning of a war. While Samuel was still praying, the Philistines attacked and "the LORD thundered with a mighty voice" against the Philistines and they were routed before Israel. Thereafter the Israelites pursued them and "smote" them "as far as below Beth-car" (1 Sam. 7:11), a site which is not known. The thunder is part of a theophany of Yahweh (cf. Exod. 19:19; Ps. 29:3ff.). The author wants to stress that Yahweh alone was responsible for the victory.

The whole Bible is saturated with the language of sacrifice. The central doctrine of the NT, the doctrine of atonement, uses the language of sacrifice. Its roots are to be found in the sacrificial order in the OT, and bears common features with the sacrificial orders in many other religions both then and now. Christians seem to find no difficulty in accepting the sacrificial teaching of the NT and in drawing inspiration from the background of the sacrificial order in the OT. Still, it is difficult to understand and appreciate similar sacrificial practices prevalent among people of other faiths. Is this not a contradiction in the Christian's own approach? Is it wrong to say that God, who used the primitive sacrifices of Israel to communicate his salvation to his people, could use similar primitive practices in other faiths towards the fulfilment of his saving purpose?

Ebenezer: Hitherto the LORD Has Helped Us (7:12)

"Ebenezer" means "stone of help" (cf. 1 Sam. 4:1b). Here is an etiological explanation of the name of the place. Stone, like rock, is a symbol of eternity and reliability (see 2:2); God, the source of lasting, reliable help, is thus known as Ebenezer. The place name reminded Israel of their benevolent God.

Peace with the Philistines and the Amorites (7:13-14)

It is assumed here that Israel had complete victory over the Philistines so that they could win back all the territories occupied by the Philistines. But we know that Ekron and Gath remained as Philistine cities even during the period of the Israelite monarchy (cf. 17:52; 2 Kgs. 18:8; Amos 1:8). These cities probably paid tribute to the Israelite kings (cf. 1 Kgs. 4:21). "Amorite" is the name for the native people of Palestine in the Elohistic (E) and Deuteronomistic (D) sources (cf. Deut. 20:17); the Yahwist (J) calls them Canaanites. That the Amorites could not be destroyed, but continued to live in peace with the Israelites agrees with the tradition found in Judges (Judg. 1:21ff.).

Samuel Administers Justice to Israel (7:15-17)

The author holds that Samuel "judged Israel all the days of his life," traveling around and visiting such places as Bethel, Gilgal, and Mizpah year by year and "administering justice to Israel."

47

1 Samuel 7:17 stresses his connection with Ramah. In saying that "he built there an altar to the LORD," the author wants to point out that it was Yahweh who was the true ruler and that Samuel was only executing Yahweh's will.

Shaphat is the Hebrew verb used here for administering justice in the sense of ruling, administering, or leading. From this verb derives the noun *shophet,* which we translate as "judge." "Gilgal" refers to a stone circle such as was to be found in many places. Here it refers to a spot near Bethel and Mizpah. On Ramah, see above on 1:1ff.

IV. ISRAEL'S APOSTASY: THE INSTITUTION OF THE MONARCHY

1 Samuel 8:1–12:25

"Let Us Be like the Nations"

Here are two traditions regarding the institution of kingship in Israel — one in favor of kingship and the other hostile to kingship. The anti-kingship tradition is found in 1 Sam. 8; 10:17-27; 12:6-25. Chapter 15 also agrees with it. In this tradition it is repeatedly stated that the people's demand for a king was an act of apostasy against the LORD, a rejection of the LORD as King over Israel (8:7; 10:19). Thus it was an act of wickedness (12:17). In requesting a king for themselves, the Israelites had thereby added to their sins.

The pro-kingship tradition is found in 9:1–10:16; ch. 11; 12:1-5. Chapters 13–14 also support this tradition. According to this second tradition, the appointment of the king was the act of Yahweh in response to the cry of his people Israel because of their affliction from the hand of the Philistines (9:16). Saul was anointed by Yahweh to reign over his people and to save them from the hand of their enemies round about (10:1; 12:3, 5).

Most scholars, following Julius Wellhausen, take the pro-kingship tradition to be the older of the two traditions. It is held that the pro-kingship tradition may well have come from positive experiences of kingship during the United Monarchy, whereas the anti-kingship tradition could have arisen out of negative experiences during the later period in the Divided Monarchy.

Such a sharp distinction seems to be doubtful. The anti-kingship tradition has its strong roots in the prophetic tradition, which probably goes back to the people's nomadic past and also continues further throughout Israelite history. According to this tradition, Yahweh is the King of Israel, capable of saving his people from all their calamities and distresses (10:19; 12:8ff.). It is for this reason that Gideon rejected the offer to become king over Israel (Judg. 8:22-23). According to Hosea, Yahweh gave Israel kings in his anger and took them away in his wrath (Hos. 13:11). According to Ezekiel, Yahweh would never again entertain such a demand as before ("Let us be like the nations . . ."), but he alone would be king over Israel (Ezek. 20:32, 33). It is possible that this anti-kingship trend was present among certain prophetic circles as an undercurrent even when the pro-kingship ideology was dominant. People belonging to this tradition seem to have tolerated kingship, though they were critical of it. This is evident from the fact that here too the king was conceded, though reluctantly, and finally appointed with divine sanction. These opponents of kingship could have felt that their stand was finally vindicated when they saw the evils happening in Israel during the later period of the Divided Monarchy.

Monarchy was felt to be a historical necessity in Israel. To defend the people from enemies and to deal with their neighbors on economic and political matters, the Israelites needed a proper administrative structure on a permanent basis. The rule of judges, the charismatic leaders who rose from time to time, proved to be inadequate. While looking for an alternative model, the Israelites were attracted by the kingship model of their neighbors, but they could not foresee the pitfalls in that model. In that Canaanite model of kingship, the king, instead of becoming the servant or shepherd of the community, could easily arrogate power to himself and become the ruler/oppressor of the community, as among Israel's neighbors. This was what the prophetic tradition feared and what later proved to be true in Israel.

Governments of world powers are necessary evils in human society. God permits these for the service of his people. In this sense, the Israelite kings were meant to be Yahweh's shepherds, his servants. But when these powers drift away from God and become self-seeking (cf. Deut. 17:14-17), they become anti-God and anti-people. This danger is present in every form of human power. Therefore the prophets, the spokesmen of God, are called to serve as watchdogs at all times to warn people when these powers become oppressive and destructive (cf. 1 Sam. 12:23).

ISRAEL'S DEMAND FOR A KING (8:1-22)

Certain internal tensions are revealed here which may be the result of a long history of traditions and reinterpretations. The people seem to have made a just demand when they asked for a king (8:4-5). Samuel was not happy with the prospect of an earthly king, because it meant the removal of his family from "judging" the people of Israel (v. 6). At first Yahweh seems to have approved of the people's demand (v. 7a), but soon the tone changes and Yahweh supports Samuel's discouraging attitude (vv. 7b-8). Yahweh's warning against kingship is explained in vv. 10-18. The words "hearken to their voice" is repeated three times (vv. 7a, 9b, 22b). The people persisted in their demands and would not listen to Yahweh's voice (vv. 19-21). Finally, Yahweh yielded and asked Samuel to make them a king. This tradition is picked up again in 10:17ff.

The Background (8:1-3)

Samuel had become old, and his sons, as judges, were not administering justice.

The historicity of this section is questioned for various reasons. In 7:15 we are told that Samuel judged Israel all the days of his life; no mention is made of his early retirement. There has been no reference to Samuel's children thus far, nor is their misconduct mentioned in Samuel's farewell (12:2). Moreover, the office of judge was not hereditary in Israel. The type of office assumed here is different from the earlier office of judges as "saviors." Quite possibly the present text was intended to be a pretext for the demand for a king.

Samuel's children Joel ("Yahweh is God") and Abijah ("My father is Yahweh") "did not walk in his ways," that is, they did not follow Yahweh as their father Samuel had. Rather, they "turned aside after gain; they took bribes and perverted justice" (8:3). This is in contrast to Samuel's administration: Samuel "walked before the people" justly, in that he did not take their ox or ass nor did he defraud anyone nor take any bribe from anyone (12:1ff.). "Walking before Yahweh" is a religious expression to characterize a life fulfilling the ethical demands of justice in the light of the commandments of God (cf. Mic. 6:6-8). Its corollary is "walking before his people." Faithful relation to God is reflected in one's faithful relation to God's people, in fulfilling one's responsibility to the community.

The Demand (8:4-6)

The elders brought forward two arguments in support of their demand for a king: (1) "your sons do not walk in your ways"; (2) "to govern us like all the nations." The second appears to be the true reason; the first is only a pretext. The second argument is further explained fully in 1 Sam. 8:20: "that our king may govern us and go out before us and fight our battles" (cf. Ezek. 20:32). Samuel brought the demand to the LORD in prayer.

The desire to conform to advanced cultures and powers is strong in every people at all times in history. It is present today in the encounter between the so-called First World and the Third World. The industrial, technocratic culture of the First World is attracting the poor and weaker Third World, and the temptation is great among many people in the Third World to copy the First World blindly. The Bible warns us against blind conformity to world powers and cultures, because in most cases such powers and cultures, instead of serving and liberating people, tend to rule over and oppress people. Jesus says, "But it shall not be so among you" (Mark 10:43).

The LORD Acknowledges the Demand with Displeasure (8:7-9)

The demand meant the rejection of Yahweh from being King over Israel. Naturally, it did not please Yahweh. Still, he conceded to the people's demand. Ever since Yahweh delivered Israel out of Egypt, the people had not been consistent in their faithfulness to Yahweh — they had often forsaken him by "serving other gods."

This is just one more instance of such backsliding (1 Sam. 8:8). Samuel should, therefore, "warn them, and show them the ways of the king" (v. 9) for whom they asked.

The Ways of the King (8:10-18)

Mishpat is the Hebrew word used here for "ways." It refers to customs and practices that were common among kings in Israel's neighborhood. According to Canaanite kingship ideology, the king was the representative of Baal. He was regarded more or less as a semi-god, and he enjoyed many arbitrary rights over his people. Samuel knew of these, and he warned the Israelites, citing examples to show what sort of consequences such arbitrary powers of the king could have for the people — forced recruitment of young men ("sons") for the service of the king as charioteers, horsemen, runners, commanders, as agricultural laborers, and as industrial workers; forced recruitment of young women ("daughters") as perfumers, cooks, and bakers; forced acquisition of fields (cf. 1 Kgs. 21); and forced levy of tithes on grains and cattle (1 Sam. 8:15-17). In short, the king would take the best of everything from the people (cf. 9:20b; 2 Sam. 11:4ff.), and the people would be treated as slaves (1 Sam. 8:17). If the people still insisted on having a king after this warning, then it is their responsibility. Later, if they should cry to the LORD because of the oppression of their king, the LORD would not listen to them (v. 18).

The heads of governments are given power to serve the people; but those who wield power when they put "self" before "people" exhibit the fact that power corrupts, and that absolute power corrupts absolutely. This is exactly the danger the people are warned about here.

The author is here perhaps writing out of the experiences of people under the reign of Solomon. Solomon tried to live like one of the oriental emperors. He used "a levy of forced labor out of all Israel" (1 Kgs. 5:13; 9:15ff.), and had a big army (10:26ff.) and a large harem (11:1ff.). The people paid the price for Solomon's extravagant living; they were oppressed (1 Kgs. 12:4). The author here draws out the lesson that was learned from the hard experiences under the reign of Solomon.

The Persistence of the People (8:19-22)

The people's desire to "be like all the nations" (1 Sam. 8:20) blinded their reason, and they insisted on having a king. So Yahweh granted their request and commissioned Samuel to "make them a king" (v. 22). So Samuel dismissed the people to go back to their respective places. This tradition continues at 10:17.

Egoistic human pursuits blind reason. People in such pursuits do not see the consequences of their decisions and actions, only to regret them later.

THE SECRET ANOINTING OF SAUL AS KING (9:1–10:16)

We have here the beginning of a completely new tradition. 1 Samuel 9:1 recalls the introduction of heroes in Judges, under the title of their fathers (cf. Judg. 6:11ff.). Thus Saul is here introduced as a charismatic leader, without a special birth narrative. Some scholars think that the birth account in 1 Sam. 1 was originally the birth account of Saul, because the etymological explanation given in 1:20 ("Because I have asked him of the LORD") suits the name Saul and not Samuel.

The account also contains inner tensions. The genealogy of Saul here does not correspond to the one found in 1 Chr. 8–9. According to 1 Sam. 9:6, Saul seems not to have heard of Samuel before; but v. 14 presents Samuel as a widely known figure. According to v. 6, an unnamed city was the residential place of the prophet; but according to v. 12 the prophet had newly arrived there just to offer a sacrifice. In v. 18, Saul asks for the seer's house, though some maidens had already told him that Samuel was only visiting the place in order to offer a sacrifice (vv. 12-13). The account has several characteristics of sagas: the exceptional nature of Saul as a leader (v. 2), the counsel of a servant (cf. Gen. 41:9ff.; 2 Kgs. 5:2ff.), young men meeting maidens going out to draw water (cf. Gen. 24:15ff.; 29:9ff.; Exod. 2:16ff.). It also bears certain characteristics of the call accounts: the call (1 Sam. 9:19-20), Saul's self-abasement (v. 21; cf. Judg. 6:15), signs confirming the call (1 Sam. 10:2ff.; cf. Jer. 1:11ff.), and the assurance of Yahweh's presence (1 Sam. 10:7; cf. Jer. 1:19). Other traditions also seem to have influenced this account: Saul's height (1 Sam. 9:2; cf. 10:23), Saul in Gilgal (10:8; cf. 13:7ff.), and the presence of the Philistine garrison in Gibeah/Geba (10:5; cf. 13:3). All these may be explained by the fact that this account had a long and complicated tradition history. Perhaps it circulated among the people as a saga for many years.

These conflicting accounts regarding the origin of kingship in Israel vouch for the fact that the kingship pattern which was known among Israel's neighbors was adapted in Israel to the faith in Yahweh. One tradition saw the demand for a king as an act of apostasy, as an act of sin on the part of the Israelites. But the fact is that God in his grace works out his purpose of salvation even through mankind's failures. Yahweh accepted the earthly kingship and transformed it into an instrument for the fulfilment of his purpose of salvation. Kings in Israel were not meant to dominate and oppress people; they were called to guide and serve people as shepherds and servants. Whenever the Israelite kings failed in this, they became guilty before God. This image of an ideal king in Israel was slowly ascribed to the messianic King, under whose rule people could live with equity and justice. The true meaning of Kingship in Israel eventually flowers in the title of Jesus, "Christ the King." Jesus is the "Servant King" who "came not to be served but to serve, and to give his life as a ransom for many" (Mark 10:45).

Saul Is Introduced (9:1-2)

Saul is introduced here as a Benjaminite, tall and handsome, suited to be a hero in every respect. The genealogy here differs from that found in 1 Chr. 8. According to 1 Chr. 8:33, Ner is the father of Kish. But here Abiel is said to be the father. According to 1 Sam. 14:50-51, Ner is Saul's uncle and Abiel is Ner's father. This confusion could have arisen in the handing down of the tradition.

The native place of Saul is not mentioned here. Perhaps it was Gibeah. 1 Samuel 11:4 speaks of Gibeah of Saul. The Gibeah of God mentioned in 10:5 may be the same place (see RSV mg).

Kish was "a man of wealth." This shows that class divisions were already emerging. A dependent class of servants was already in existence (9:3). When wealth accumulates in the hands of a few in the form of land, cattle, and the like, it often happens at the cost of the weaker elements in the society. Small farmers and small cattle breeders are compelled at times of crisis to sell their possessions to the rich and thus become dependent on the rich for their survival.

Saul on His Father's Mission (9:3-14)

Saul takes one of the servants and goes in search of his father's asses. When they cannot find them after long searching, the servant advises Saul to consult the seer (9:6). Servants bringing good news to their masters is characteristic of ancient sagas (16:16; 25:14; cf. Gen. 41:10ff.; 2 Kgs. 5:3). The "maidens coming out to draw water" give them a hint as to where Saul could be found (1 Sam. 9:11).

The Hebrew word used here for "servant" is *na'ar.* Perhaps this is different from "slave" (*'ebed*). The fact that the servant sat at meals with Saul at the high place (9:22) indicates that these servants enjoyed some social status in Israelite society, unlike slaves. The "land of Shalishah" and the "land of Shaalim" (v. 4) are not identified. Shalishah is taken to be the Baal-shalishah mentioned in 2 Kgs. 4:42, and Shaalim to be either the Shaalabbin mentioned in Josh. 19:42 or the Shaalbim mentioned in Judg. 1:35; 1 Kgs. 4:9.

Saul was at the point of giving up his search when divine assistance came through this servant. Divine assistance may come when all human efforts fail; this motif runs throughout much Deuteronomic thinking. Bearing gifts when visiting religious leaders (saints or gurus; 1 Sam. 9:7ff.) is a custom widely practiced in oriental countries to this day.

In v. 9 the redactor tries to clarify a point regarding prophecy in Israel. He does not want his readers to identify Samuel as one of the "prophets" among the Canaanites. He wants to point out that prophecy in Israel was different from prophecy among Israel's neighbors, different from the cultic, ecstatic prophecy of the

Canaanites (1 Kgs. 18:26ff.). The redactor holds that Israelite prophets such as Samuel did not belong to the tradition of ecstatic cultic prophecy but to the "seer" tradition of the Israelites. The Hebrew word here is *ro'eh* (also 1 Sam. 9:11, 18-19). Another Hebrew word with much the same meaning is *hozeh* (Amos 7:12). It comes from the verb *hazah,* which means to possess insight into the ways of God. David had such a seer in his court (2 Sam. 24:11). Perhaps with Samuel we have the beginning of an independent tradition of prophecy which distances itself from the ecstatic type; this new tradition develops more towards finding (divining) God's will and proclaiming it to his people. Thus the seer/prophet is the "man of God" who is able to see beyond the horizon of human perception and see things in depth, in the realm of the divine. The *yogis* and the *rishis* in Hinduism are known to be such seers, people who are able to look into the realm of the divine, particularly by realizing their identity with the divine.

Through the words of the "maidens" the author explains the nature of the sacrifice that was to be offered (1 Sam. 9:12-13). Samuel is here represented as a prophet/seer and as a priest and a judge who travels from place to place to bless people's sacrifices and to administer justice. What we have here is a sacrificial feast. Samuel is not involved in its preparation; he is there only to bless the sacrifice. This is perhaps an indication of the superiority of the prophet. He can curse or bless (cf. Num. 22–24). Only after the blessing will the people participate in the meal. Such sacrificial meals are meant to strengthen the people's participation in the divine and in their communion with God. The eucharistic meal of the NT follows in this tradition.

The sacrifice is here offered on "a high place" *(bamah)*. This was an altar of Canaanite heritage, later condemned after the centralization of worship in Israel (2 Kgs. 23:8ff.). This shows us how people's understanding of their own religious heritage can change from time to time depending on changed situations. At a time when the Israelites believed that Yahweh, like Baal, could be worshipped in every place, worship in high places was allowed. But when King Josiah centralized worship in Jerusalem and banned worship in high places, people began to believe that God was not pleased with worship in high places.

Saul's Call for God's Mission (9:15–10:1a)

The LORD has already revealed to Samuel what was to happen. In this sense, Samuel stands in the true tradition of the classical prophets in Israel: "Surely the LORD God does nothing, without revealing his secret to his servants the prophets" (Amos 3:7). The LORD had already chosen Saul, so now he leads Saul to Samuel. Samuel anoints Saul as a "prince" over Israel (1 Sam. 9:16; 10:1; 13:14).

The Hebrew word used here for "prince" is *nagid*. The root *ngd* is only known from its hiphil (causative) form, so a possible meaning for *higgid* is "one who tells forth," perhaps "the word of God" (i.e., a charismatic figure), or one who "professes faith in Yahweh." The root in its substantive form means "counterpart" and as a preposition means "before." If we derive *nagid* from the preposition, it may imply that the term designates one who stands before the LORD. However, as Brown-Driver-Briggs suggests, it may simply mean "one who stands out in front," and so "a ruler" (cf. 2 Sam. 5:2).

The purpose of anointing Saul as prince was to "save my people from the hand of the Philistines; for I have seen the affliction of my people, because their cry has come to me" (1 Sam. 9:16). Kingship in Israel, according to this tradition, met a legitimate need.

The God of biblical revelation is a God who hears the cry of all afflicted people and intervenes in history to liberate them from their distress. The anointing of Saul as *nagid* was one such act. It is faith in this liberating God that gives hope to millions of suffering people in the world today and sustains them in their struggle for liberation.

Saul Meets Samuel (9:18-21)

Even before Saul's asking, Samuel reads Saul's mind and gives him the answer — a real proof to vindicate the authority of a true seer (Dan. 2:2-9). The asses were already found. Saul was then asked to follow Samuel and could not resist the prophet's word (cf. Amos 3:8). He followed without raising a question.

Samuel says that "all that is desirable in Israel" is for Saul and his father's house (1 Sam. 9:20). This is a popular notion about kingship which fits well with the Canaanite conception of kingship, but contradicts what was given as a warning in ch. 8.

Saul understood Samuel's intention in this subtle saying. He knew he was called to take up the kingship in Israel. As a true leader in the tradition of Moses and Gideon, he acknowledged his unworthiness for such a recognition (9:21). Benjamin was the least of the twelve tribes in Israel (Gen. 49:27); moreover, it had a bad reputation among the other Israelites (Judg. 21:18). Among the Benjaminites themselves, Saul says, his family was "the humblest."

Saul at the Feast (9:22-24)

Saul had a special seat of honor at the feast (1 Sam. 9:22), and special portions were served to him (v. 23), an action which ought to have revealed to the "thirty persons" Samuel's intentions. These were probably the elders of the city. David, too, had thirty chiefs (2 Sam. 23:13). Samuel seems to have planned every detail beforehand (1 Sam. 9:23).

Saul is Anointed (9:25–10:1a)

As Saul and his servant prepare to return home, Samuel asks Saul to stay behind for a while that he may make known to him the word of God (9:27). Then Samuel secretly anoints Saul and reveals to him the LORD's purpose in anointing him (10:1a).

The Signs and Their Fulfilment (10:1b-13)

As a proof of all that has been said and done, Samuel gives to Saul three signs; all these signs are later fulfilled. It is possible that all the three places where these signs should happen were places of cultic importance. The first is Rachel's tomb (10:2). According to Jer. 31:15, as the captive Israelites marched northward from Jerusalem on their way to Babylon, Rachel wept for her children, Joseph and Benjamin, as they passed her tomb. The contrast here may be that Rachel is happy now, centuries before the Babylonian exile, as Saul the Benjaminite passes that way as the newly appointed king over Israel. So Rachel brings him the good news that the asses have been found. The second place is the oak of Tabor (1 Sam. 10:3). This was possibly a cultic tree like the oaks of Mamre in Gen. 18:1 (cf. 1 Sam. 14:2). Most trees in Palestine are deciduous, shedding their leaves annually. However, the holm oak is evergreen and never seems to "die," so in early centuries a god was thought to inhabit it. The third place is Gibeath-elohim, which means "the hill of God" (10:5). As the name suggests, this too should have been a cultic place. The band of prophets were probably coming from the high place on this hill. The giving of food would suggest that the men recognized Saul as their superior.

The "band of prophets" (vv. 5-6) mentioned here are the ecstatic prophets belonging to prophetic guilds. These were the cultic prophets who worked themselves into ecstasy at the inducement of music and dance (cf. 19:20ff.; 1 Kgs. 18:26ff.). In this state of ecstasy, it was believed, they were possessed by the spirit of the deity they worshipped (cf. 1 Sam. 10:10), and whatever they uttered in such a state would be taken to be the words of that deity.

The same phenomenon of ecstatic prophecy is still known and practiced in many places in Asia, in India in particular. In Madurai in South India is an ancient village temple called Pandi Koil. If one visits this temple on Fridays one will be able to see even today how ordinary people coming to worship can be infected by ecstasy and the spirit of prophecy.

The three signs, then, are the proof Saul needs to know that he has been appointed by the LORD as prince over Israel, so that he has the authority to do whatever he is moved to do and that God is with him (v. 7). Samuel's promise that "the Spirit of the LORD will come mightily" upon him and that Saul shall "be turned into another man" (v. 6) was fulfilled. Saul was a charismatic leader endowed with the gift of the Spirit of God.

But the commandment in v. 8 to wait till Samuel returned contradicts what is said in v. 7. Verse 8 does not belong to this place. It is part of the tradition given in 13:7b-15a. A later redactor could have put it here trying to find a link between these two accounts.

In 10:9, the fulfilment of all the signs is summarized when it is said, "God gave him another heart." This apparently happened after "the spirit of God came mightily upon him" (v. 10). Later, when Saul's kingship was rejected, the spirit left him (16:14), but it came upon David (v. 13). This shows that the Israelite kingship was originally meant to be a charismatic kingship and not a hereditary monarchy as it later turned out to be. The "heart," according to Israelite psychology, was the seat of all thinking, feeling, and emotions.

1 Samuel 10:10-13 etiologically explains the origin of the proverb, "Is Saul also among the prophets?" This probably was an independent tradition, as is evident from 19:24 where the proverb is placed in another context. Perhaps the paradoxical nature in Saul gave rise to this proverb. In the book of Samuel, Saul is presented at one time as a cowardly man who could not face people (10:22) and at another time as a man of great valor (11:5ff.). Neither of these reveals the nature of an ecstatic prophet.

After finishing prophesying, Saul is said to have gone to "the high place" (10:13). It is not said to which place he went. Probably it was the one in Gibeah (LXX reads Gibeah). However, most scholars read here "he came back to his house," reading Heb. *habbayetah* ("to the house") instead of *habbamah* ("to the high place") (see *Biblia Hebraica*).

A servant of God, when called to serve his people, is thereupon endowed with the spirit of God, in order that he or she may carry out the will of God: ". . . no one comprehends the thoughts of God except the Spirit of God. Now we have received not the spirit of the world, but the spirit which is from God . . ." (1 Cor. 2:11-12).

Saul Meets His Uncle (10:14-16)

Saul tells his uncle only what Samuel had told him about the asses, "but about the matter of the kingdom . . . he did not tell him anything." This probably is an independent tradition from a redactor who wanted to heighten the secrecy of God's revelation to Saul.

SAUL'S ELECTION BY LOT (10:17-27)

In 1 Sam. 10:18-19 the account picks up the anti-kingship tradition left in 8:22. Samuel hearkens to the voice of the people, as per Yahweh's instruction (8:7, 9, 22) and assembles the Israelites at Mizpah for the task of electing a king.

The early tradition is interrupted in order to provide room for Saul's election by lot. An election by lot after anointment is not only unnecessary, but also would be sacrilegious. This means that originally both belonged to two different traditions. Here Saul is mentioned by the title "king" *(melek)*, whereas in the early tradition he is mentioned only as a "prince" *(nagid)*. This points to the fact that the present tradition is late, coming from a period when the early *nagid* had become firmly established as *melek*.

Internal tensions are also found in this late tradition. 1 Samuel 8:4 speaks of "elders of Israel," whereas 8:7, 10; 10:17 speak of "the people" and 8:22 mentions "men of Israel." In 8:4 Ramah is given as the meeting place, whereas 10:17 mentions Mizpah. Ramah and Mizpah may have been close together so that they could almost be identified. Thus in Josh. 13:26 we come across a place Ramath-mizpeh. These differences may be due to different phases in the development of the tradition.

Saul Is Elected (10:20-24)

Saul was elected through the process of casting lots, most likely using Urim and Thummim (cf. 1 Sam. 14:41). It was a process of elimination — first of the tribes, then of the clans, and then of the families. The lot could give only a "yes" or a "no" answer. How it could give a detail such as "Behold, he has hidden himself among the baggage" (10:22) is not clear. It is possible that this is a late addition intended to underline the mysterious way in which God works. According to this author, Saul was by nature a shy, cowardly man who could not face people, and that was why he hid behind the baggage. The skepticism expressed by some "worthless fellows" about Saul's ability to save the people (v. 27) was also intended to strengthen this impression. But if God chooses such a person, God turns that person into a hero, an effective instrument in God's hand to bring salvation to his people (cf. 11:12; 16:1-13). We are here reminded of Paul's words in 2 Cor. 4:7: "But we have this treasure in earthen vessels, to show that the transcendent power belongs to God and not to us" (cf. 1 Cor. 1:27-28).

The Matrites (1 Sam. 10:21) were possibly a clan of Benjamin to which Kish's family belonged. In physical stature Saul had all the qualities of a hero (v. 24; cf. 9:2). The author apparently wants to tell the reader that Saul's inward shyness and cowardice would be overcome by the gift of the spirit of God (cf. 11:6). "Long live the king" were the words of acclamation and salutation to a king, used by the Israelites and also, quite likely, by their neighbors. The same has gone into all royal traditions right up to modern times. It is an invocation of God's protection and blessing upon the king.

The Constitution for the Kingship (10:25a)

Samuel wrote "the rights and duties of the kingship . . . and laid it up before the LORD." The institution of the kingship is here placed in the context of a covenant between the LORD and the people. The terms of the covenant, the constitution of the kingship, are written in a book and kept in the temple (before the LORD), thereby following the covenant-making tradition in Israel. It is not said what "the rights and duties of the kingship" were. Deut. 17:14-20 probably gives some indication as to what they could have been.

Samuel is now ready to hand over the administration to the newly elected king, Saul. This tradition is further continued in 1 Sam. 12, where we have Samuel's farewell speech.

"How Can This Man Save Us?" (10:25b-27)

This section seems to come from a harmonizing redactor who wanted to link the preceding section to ch. 11, where Saul is still presented as a civilian. The heroic adventures of Saul in ch. 11 are given as an answer to the question raised by "some worthless fellows": "How can this man save us?" It is recalled again in 11:12.

Saul returned to "his home at Gibeah," and "men of valor" went with him to be his warriors. How this was possible at this stage when there was no infrastructure to support such an army gathered in one place is not clear. Apparently people brought to the king "presents" (10:27), and that was the source of income for Saul, at least during his early period. The "worthless fellows," who questioned Saul's competence to be king, did not bring gifts. Nevertheless, Saul "held his peace," which was a sign of maturity and leadership.

SAUL'S VICTORY OVER THE AMMONITES AND THE RENEWAL OF THE KINGDOM (11:1-15)

The early source which was interrupted in 10:16 is resumed here. But ch. 11 in itself is not from a single hand. Verses 1-11 seem to be an independent account in the tradition of the judges, and Saul is here presented as a judge/savior like Jephthah or Samson (v. 6; cf. Judg. 11:29; 13:25). Here Samuel plays no active role, except that his name is put into Saul's mouth once (1 Sam. 11:7). The enemies in the earlier and later accounts are the Philistines, but here the enemies are the Ammonites. This was probably part of a Saul tradition dealing with Saul's adventures. The redactor fits it into his account here to show his readers that what Samuel promised to Saul in 10:7 has come true. Saul, as a true leader, plans and executes the attack against the Ammonites.

The Ammonites were one of the neighbors of Israel, living in a relatively fertile but limited area across the Jordan. They seem to have had land disputes with Israel (Judg. 10:9), for there was constant tension between Israel and the Ammonites (2 Sam. 11:1; 12:26). Unlike the Philistines, the Ammonites were a Semitic people, closely related to the Israelites. This affinity was explained by their common origin in the Lot saga (Gen. 19:30ff.). Unlike the Israelites, the Ammonites already had a king and were constituted as a nation. They were therefore militarily stronger and could pose a constant threat to the Israelites. In a similar attack from the Ammonites earlier on, Jephthah the Gileadite had saved Israel (Judg. 10:17ff.).

Nahash was the king of the Ammonites (cf. 2 Sam. 10:1-2).

The name means "serpent" (as also in Sanskrit). Perhaps the Ammonites worshipped a snake-god, as was widely practiced in the ancient Orient.

The people of Jabesh-gilead pleaded to Nahash to make a vassal treaty with them, as a sign of their conditional surrender. This points to the loose structure of the Israelite tribes at this time, where every tribe was left to take care of its own affairs, except when matters went beyond their control. Nahash rejected the offer and ridiculed the Jabeshites with the threat that he would pluck out one of the eyes of every one of the people in order to insult Israel as a whole. That would prove that in the whole of Israel there was no one to exercise his right of *go'el* ("redeemer") to deliver their kin in Jabesh. Nahash's intention was more to insult Israel than to have control over the place. Captives of war were blinded to humiliate the enemy; this act was practiced by many in ancient times (cf. Judg. 16:21; 2 Kgs. 25:7).

The Jabeshites ask Nahash for "seven days" respite in order to find if anyone from Israel could exercise his right of *go'el* and thus save them. The historicity of this event is doubtful. It is strange that any Israelite would make such a request to Nahash when he was not prepared even to accept their surrender offer. The mystic number seven is here introduced to indicate a complete period of preparation for the holy war (cf. 1 Sam. 6:1). The fact that the messengers came to "Gibeah of Saul" (11:4) indicates that this account belonged originally to the legends around Saul. When the messengers brought the news, "all the people wept aloud." This was perhaps a communal mourning.

Saul Takes Up the Challenge (11:5-6)

That the Jabeshites had some special relationship with the Benjaminites is suggested by the account in Judg. 21:11ff. That would be the reason why the message was first sent to the Benjaminites. Saul was "coming from the field behind the oxen." Kish, being a man of wealth (1 Sam. 9:1), could have possessed many fields. This suggests that the nomadic Israelites had by this time adapted to settled agricultural life to a large extent. It is possible that a "call" motif is hidden in the phrase "behind the oxen." One who led the oxen was called to lead God's people; one who shepherded the sheep was called to shepherd God's people; those who were fishermen were called to be "fishers of men" (Mark 1:17).

On hearing the threat of Nahash, "the spirit of God came mightily upon Saul," an indication that the LORD had indeed appointed Saul to be the savior of the people (cf. Judg. 11:29). That Saul's righteous "anger was greatly kindled" means that Saul was stirred to act against the Ammonite oppression and to deliver the people.

"Where the Spirit of the Lord is, there is freedom (liberation)" (2 Cor. 3:17). The Church is the body of Christ in which the Spirit of God is believed to be active. As the bearer of this Spirit of freedom, how does the Church respond to the cries of oppression and exploitation all over the world today? Is its righteous anger kindled against the forces of oppression and exploitation today? The oppressed in the world are looking to the Church with great hope for the liberation of the Spirit in Jesus Christ.

The Preparation and the Attack (11:7-11)

Through the symbolic act of sending a piece of oxen meat Saul drives home the message to the people of Israel (1 Sam. 11:7). It is said that "the dread of the LORD fell upon the people." This united the people "as one man." The "dread of the LORD" is an important element of the holy war motif (see above on 4:6-8). Saul's social status as a man of wealth and his imposing physical stature could have given him a social standing which made the people take his words seriously. For the author, however, all these were the workings of the Spirit of God. The figures in 11:8 are exaggerated as usual, perhaps to show the greatness of Saul's obedient action.

The message of deliverance was sent to the people of Jabesh (v. 9). The men of Jabesh then sent word to Nahash that they would hand themselves over the next day (v. 10). Saul, as an experienced military strategist, divided his people "in three companies" and began the attack on the Ammonites "in the morning watch," at a time when the enemy was the least prepared. He "cut down the Ammonites until the heat of the day" (v. 11). Perhaps the fighting took place in a desert area and the unprepared enemy could not stand the midday heat, and so were scattered.

The Vindication of Saul's Kingship (11:12-15)

The author of the earlier source takes a story from the "Saul sagas" and connects it with his main story. It is only at this stage that Samuel appears. Verse 12 picks up from 10:27. Those who saw Saul's victory over the Ammonites were convinced that Saul was truly elected as king over Israel and wanted to put to death those who had questioned his election (11:12). It is surprising that, instead of Samuel, Saul responds. This, too, shows that Samuel's name has been secondarily added at this point.

As a good leader, Saul showed his magnanimity and ruled out any act of vengeance on anyone that day (v. 13). The redactor seems to be aware of Saul's secret anointing in Mizpah (10:1-2). In order to reconcile it with Saul's public appointment in Gilgal, he talks of the renewal of the kingdom in Gilgal (11:14).

Verse 15 seems to be the original ending of the account, following immediately after v. 11. Samuel does not appear here. It was the people who made Saul king in Gilgal and offered a sacrifice of "peace offerings." Here again, the account follows the pattern in the book of Judges. When Gideon won the victory over the Midianites the people offered to make Gideon king, but Gideon rejected that offer. In a similar way, when Saul was victorious over the Ammonites the people offered to make Saul king, and Saul accepted that offer.

SAMUEL SPEAKS TO THE PEOPLE (12:1-25)

This chapter is of complex composition. 1 Samuel 12:1-5 alone can be considered a farewell speech; vv. 6-25 bear the characteristics of prophetic admonition. Verses 1-5 present Samuel as a judge, but vv. 6-25 present him more as a prophet. The only thing that connects these two sections is the reference to "witness." "The LORD is witness" in v. 6 picks up from the words "he is witness" in v. 5. We note that the words "is witness" are missing in the Hebrew of v. 6, and without these words the narrative runs smoothly and makes good sense. We may therefore gather that later versions bring together here two originally independent accounts, linking them by inserting the words "is witness" in v. 6.

Verses 1-5 are a proper conclusion to ch. 11, where Samuel resigns from his responsibility as judge and Saul is openly acclaimed as king. 1 Samuel 12:6-25 picks up the anti-kingship theme and gives a prophetic admonition against Israel's conduct in history, starting from the days in Egypt up to the present times.

Samuel the Judge Bids Farewell (12:1-5)

It is interesting to note that Samuel, the leader of a cultic community, defends his integrity by citing his just dealings in that society, his day-to-day dealings with people. There is no mention of a cultic-ritual piety. This prophetic trend we find strongly established in the Bible, running throughout the OT and leading to the teachings of Jesus Christ in the NT. The religion of the Bible is a down-to-earth religion; it speaks about mundane things of the world here and now — stealing, defrauding, oppression, bribery, and corruption, and it does not speak about other-worldly eschatological things alone (cf. Isa. 1:12-17; 58:1ff.; Amos 4:4ff.; 5:10ff.; Mic. 6:6-8). Jesus also stands in this tradition when he talks about the coming of his kingdom. The this-worldly character of Jesus' teachings should not be spiritualized and watered down (cf. Matt. 25:31ff.; Mark 10:42-45; Luke 4:18-21). The kingdom of God which Jesus proclaimed begins here and now, and people are called to fulfil the righteousness of the kingdom.

Samuel's words, "I have hearkened to your voice" (1 Sam. 12:1), recall 8:7, 9, 22 and show that the author is aware of the events narrated in ch. 8. On "walking before" people (12:2), see above on 8:3. Saul as king has now taken the place of Samuel. The people acknowledge Samuel's integrity. He is portrayed here as a righteous judge (12:4). The social evils that were common in secular administration in those days are listed here — stealing (of cattle), cheating (cf. Amos 8:5-6), oppression (cf. Amos 5:11; 8:4), corruption (bribery), false witness (perversion of justice). Bribery blinds the eyes of justice. The same evils continue in our modern society as well, in spite of other great advances the human race has made.

Samuel's integrity is vindicated before the people, and Samuel invokes "the LORD" and "his anointed" as witnesses (1 Sam. 12:5). "His anointed" is a designation for the king. This recalls Saul's secret anointment in 10:1ff.

Samuel's Admonition to the People (12:6-25)

Reference to Israel's past history has already been made in 8:8 and 10:18, but here it is mentioned in detail. Samuel reminds the people "concerning all the saving deeds of the LORD" in history (12:7). The scheme of history found in Judg. 2:11-19 is also found here — deliverance by the LORD, apostasy of the people, punishment in the hands of the enemies, and the people's cry in suffering followed by the LORD's response. The reference to Gideon by the name Jerubbaal and the mention of the unknown judge Bedan in the MT of 1 Sam. 12:11 indicate that we have here an independent tradition. The account probably comes from a Deuteronomistic redactor.

Samuel recalls here God's deliverance of Israel from the bondage in Egypt (v. 8); Israel's apostasy and the consequent punishment at the hands of the Canaanites, Philistines, and Moabites (v. 9); Israel's cry of repentance and the LORD's deliverance through Jerubbaal (Gideon, Judg. 6–8); Bedan (RSV, following Greek and Syriac manuscripts, reads Barak; Judg. 4–5); Jephthah (Judg. 10–11); and Samuel (1 Sam. 12:11). At this point the demand for a king is introduced, obviously as an act of apostasy fitting into the above Deuteronomistic scheme of history. The Ammonite attack under Nahash is seen as the immediate occasion for the demand for a king (vv. 12-13), though in the other accounts the Philistine menace was seen as the main reason for the demand of a king.

"All the saving deeds of the LORD" in v. 7 literally means "all righteousness of Yahweh" according to the Hebrew text. Hebrew *tsedaqah* is the word used for "righteousness"; it comes from a root *ts-d-q*, which means "to be firm or strong." Thus *tsedaqah* means to be firm in observing the accepted norms of a relationship. Here it refers to the covenant relationship between the LORD and his people. The LORD remains faithful in his relationship to his people, even when they go away from him. This is his righteous-ness. Yahweh's saving deeds in history are thus part of his acts of righteousness. Thus "righteousness" and *hesed* ("covenant love") are related concepts.

In response to their demand, God had given Israel a king (vv. 12-13). Though the king is given in displeasure, the LORD can still use him, provided he and the people follow the LORD faith-fully. This means fearing the LORD and serving him and hearkening to his voice and not rebelling against his commandments (v. 14). If Israel rebels against his commandments, then the LORD will be against the people and the king (v. 15). The whole nation must bear responsibility for the king's foolish lead.

A Sign from the Lord (12:16-18)

Samuel gives the people a sign to authenticate all that he said as the word of God. Wheat harvest is normally a dry season in Israel; hardly any rain could be expected. Having rain and thunder in such a season is therefore a miracle from the LORD. Making things happen against the law of nature is characteristic of OT miracles (cf. Judg. 6:36-40).

The demand for a king is again singled out and underlined as the climax of Israel's history of apostasy. The fact that "the LORD sent thunder and rain" (1 Sam. 12:18) is also meant to be a warning against "vain things" (v. 21), obviously a reference to the idols of the Canaanite fertility cult. One reason why the Israelites turned towards the Canaanite fertility deities, Baals and Ashtaroths (see above on 7:3-4), was that the people believed that these fertility deities were responsible for rain, which was very much needed for agriculture (cf. Hos. 2:8ff.).

Samuel's Call for Faithful Following (12:19-25)

The people admit their mistake and see that their demand for a king was an evil thing before the LORD. They plead Samuel to intercede for them (1 Sam. 12:19). Repentance brings reconcil-iation. Samuel comforts the people with the words "fear not" (v. 20), which normally introduce oracles of salvation (cf. 4:20).

Now the message for the people is "do not turn aside from
following the LORD, but serve the LORD with all your heart"
(v. 20). It means turning away from "vain things" which were the
cause for Israel's sins (v. 21). In Hebrew the word used here for
"vain things" is *tohu,* the same word used in Gen. 1:2 to indicate
the state of chaos, the situation before God created the cosmos,
the world of order.

It has always been a temptation for mankind in history to drift
away from God and to follow other forces such as wealth, science,
and technology in the hope that they would ultimately profit them
and save them. But the Bible repeatedly warns mankind against
the fallacy of such a hope and reiterates that by being away from
God mankind is doomed to chaos and self-destruction.

As a priest/prophet Samuel has a duty to instruct the people
"in the good and the right way" and "to pray" for them (1 Sam.
12:23). Not to do that would be a sin on his part. As for the
people, they should "fear the LORD, and serve him faithfully"
(v. 24).

Verse 25 is an oracle of doom, warning against any false hope.
If the people "still do wickedly," they and their king will be "swept
away." This reminds us of Amos's oracle of doom. The verse stands
independently. It was perhaps added later.

V. THE RISE AND FALL OF SAUL AS KING

1 Samuel 13:1–15:35

"To Obey Is Better than Sacrifice"

1 Samuel 13–14 belongs to that tradition which deals with Saul and Jonathan. Here Samuel does not play a major role except in 13:8-15. Chapter 15 comes from another tradition which deals with Saul and Samuel. The passages are placed side by side because both deal with the common theme of the rejection of Saul's kingship, though they give different reasons. 1 Samuel 13:10-15 gives Saul's disobedience in terms of his failure to wait for Samuel as the reason, whereas ch. 15 explains it in terms of Saul's failure in fulfilling Samuel's command regarding the *herem*, the law on total destruction (see below on 15:3) of the Amalekites.

In chs. 13–14 we have a basic Saul-Jonathan tradition which had undergone changes by the hand of redactors in the course of history. There are certain internal tensions. 1 Samuel 13:2 says that Jonathan was at Gibeah; v. 3 says that he defeated the Philistines at Geba. According to v. 3, Jonathan was responsible for the defeat of the Philistines, whereas according to v. 4 Saul was responsible for the Philistine defeat. But the two chapters stand together in that they both introduce the new character Jonathan.

1 Samuel 13:8-15a picks up what was said in 10:8, and it appears to be an interpolation in this context. The narrative flows smoothly from 13:7 to v. 15b, whereas in v. 14 the conversation between Saul and Samuel ends rather abruptly. After Samuel's announcement of Saul's rejection, one would normally expect Saul's repentance and plea for forgiveness, as

is the case in 15:24ff. Moreover, the rest of the account in chs. 13–14 does not reveal that Saul had already lost the favor of the LORD. Saul is here presented as a zealous follower of the LORD (cf. 14:41ff.).

1 Samuel 14:47ff. winds up Saul's biographical account, and chs. 16–31 deal with Saul's downfall and David's rise. Chapter 15 stands as a link between these sections. It prepares the ground for the introduction of David. We do not find here much reflecting Deuteronomistic ideas. Here kingship is not rejected; Saul alone is rejected. Samuel is presented here in the line of the later prophets, not as a judge. The subject matter of the chapter is the law of *herem,* about which nothing was mentioned earlier, though wars with Philistines and Ammonites were mentioned. This, too, confirms that an independent tradition lies behind ch. 15.

WAR WITH THE PHILISTINES (13:1-23)

Saul's Reign (13:1)

Here we have an editorial insertion like those which have been supplied for other Israelite kings (cf. 14:21). But the numbers here are missing. Evidently the Deuteronomistic redactor was unwilling to insert them here, because for him Saul's kingship was invalid, so that the judgeship of Samuel was followed rather by the reign of David. Many commentators have suggested changing the "two" into "twenty," but with no justification; unlike English, in Hebrew "two" and "twenty" have no similarity, so we cannot assume that twenty was mistaken for two. An exact period for Saul's reign is difficult to fix. In the beginning he was only the leader of the Benjaminite tribe, but slowly his influence became stronger until it spread over the whole people of Israel. The unification of the people of Israel was actually the result of Saul's reign and not its precondition. That Saul's reign had a lasting impact is underscored by the fact that later on there was an attempt to confirm his dynasty (2 Sam. 2:9ff.). David tried to legitimize his kingship by marrying Saul's daughter Michal (cf. 2 Sam. 3:12ff.).

Initial Victory (13:2-4)

It is possible that here Jonathan's victory is credited to Saul. The leader gets the credit for the victory of his subordinates. Michmash is about 3 km. (2 mi.) NE of Geba. It was an area of Philistine influence (1 Sam. 13:5, 16; 14:4). Gibeah of Benjamin is perhaps the same as Gibeath-elohim in 10:5 and Gibeah of Saul in 11:4, the native place of Saul. Geba is said to be about 5 km. (3 mi.) NE of Gibeah.

It is strange that in 13:3 Saul addresses the Israelites, saying, "Let the Hebrews hear." Except for here, the Israelites never call themselves "Hebrew" except when introducing themselves to foreign authorities (see above on 4:6). It is possible that Saul's call was addressed to all who were socially discriminated against and other oppressed groups, of whom Israel was only a part. Such groups are found in 14:21.

Countermeasures by the Philistines (13:5-7)

Seeing that the Israelites defeated their garrison in Geba, the Philistines tighten their security measures and strengthen their offense so that "the men of Israel saw that they were in straits" (13:6). They were seeking shelters in which to hide from the Philistines. According to v. 2 Saul was in Michmash, but here he is said to be "still at Gilgal" (v. 7). Beth-aven (v. 5; cf. 14:23) is taken to be another name for Beth-horen (Josh. 18:13-14) near Ai. They so lacked faith that they abandoned the land which God had given them.

Saul's Controversy with Samuel (13:8-15)

This section continues the tradition from 1 Sam. 10:8, where Samuel asked Saul to wait for seven days. The assumption here is that Saul was not able to hit back at the Philistines because of Samuel's command to wait. But 13:3-4 shows that Saul had already acted independently. This confirms the secondary nature of vv. 8-15 in the present context.

According to this account Saul waited for seven days, but

Samuel failed to turn up. Accordingly the people who gathered around Saul for defense against the Philistines were beginning to leave, and Saul was under pressure to take defense initiatives. As a God-fearing man, he wanted to "entreat the favor of the LORD" (v. 12) before going to war. So he offered sacrifice — a legitimate response according to our thinking. However, according to Samuel Saul had acted foolishly, because he was not an ordained priest and had no right to offer sacrifice. Had he just (blindly) obeyed Samuel's command to wait, despite Samuel's failure to turn up at the appointed time, the LORD would have established Saul's kingdom (v. 13). But now because Saul did not keep to that commandment of the LORD, the LORD rejected him (v. 14).

The real king of Israel was Yahweh. According to v. 15b and 14:2, Saul had with him "six hundred men," but according to 13:2 Saul chose "three thousand men of Israel." Perhaps the figure six hundred stems from the influence of the Davidic traditions (cf. 23:13; 27:2; 30:9; see below on 23:13).

This account, together with several such instances in the OT, shows that at this stage of Israel's history the faith response in Israelite religion lacked in rational and moral content. God's words (commandments), whether they are rationally acceptable (explainable) or not, whether they sound moral or amoral (e.g., the laws regarding the *herem*), must be obeyed. Obedience was thus regarded as the highest virtue in religion (cf. 15:22ff.). Such a blind obedience was reckoned to be righteousness in Abraham's case (cf. Gen. 15:6). Abraham was prepared to sacrifice his only son Isaac, even though he could not understand or explain how he was to have descendants to inherit the Promised Land if Isaac were to be sacrificed. Yet God made use of such primitive conceptions and did not expect more of his covenant people at that stage in their history.

Much of such primitive conceptions about God and his dealings has undergone change in the ongoing biblical revelation. Still, many who hold hierarchical positions in the Church today are influenced by this primitive conception of piety and demand from their subordinates uncritical obedience as the highest virtue.

Philistine Raiders on the March (13:16-18)

The details here differ from what was said in 1 Sam. 13:2ff. Here both Saul and Jonathan are said to be in one place and the number of men with them are only six hundred. The Philistines, on the other hand, strengthen their position in Michmash. Dividing themselves into three companies of raiders, they move off in three directions — towards the north, west, and east — obviously to plunder Israelite territories and to occupy strategic positions.

In v. 18, "the border" means the boundary between Ephraim and Benjamin. Ophrah (v. 17) is identified with modern et-Taiyibeh, approximately 10 km. (6 mi.) N of Michmash. According to Josh. 18:23 it belonged to Benjamin. However, according to Judges Ophrah belonged to Manasseh and was the birthplace of Gideon (Judg. 6:11, 24; 8:27, 32). "The land of Shual" is not known for certain; perhaps it refers to "the land of Shaalim" mentioned in 1 Sam. 9:4. Beth-horon (13:18) is identified with Beit 'Ur, about 19 km. (12 mi.) W of Michmash. The name means "the house of Horon." Perhaps Horon was the name of a Canaanite god. The valley of Zeboim has not been identified (cf. Neh. 11:34).

Cultural Superiority of the Philistines (13:19-23)

The Philistines were technologically advanced, and the Israelites were totally dependent on them for all their metal implements, agricultural tools as well as weapons of war. In wartime such as this, the Philistines may have withdrawn their craftsmen from the territories of the Israelites or strictly ordered them not to make tools and weapons for the Israelites. This would explain the improvised nature of the Israelite army. It is said that only Saul and Jonathan had swords (1 Sam. 13:22). The historical credibility of this is questionable, because at least out of the spoils of their earlier wars the Israelites could have acquired some weapons. Later accounts also show no evidence of the scarcity of swords among the Israelites (cf. 14:20). The purpose of the author in stressing the helplessness of Israel is to show that "nothing can hinder the LORD from saving by many or by few" (14:6), with swords or without swords.

A modern analogy to this is found in the relationship between the technologically advanced First World countries and the less developed Third World countries. The rich countries of the North and the West literally blackmail the weaker countries because of their superiority in technology and armaments. But our account says that God stands on the side of the weaker and the less-developed people of this world.

A pim (13:21) is two thirds of a shekel. Verse 23 is generally taken to be the continuation of vv. 15b-18; but some take it to be a verse from the redactor for the purpose of leading into ch. 14.

VICTORY THROUGH JONATHAN AND SAUL'S OATH (14:1-46)

Again we have an independent account of Saul's campaign against the Philistines. As in ch. 13, here also Jonathan is in the forefront. Saul is presented here as a cultic person who takes the utmost care for the observance of the cultic rules. However, God acts outside the cult through Jonathan. Such a notion is strange in Israel, and it is difficult to localize it. Some scholars think that it could have arisen from the successful era of the Omride dynasty in the northern kingdom around the 9th cent. (Fritz Stolz, *Das erste und zweite Buch Samuel,* 90). It is possible that we have in the chapter different independent traditions brought together through several redactions.

Victory through Jonathan (14:1-23)

Until the Philistine defeat was wrought by the LORD through Jonathan, Saul played a passive role. He did not know what was happening. Only at the point of consolidating the victory over the enemy did Saul and his men and also the Ephraimites join the battle. The writer sees the whole campaign as a holy war. The holy war motif that "nothing can hinder the LORD from saving by many or by few" (14:6) is at the center of the account. The "great panic" and the accompanying earthquake (v. 15) also belong to the holy war motif (cf. 5:6ff.; 7:10).

14:1-3   While Jonathan and his armor-bearer left for the Philistine garrison, Saul was staying in the outskirts of Gibeah, under "the pomegranate tree" (14:2). Perhaps this was a cultic tree (cf. 10:3; 22:6) and Saul was waiting for an oracle. On "six hundred men," see above on 13:15b. Migron is not known. G. B. Caird suggests a small emendation and derives it from Heb. *goren*, reading then "which is in the threshing floor" (*IB* 2:950). A pomegranate tree at a threshing floor is proper for a cultic center (see above on 6:14).

The details of the Priestly genealogy are given mainly to introduce the ephod, which Saul needed for receiving an oracle from the LORD (14:3). Ahijah was bearing the ephod, and his priesthood is here traced back to Eli. Ahijah is said to be the son of Ahitub, the brother of Ichabod, the son of Phinehas. The account of Ichabod's birth in 4:19-21 gives no indication that Ichabod had a brother. The mention of a brother's name in a genealogy is also unusual. Ahitub's grandson Abiathar was David's priest. Thus it is hardly credible that Ahitub was Ichabod's brother. "Wearing an ephod" should be read as "bearing an ephod." It is not the priestly dress but a cultic object for receiving oracles that is referred to here (see Introduction).

14:4-5   Jonathan and his armor-bearer go through a straight pass, between the hills Bozez and Seneh. Bozez means "shiny," and Seneh means "thorny." Perhaps Bozez was exposed to the sun and was barren because of the heat, whereas Seneh had some shade and thus had some thorny bush on it. Neither place has been identified.

14:6-10   Jonathan is presented here as a charismatic leader who puts his trust in the LORD. He acknowledges that it is Yahweh who is fighting on their behalf (14:6). To make sure of the will of the LORD, both Jonathan and his armor-bearer agree on a strategy. When they approach the Philistines, if the Philistines were to respond arrogantly and say "Come up to us," that would be the sign that the LORD had handed over the Philistines to them (cf. 17:44). But if the Philistines should say, "Wait until we come to you," then that would be a sign that the LORD did not want them to attack the Philistines.

14:11-15   As agreed, Jonathan and his armor-bearer show themselves to the Philistines, and the Philistines in an insulting manner call upon them to come forward; thereby the two know that the LORD has handed the Philistines over to them. Both then crawl into the Philistine camp and take the Philistines by surprise. Perhaps the Philistines thought that both men had gone away after hearing their insulting response and so were not prepared for an attack. Jonathan and his armor-bearer kill twenty men in the "first slaughter" (14:14). This implies that there were several such campaigns by Jonathan. The number of people killed is not exaggerated, because the focus here is not so much on the number of people killed but on the "very great panic" (v. 15) it caused among the Philistines. Verse 15 is taken to be a redactional interpolation. According to this redactor, the war is the war of the LORD and the initiative taken by Jonathan has been taken over by the LORD, who leads his people to victory.

Whether human initiatives have any place in the fulfilment of God's purpose in the world is a question often raised in the context of Reformation theology today. However, the Bible has enough examples to show that human response and participation are important in God's work in this world.

14:16-20   Saul's watchman, perhaps standing on a watch tower, sees the confusion in the Philistine camp and brings the news to Saul. Saul guesses that the confusion may have been caused by someone from his people and asks them to count and find out who had gone away. Thus it is discovered that Jonathan and his armor-bearer are absent. Saul asks Ahijah the priest to bring "the ark of God" (v. 18), perhaps to consult the LORD before joining Jonathan in the battle. But before Ahijah could find out the will of God, the "tumult" in the Philistine camp increases (v. 19) and "Saul and all the people who were with him" (v. 20) join in the battle.

In v. 18 it is possible that originally "ephod" stood in place of the "ark of God" (cf. v. 3; see also Introduction). The redactor here seems to know that the ark had been withdrawn from Israel for a period (cf. 6:21; 7:1), and wants the reader to know that at this time it went "with the people of Israel" (14:18). Saul's instruction to the priest to "withdraw your hand" (v. 19) indicates that the oracle-finding ephod must have been a box or a bag in which the Urim and Thummim were kept and shuffled, as we shake dice today. "Confusion" among the enemy (v. 20) is also part of the holy war motif.

14:21-23 The "Hebrews" and the Ephraimites also join Saul and his forces and pursue the fleeing Philistines beyond Beth-aven. On "Hebrews," see above on 4:6. Use of the designation here indicates that it did not refer to the Israelites alone but to several groups of people who may have experienced the same status in society. "Hebrews" seems to be people who were dependent on other richer and stronger communities. Thus the Hebrews mentioned here are people who were dependent on the Philistines. It is natural that such groups are always disgruntled against the stronger groups who oppress and exploit them. When these people saw that the Israelites were winning the battle against their oppressors, they changed sides, joined the Israelites, and fought against the Philistines.

These Hebrews may be compared to the Dalits of India, the Minjungs of Korea, the Burakus of Japan, the Aborginals of Australia, the Blacks of South Africa, and similar groups in other parts of the world today. The God of the biblical revelation is the God of the "Hebrews," the God of oppressed people all over the world.

Likewise the Israelites who were hiding "in the hill country of Ephraim" also joined in the battle (cf. 13:6). 1 Samuel 14:23 is from the redactor. It links what precedes with what follows. That it is the LORD who "delivered Israel that day" — not Saul — is the focus of the whole account.

Saul's Oath (14:24-46)

Verses 31-35 do not belong to this section originally. They reveal no knowledge of Saul's oath of abstinence from eating and interrupt the oath account. Rather, they deal with the matter of eating meat with the blood.

Oath-making, especially in times of crisis such as war, was

common among the Israelites (cf. Judg. 11:30). It was feared that breaking an oath would bring adverse consequences. That is why "the men of Israel were distressed that day" (1 Sam. 14:24).

14:25-28   Jonathan was not aware of the oath; perhaps Saul pronounced it when Jonathan was away in the Philistine camp. Jonathan was informed of the oath only after he had tasted the honey (v. 28). Nevertheless, Jonathan was held guilty of breaking the oath (vv. 36ff.). Behind this may lie the Hebrew understanding of corporate personality. The individual shares in the corporate personality of the community; what he or she does affects the community and vice versa.

14:29-30   Jonathan, as a member of the younger generation, questions the wisdom of Saul in introducing a practice which does not bring much good to the people. To forbid eating at a time of war would make people weak; and that, according to Jonathan, was an unwise thing to do. Jonathan ascribes to this oath the fact that the defeat of the Philistines was only partial (v. 30). Had the oath not been there, the possibility of eating the spoils could have given the people the motivation to inflict greater destruction on the Philistines. This, however, does not agree with the holy war motif, according to which total destruction was demanded. This, as well as the following section on spoils, is secondary in the present context.

14:31-35   The Israelites defeated the Philistines "from Michmash (cf. 13:2, 11) to Aijalon." Because they were "faint" (14:31), they took the cattle of the Philistines as spoil and "ate them with the blood" (v. 32). Saul, as a zealous cultic leader, stops them from doing this and sees to it that they slay the animals on a stone, shed the blood, and only then eat. Saul is said to have built his "first altar" to the LORD (v. 35). This was probably the "great stone" (v. 33) on which the animals were slain.

"Eating meat with the blood" was forbidden because it was believed that blood was "life" (Lev. 17:10-14; Deut. 12:23) and that all life belongs to God. Whether we have here a trace of pantheistic belief as in Vedantic Hinduism — according to which the life of all beings is essentially the same and is the manifestation of the ultimate reality, the Brahman — is a question that needs to be probed further.

14:36-39 Saul wants to pursue further the campaign against the Philistines, and he seeks the counsel of the LORD. However, the LORD gives no answer. Saul immediately realizes that something has gone wrong in Israel, that some sin has been committed.

Obviously the oracle was sought through the device of casting lots (cf. 1 Sam. 14:41; 28:6); but it is not clear how the LORD's silence could be indicated by casting the lot. Perhaps there was a blank dice or a blank side on the dice to indicate that!

14:40-45 Saul seeks God's guidance through Urim and Thummim (14:41) to find out who in Israel committed the sin. Through the usual process of elimination Jonathan is identified as the sinner. Jonathan admits his mistake and offers himself to be punished according to the law.

In early times the event alone was all that mattered; how it happened was not a matter for serious consideration. In later times, however, some lenience was shown on sins committed unwittingly (cf. Num. 15:24). The lenience with which Jonathan is handled here may be due to the fact that he committed the sin unwittingly.

Because of the great victory that Jonathan brought to Israel, the people would not let him die. They "ransomed" him (1 Sam. 14:45). Following the ransom provision for unwitting sin in Num. 15:24, the people may have offered a young bull as a burnt offering with its cereal offering and drink offering, as well as a goat as a sin offering.

14:46 A decisive defeat of the Philistines did not take place. Both the Israelites and the Philistines returned to their respective places. Thus God overruled the follies of humans.

SAUL'S RULE AS KING: A BRIEF SUMMARY
(14:47-52)

This section probably comes from the Deuteronomic historian. It could not have come from the same editor who worked on the late account of the institution of kingship in Israel. According to that author, the Philistine menace had already been brought to an end by Samuel (1 Sam. 7:13), and Saul's reign was invalid.

14:47-48   Israel's enemies listed here are the same as those in the time of David (cf. 2 Sam. 8). About Saul's attack on the Ammonites (1 Sam. 11), the Philistines (chs. 13–14), and the Amalekites (ch. 15) we have reliable information; but we have no information regarding his campaigns against Moab, Edom, and Zobah. Edom and Zobah are far from the area of Israel's military engagements. Saul was more active in the middle of Palestine. Perhaps someone has set both Saul and David as parallel figures in order to stress the continuity of kingship. What Saul began, David completed.

14:49-51   Here is presented information about Saul's family. Saul had three sons (Jonathan, Ishvi, and Malchishua) and two daughters (Merab and Michal). According to 31:2, 6, the Philistines killed the three sons of Saul, whose names are given there as Jonathan, Abinadab, and Malchishua. In 2 Sam. 2:8, Ishbosheth is mentioned as one of the sons. Perhaps Ishbosheth is identical with Ishvi. Whether Saul had a fourth son by the name Abinadab is not clear. We know that one of David's brothers was known as Abinadab (1 Sam. 16:8) and that David's brothers were fighting in Saul's army (17:17ff.). It is therefore possible that Abinadab, David's brother, was one of those slain in the war and, because of his status as king's brother, in later traditions his name came to be associated here. Saul's daughters Merab and Michal are the focus of 18:17ff. Ahinoam (14:50) was perhaps Saul's queen; Saul's concubines are mentioned in 2 Sam. 21:8. Abner was Saul's commander and was the son of Ner, Saul's uncle (cf. 1 Sam. 10:14ff.). Abner plays an important role later in the Succession narrative.

14:52 This verse comes from a redactor. Only one enemy is mentioned here, as against what is said in v. 47. This serves as a link between 14:46 and 16:14.

"When Saul saw any strong man, or any valiant man, he attached him to himself." Saul was obviously building up a regular army (10:26). David's recruitment to "his service" (16:21) was also part of this plan.

WAR AGAINST THE AMALEKITES AND SAUL'S SECOND REJECTION (15:1-35)

It is possible that we have here a historical core, which is placed in a framework of tension between Samuel (representing the old sacral ideology) and Saul (representing the new kingship ideology). Saul swings between the old and the new, and that is his tragedy. Some scholars question the historicity of the core account on the ground that Saul's influence never reached as far south as Judah. Others argue from the fact that David met with a quick response in the south because of Saul's earlier campaigns there. This seems to be more likely.

Amalek was a tribe of Bedouins living south of Judah, listed among the enemies of Israel ever since the time of the Exodus (cf. Exod. 17:14; Num. 14:45; Deut. 25:17-19). Like the other Bedouin tribes, Amalek was a constant threat to the security of Israel (cf. Judg. 7:12). The overthrow of King Agag is mentioned in Balaam's oracle in Num. 24:7. The man who later killed Saul was an Amalekite (2 Sam. 1:8). Judah was immediately exposed to Amalekite threats, and Saul's attack on the Amalekites could have strengthened his influence in the south. But Saul's victory was only limited; the decisive victory was left for David (1 Sam. 30).

Samuel's Instruction regarding the Herem (15:1-3)

Samuel was "sent" to anoint Saul king over Israel (15:1). The idea of "sending" is a prophetic element. Saul is thus commissioned here by God through his prophet for a special task. "Hearken to the words of the LORD" and "thus says the LORD of hosts" both are oracle introduction formulas. The second formula is redundant here. The prophet as the messenger of God speaks on behalf of God. (On "the LORD of hosts," see above on 1:3.) This goes with the demand for *herem*, "total destruction," here. The reason why the Amalekites should be totally destroyed is that they had opposed Israel "on the way, when they came up out of Egypt" (15:2; Exod. 17:8ff.).

Saul is here instructed to "utterly destroy" (1 Sam. 15:3) the Amalekites. What lies behind this is the institution of *herem* ("ban") in Israel, which is grounded on the Israelite understanding of holiness (see above on 6:7). The war that the Israelites fight is the war of Yahweh. As such, the spoils of the war belong to Yahweh and thus become holy. What is thus holy to Yahweh is "ban" to human beings, and so becomes *herem*, as objects to be destroyed utterly. One other practical reason could have been that, when the enemy were utterly destroyed with all their belongings, the Israelites could then be guarded from contamination by their idolatrous religion and culture. This appears to have been the main concern of the Deuteronomic legislation on *herem* when it tried to limit the destruction to human spoils (cf. Deut. 7:2ff.; 20:17-18).

Whatever its origin, *herem* was a primitive religious institution practiced by the Israelites and some of their neighbors. It still finds its echo in the concept of *jihad* in Islam. However, for Christians it appears today as a gruesome primitive religious practice. We marvel at the profound love of God which has used even such practices as part of his overall revelation to lead humankind to the fuller understanding of the salvation which he brings them — that it is wrought forth not by utterly destroying others for the sake of oneself, but by destroying oneself for the sake of others (cf. Isa. 53:4ff.; John 3:16). This should help us to look sympathetically at similar practices found among people of other faiths. In modern times under the guidance of the Holy Spirit we should invoke the law of *herem* against the "principalities" and "powers," against "the unfruitful works of darkness," about which Paul speaks (cf. Eph. 5:11; 6:12). We need *herem* against the forces of death that threaten human life today — greed, corruption, exploitation, manipulation, oppression, injustice, racism, casteism.

Saul Fails in Executing the Herem (15:4-9)

Saul "numbered" the people in preparation for the war (1 Sam. 15:4). Perhaps this numbering itself was considered to be a sin on the part of Saul, as in the case of David who committed a similar sin when he numbered the people (2 Sam. 24:10). It was a sign of mistrust in Yahweh, for Yahweh is capable of "saving by many or by few" (1 Sam. 14:6). The figures here are exaggerated and stand in contrast to those found in 13:2, 15. Saul told the Kenites, who were living in the midst of the Amalekites, to leave so that they might be spared from the total destruction. This was because of the kindness of the Kenites, in contrast to the Amalekites, which they showed to the Israelites on their way from Egypt (15:6). The Kenites also were a nomadic tribe, historically having friendly relationships with Israel and also worshipping Yahweh (cf. Exod. 3; 18:1ff.; Judg. 1:16; 4:11). In the latter two passages, Moses' father-in-law was said to be a Kenite, whereas according to Exodus he was a Midianite. Perhaps the Midianites and the Kenites were in fact the same people. The Kenites, it seems, joined the Israelites in their invasion of Canaan (Judg. 1:16), but later abandoned the settled life and resorted to their old nomadic life; and so they seem to have joined the Amalekites (cf. 1 Sam. 27:10).

Saul defeated the Amalekites from "Havilah as far as Shur" (15:7). These names occur in Gen. 25:18, where they define the territory of the Israelites. Havilah is in Arabia, far from the territory of the Amalekites. It has not been possible to conjecture what the text may have read originally here. Shur means a wall, and refers either to a border city between Egypt and Palestine or to a route marking the border.

Saul took the best of the cattle along with King Agag and destroyed all the rest (1 Sam. 15:8-9). Thus Saul only partially fulfilled the *herem*-commandment. This account is meant to show that Saul followed the LORD only half-heartedly. The LORD calls his servants to love him and to follow him "with all your heart, and with all your soul, and with all your might" (Deut. 6:4). Half-hearted following is not what the LORD requires (cf. Rev. 3:15).

The LORD's Displeasure and Saul's Rejection (15:10-23)

The LORD was displeased with Saul because the king did not fully carry out Yahweh's word regarding the *herem* of the Amalekites. Instead of killing Agag the king, Saul took him prisoner and allowed the people to take the best of the cattle as spoil. This act of disobedience led to Yahweh's rejection of Saul. The LORD "repented" about making Saul king (1 Sam. 15:11). Saul's disobedience made God change his plan of action, which is what "repented" means here.

The concept of *herem* derives from the belief, enunciated by Moses, that Israel is to act towards Yahweh with total loyalty. The significance of the word "total" was only gradually worked out by Israel as its theologians, the prophets, came to recognize that total dedication included not only loyalty but love, care, and compassion. These represent what is implied in the word *hesed,* translated in the RSV as "steadfast love." This *hesed* God showed towards Israel through the covenant he had "cut" with his people. Israel, in return, was meant to show total *hesed* to God in response to his gracious gift in this unique fellowship experience, and Israel was to show similar *hesed* to their neighbors. Before the time of David, all that Israel could understand about the *herem* was what is evident here and in the book of Joshua. Thus we cannot blame Saul for not having reached a full understanding of what loyalty and obedience should mean. He could put no moral content into his covenant obedience. Such an understanding of commitment and obedience would not be fully understood until addressed by the great prophets several centuries later. Psalm 136 could only have been written at a late period, when Israel could look back and see the content God had poured into the covenant relationship throughout their history. Saul was evidently living up to his honest interpretation of his duty to God as his people's leader when he dealt with the *herem* as told here. In fact, even Samuel understood that the idea of *herem* meant the priest had to "hew Agag in pieces before the LORD" (1 Sam. 15:33).

Through the events witnessed here God is "paving the way" for his chosen one, David, coming to the throne as Yahweh's own choice of king over all Israel.

Whether our human actions influence God's work is a theological question disputed among scholars. Many Protestant theologians, influenced by Martin Luther's teaching on "justification by faith alone," tend to argue that God's actions are quite independent of human actions. This view, however, rules out the scope of human freedom and leads to predestination. While affirming that God is in control of his overall program of salvation and would not allow it to be thwarted by any human effort, it makes sense to believe that God's acts are not independent of human activity. Rather, in and through human deeds, in and through human acts of obedience and disobedience, God continues to evolve his plan.

"The word of the LORD came to Samuel" is another form of the oracle-introduction formula (cf. v. 1). Samuel "was angry" about God's change of mind, and he "cried to the LORD all night" (v. 11), true to his character as a man of prayer (cf. 12:23). This account reminds us of Moses (Exod. 32:31-32) and Jeremiah (Jer. 14:11; 15:11), who in similar conflicts, standing between God and his people, prayed on behalf of the people before announcing God's message of judgment. Moses and Samuel are remembered as legendary figures of prayer (cf. Jer. 15:1).

After praying to the LORD "all night," Samuel believed himself to be clear about the will of God, and so he proceeded "to meet Saul" (1 Sam. 15:12a) to expose his sin and to reveal to him God's will. The sinner being confronted by the word of God through the prophet is a special characteristic of prophetic writings — Nathan meeting David (2 Sam. 12) and Elijah meeting Ahab (1 Kgs. 21:17ff.)

1 Samuel 15:12b talks about Saul's setting up "a monument for himself" in Carmel; this probably belongs to another tradition. The redactor is interested in including it here in order to underline the intensity of Saul's sin. Saul's "turning back" from following Yahweh was not because of his avariciousness regarding the spoils, but because he was concerned only with his own glory. Instead of giving glory to Yahweh, who alone was responsible for Saul's victory over the Amalekites, the king attempted to claim the glory for himself. In other words, he tried to project himself in the place of God, and this was indeed his basic sin. That burial memorials were common in Palestine is attested archaeologically. Here it is

a victory monument that is described. 2 Sam. 18:18 speaks of Absalom's "monument." Carmel is ca. 13 km. (8 mi.) S of Hebron; it figures prominently in the history of David (cf. 1 Sam. 25:2ff.). Why did Saul choose Carmel as the site for the monument? Perhaps it had some connection with the Canaanite sanctuary in Carmel (1 Kgs. 18:20ff.); if so, it could have symbolically meant Saul's turning away from the LORD. From Carmel Saul came to Gilgal, the scene of his second rejection, the very place where he had been made king publicly (1 Sam. 11:14-15).

Saul greeted Samuel and told him that he had "performed the commandment of the LORD" (15:13). Hebrew *dabar* is used here for "commandment." On the use of *dabar* as the concretization or realization of the word of God, see above on 3:1ff. Either Saul was naive and innocent and took Agag and the best of the spoils with the good intention of sacrificing to the LORD (15:15), or he was an avowed fraud and intended only to hide the facts from Samuel. We are not in a position to find his true intention, though many speak in favor of the former. The redactor of the present account would want to stress the latter and claim that Saul wantonly disobeyed the LORD. According to the redactor, "the bleating of the sheep" and "the lowing of the oxen" in the camp (v. 14) exposed Saul's dishonesty. Samuel rejected Saul's excuse (v. 16) and maintained that Saul "swooped on the spoil" because of his avariciousness (v. 19). So Samuel announced to Saul the word of judgment: "Because you have rejected the word of the LORD, he has also rejected you from being king" (v. 23).

Verse 17 is reminiscent of 9:21. In 15:20-21 Saul defends his case by repeating the same arguments as before, that he took the Amalekite king Agag and the best of the spoils for sacrifice to the LORD. This seems to be what happened later: "Samuel hewed Agag in pieces before the LORD in Gilgal" (v. 33). The expression "before the LORD" is characteristic of Priestly writings, used mostly in the context of sacrifices offered to the LORD. Agag was offered as a human sacrifice to Yahweh. That human sacrifice was known in Israel at this time, at least to a limited extent and under special circumstances, is indicated by the sacrifice of Jephthah's daughter (Judg. 11:30ff.). What happened to the cattle is not mentioned; perhaps they too were offered in sacrifice.

1 Samuel 15:22-23 appears to come from an independent prophetic tradition which seeks to underline the priority of the prophetic word over cultic rituals and sacrifices. This trend is attested in all the writings of the ethical prophets (cf. Isa. 1:11-15; Hos. 6:6; Amos 5:21-27; Mic. 6:6-8). Disobedience to the word of God is paralleled with the sin of "divination" and "idolatry," for these went hand in hand (see below on 1 Sam. 19:13). The redactor, by introducing these verses here, accepts Saul's argument that the best of the spoils should have been sacrificed to the LORD. Nevertheless, he holds that "to obey is better than sacrifice," that Saul had no right to interpret or change the word of God; he should have obeyed it literally.

We have seen above (3:1ff.) how the word of God is at the same time the revelation of God's will — the medium of its revelation and also its concretization. The cult and all that goes with it are expected to help the people of God to receive the word and to do it. The cult is thus only a means to receive and to realize the word of God. However, the religion of the Israelites made the means an end in itself, giving prominence to the cult and forgetting the word of God (cf. Jer. 7:21-27). The Church with its complex orders, structures, personnel, and wealth is also in danger of becoming a "cult" for its own sake, its structures and wealth becoming "gods" (idols) in themselves where the actual word of God cannot be heard and followed. The Church is constantly warned against such a danger.

In 1 Sam. 15:23a the Hebrew text reads, "The sin of oracle is rebellion, and iniquity and *teraphim* are . . . (meaning uncertain)." English versions reverse the order and introduce an element of comparision which is not present in the original. It is highly improbable that the late source made Samuel condemn divination as sinful when it had already portrayed him as presiding over the operation of the ephod oracle (cf. 10:17-24). This too confirms that these verses come from a late hand.

1 Samuel 15:23b reads, "Because you have rejected the word of the LORD, he has also rejected you from being king." The same argument appears in v. 26 as well. Behind this argument of *lex talionis* lies the Deuteronomic principle of "reward and retribution" (cf. Deut. 28:1ff.). This influenced the popular piety of many

Israelites, and has also influenced the popular piety of the Christian Church. For many Christians the motivation for doing good is the assurance that their good deeds will be rewarded by God, if not here in this life at least in the life after death. This equation of earthly blessings with one's good deeds and sufferings with one's bad deeds came to be questioned in the OT itself (Job; Ps. 73; Isa. 53). The OT asserts that Yahweh is God and not human (Hos. 11:9) and that he does not do as humans do. God's (covenant) love knows no bounds, but flows towards the sinner (Hos. 11:8). The New Covenant spoken of in the OT is a covenant based on forgiveness (Isa. 54:6-7; Jer. 31:31-34; Hos. 2:16-20). In Jesus Christ this New Covenant is then fulfilled and salvation is effected by the grace of God alone. Good deeds are not the pre-condition for receiving God's grace, but are the fruits of God's grace, the fruits of being in Christ.

Saul's Repentance (15:24-31)

This section also seems to come from a later edition. 1 Samuel 15:29 says, "the Glory of Israel will not lie or repent; for he is not a man, that he should repent." This is inconsistent with vv. 11 and 35, where it is said that the LORD "repented" for making Saul king. Also, the nature of Saul as presented here differs from that offered earlier. The person who had strongly defended his case is made to surrender here as a weak person; he could no longer command his people, but was rather commanded by the people. Saul confessed that he had sinned "because I feared the people and obeyed their voice" (v. 24). "Obeying the voice" of the people was not brought as a charge earlier in the story. Thus we gather that this section along with vv. 22-23 comes from a pro-Davidic redactor who wanted to portray gradually the decline of Saul and the rise of David.

Saul repented and pleaded for forgiveness (v. 25). He begged Samuel to return with him; but Samuel first resolutely refused to do so. The argument that had been put forward earlier (v. 23b) was repeated (v. 26). Saul persisted in his pleading, holding Samuel by his robe, and "the skirt of his robe" tore off (v. 27)! Samuel interpreted this as a prophetic symbolic act foreboding the removal of the kingdom from Saul and its being given to Saul's neighbor "who is better than you" (v. 28), evidently referring to David. Saul confessed his sin once again. He pleaded with Saul to return with him so he might not lose face before his people and so he might worship the LORD (v. 30). Samuel finally yielded and went with Saul, and "Saul worshipped the LORD" (v. 31).

This whole episode of Saul's sin and repentance reminds us of the account of David's sin and repentance in 2 Sam. 12:1-13. Though both confessed their sins, it is said that only David received absolution from the prophet — "The LORD . . . has put away your sin" (2 Sam. 12:13) — though David's sin was more heinous than Saul's. Here may be evidence to show how a historian's subjective presuppositions and prejudices can influence his writing of history and affect the characters in history positively or negatively. The history written by the conqueror is never the same as that written by the conquered; the history written by the colonizers is never the same as that written by the colonized. For the biblical historians, David was the king par excellence, and this bias towards Davidic kingship influenced their value judgments both before and after events.

"The Glory of Israel" is one of the titles for Yahweh (1 Sam. 4:21). That "Yahweh 'is not a man' but God" is an important theme in the OT (15:29; cf. Hos. 11:9).

Execution of Agag (15:32-33)

The fact that the execution of Agag took place "before the LORD" and that Samuel himself did the killing indicates that it was done in temple precincts and had sacrificial significance.

Agag was killed not so much because he was part of the *herem*, but in retribution for what he had done to the Israelites earlier: "As your sword has made women childless, so shall your mother be childless among women." A woman's being barren or becoming childless was considered to be a curse in Israel. The crude justice exercised here is beyond our modern understanding. Behind this lies the Israelite belief in the inseparableness of the act from its consequence and also their belief on bloodguilt and blood revenge (cf. Gen. 4:10-11; 9:6; 1 Kgs. 2:33).

Final Rift between Samuel and Saul (15:34-35)

The author says here that "Samuel did not see Saul again until the day of his death" (1 Sam. 15:35). This contradicts 19:23-24, according to which Saul met Samuel once again at Naioth in Ramah. The author's purpose here in asserting that the two did not see each other afterwards is to show that the rift between them was final and complete. From this moment on Saul was left alone; there was no more guidance from the LORD.

Here may be a spiritual lesson for us. As long as we live in fellowship with God we are warned, disciplined, corrected, and guided by the word of God. When we drift away from the fellowship of God, we reject the word of God and are left with no one to lead us — to warn, to correct, or to guide. This is the tragedy of every sinner. This was also the tragedy of Saul.

The words "Samuel grieved over Saul" (15:35) are intended to serve as a link to ch. 16.

VI. THE DECLINE OF SAUL
AND THE RISE OF DAVID
1 Samuel 16:1–31:13

"You Are More Righteous than I"

"You are more righteous than I" are the words of Saul to David in 24:17. In these words we have the clue to the understanding of the whole account that follows, which narrates step by step the decline of Saul and the rise of David. The purpose of the historian(s) here is to portray David as more righteous than Saul and as one who was loved by all (18:16), including the enemy and his family (16:21; 18:1-3, 16, 20). We see this more as an attempt to legitimize the Davidic kingship by an author who lived in immediate contact with it and who saw the popularity of that kingship among the people. The author ascribes David's success to his "righteousness," i.e., to his faithful relationship to God and to his people, and the decline of Saul to his unrighteousness, to Saul's strained relationship to God and to his people. Because Saul disobeyed the LORD the Spirit of the LORD deserted him, and an evil spirit took control of him and led him to his downfall (16:14; 18:12). From that moment onward "the Spirit of the LORD came mightily upon David" (16:13), and "the LORD was with him" (18:12, 14; 20:13) and led him to victory after victory until the kingdom was finally established.

Looking at the sagas around Saul, one gets the impression that Saul was an able leader. However, because he was Israel's first king, Saul had to face many odds — a disorganized people divided into several tribal groups. These had first to be united. They were a people with no military training and with no up-to-date weapons, with powerful enemies round about, and experiencing conflict with the old power structure of the judges. In addition, there were

94

the coup by Samuel when he anointed David, a conflict of cultures, and the anti-kingship trend in the prophetic circles. Finally, Saul's own son and daughter turned against him. By the time David assumed power, the threat of the old order of the judges was no longer present; the kingship was now more or less accepted by the people. David had the advantage also of being trained in Saul's royal circle as an "armor-bearer" (16:21) and a commander over "the men of war" (18:5, 13), as well as being the king's son-in-law (18:20ff.). Consequently, from an organizational standpoint David did not have to start from scratch; much of what Saul had built up was now available for David's use.

DAVID'S ANOINTING (16:1-13)

This account was meant to legitimize the kingship of David and to discredit that of Saul. Even when Saul was still ruling, it was not Saul but David who was the legitimate king. "The Spirit of the LORD departed from Saul" (16:14), but it "came mightily upon David" (v. 13).

There are some inconsistencies in this account. Samuel invites the elders of the city to come for the sacrifice (vv. 4, 5a), but later the people do not appear; only Jesse and his sons appear. People are invited for a sacrifice, but there is no mention later of any sacrifice. According to v. 5, "Jesse and his sons" are consecrated by Samuel; but according to v. 11, David was not present among the sons. According to v. 7, the LORD does not look on one's outward appearance, but v. 12 praises David's outward appearance. Perhaps we have here a redactional piece intended to bring together different traditions about Saul and David.

16:1-3   Samuel hesitates at the LORD's commandment to anoint one of Jesse's sons as king because it would amount to a coup d'état against Saul. Accordingly, if Saul should come to know of it he would put Samuel to death. Thus the LORD is said to have advised Samuel to go, on the pretext of offering a sacrifice. That God guides people even in human intrigues was clearly part of the thinking of the period.

16:4-13   Samuel now carries out the LORD's command to anoint David. Here again Samuel uses the method of elimination to find out the person the LORD has chosen, as he did in the case of the election of Saul (10:20ff.). However, here the lot device is not used; instead the candidates are asked to pass before Samuel, and then the LORD himself would "name" the candidate to Samuel (16:3). In the rejection of Eliab (v. 6), the redactor perhaps sees the rejection of Saul: "man looks on the outward appearance, but the LORD looks on the heart" (v. 7). This verse possibly comes from the wisdom circle, as the account was being edited by a later generation.

All the "seven" sons of Jesse passed before Samuel, and none was selected (v. 10). On "seven," see above on 6:1. With the seven sons Jesse's family was complete. In Jesse's reckoning of his sons David was left out; evidently Jesse did not count him as being of any significance: he was "the youngest" (16:11). Perhaps the author wanted to underscore the fact that the LORD may choose the least to be his servant — an important theological motif throughout the Bible (cf. Gen. 37; 1 Cor. 1:27; 2 Cor. 4:7). The anointing of David takes place "in the midst of his brothers" (1 Sam. 16:13), so it seems to have been a secret anointing. Later on, however, David is publicly anointed, this time at Hebron as the first "king over the house of Judah" (2 Sam. 2:4) and later again as "king over Israel" (5:3).

The gift of the "Spirit of the LORD" is here associated with the act of anointing. Baptism and the gift of the Holy Spirit encountered in the NT is to be understood against this background. The name David occurs here for the first time; it probably means "darling" (Martin Noth, *Die israelitischen Personennamen,* 223), which suits the description given in 1 Sam. 16:12. David was the darling of all the people (18:16), including Saul (16:21), Jonathan (18:1), Michal (18:20), as well as of the LORD (16:3).

DAVID INTRODUCED TO THE COURT OF SAUL
(16:14-23)

This section shows no knowledge of David's anointing nor of the coming of the Spirit of the LORD upon him. Perhaps it comes from a redactor who wanted to contrast David, who was filled by the Spirit of the LORD (v. 13), with Saul, who was filled by an "evil spirit from the LORD" (v. 14). The rise of David and the decline of Saul are thus ascribed to the working of both good and bad spirits from God.

16:14   Saul becomes here an example of the parable of the empty house in Luke 11:24-26. As soon as "the Spirit of the LORD departed from Saul," "an evil spirit from the LORD" entered him. As G. B. Caird notes, "A bad conscience produced by his own disobedience to what he believed to be the will of God, and his consequent break with the man who had been instrumental in bringing him to the throne, robbed Saul of his self-confidence and his sense of the presence of God" (*IB* 2:969). Saul's mental sickness was ascribed to the working of the evil spirit. At a time when people had no access to the modern scientific understanding of human personality, all unexplainable human behaviors were ascribed to the working of the spirit of God. In early times the Israelites, being true to their monotheistic faith, saw Yahweh as the author of both good and evil. This belief continues throughout the OT (cf. Isa. 45:7). Thus Satan, who seduced David to commit sin and tested Job, was seen to be an angel of God (2 Sam. 24:1; 1 Chr. 21:1; Job 1:6ff.).

16:15-18   The servants of Saul diagnose the king's disease and suggest music as the necessary therapy. One of them advises Saul that he should get David to play sweet music for him. On servants bringing good news to their masters, see 1 Sam. 9:6. 1 Samuel 16:18 appears to be secondary in this context. Whereas in vv. 15-16 the Hebrew word used for "servants" is *ʿabadim,* in v. 18 the word *neʿarim* (RSV "young men") is used. In v. 19 David is presented as a man "with the sheep," but in v. 18 he is presented as "a man of valor, a man of war." Through the words of the servant, the pro-Davidic redactor here portrays David as the best choice for a king in all respects. He was not only good at playing music, but he was also "a man of valor," "a man of war," "prudent in speech," and "a man of good presence."

16:19-23   Taking his servants' advice, Saul sends messengers to Jesse and brings David into his service. Here two traditions appear to have been fused together. According to one tradition David was primarily recruited into Saul's military "service" (v. 21), true to what was said about Saul in 14:52. That Saul later "set him over the men of war" (18:5) to become "a commander of a thousand" (18:13) speaks in support of this tradition. According to the other tradition, the musician-cum-shepherd David was brought to Saul's court mainly to play music whenever the evil spirit tormented Saul (16:23). According to vv. 22-23, David entered Saul's service permanently; this contradicts the account in ch. 17, where David is found still with the sheep. Chapter 17 may represent an independent tradition.

Here is one of the important election motifs in the OT. The elected one is to be the source of blessing to others (cf. Gen. 12:3). David, the LORD's anointed one, thus becomes the source of blessing to all people, including even his rival Saul (cf. 1 Sam. 23:1-5).

DAVID'S VICTORY OVER GOLIATH AND THE DEFEAT OF THE PHILISTINES (17:1-58)

This chapter seems to have had a complex literary history. The Vaticanus manuscript of the LXX appears to have had a shorter text here; it omits vv. 12-31, 41, 48b, 50, 55-58, and 18:1-5. We are therefore faced with the question as to which text is original, the longer or the shorter. Within the present text also there are internal tensions. Verses 31ff. contradict vv. 55ff., for David is here introduced to Saul twice. We must suppose either that the LXX translators had before them the longer text and, finding it self-contradictory, they tried to make the story consistent by judicious omissions, or that they had before them the shorter text and that the disputed passages were added to the Hebrew text at a later date after the formation of that text from which the LXX version was made. The disputed sections form a continuous story of themselves, and they bear a striking resemblance to 16:1-13. It is possible that two originally independent traditions have been brought together in the course of a long and complicated redaction history. One account introduces David as Jesse's son and goes on to tell about David's visit to the Philistine camp and his inquiry regarding the reward for the one who defeats the Philistine (17:12-29, 55-58). The second account has its focus on the unequal fighters (vv. 1-11, 32-54). Only here is David described as a boy.

17:1-11 The armies of the Philistines and the Israelites are set against each other in battle array (vv. 1-3). Goliath, the Philistine "champion," challenges the Israelites to a duel (vv. 4-7). The custom of beginning a war with combat between individuals was known in Israel (cf. 2 Sam. 2:14ff.). The name Goliath is a foreign word and occurs here only twice (1 Sam. 17:4, 23). Many scholars hold that the Philistine champion was originally anonymous and that he was wrongly identified with the Goliath who was killed by Elhanan (2 Sam. 21:19); in both cases the shaft of their spears was likened to a weaver's beam.

Socoh and Azekah (1 Sam. 17:1), the scene of the battle, lie in the Shephelah, the high plains between the coast and the Judean mountain region (cf. Josh. 15:35; 2 Chr. 11:7, 9). Ephes-dammim is perhaps the same as Pas-dammim in 1 Chr. 11:13. The valley of Elah (1 Sam. 17:2; 21:9) is about 20 km. (12 mi.) SW of Bethlehem. It was waterless during summer and was therefore suitable as a field of battle.

A cubit is the distance from the elbow to the tip of the middle finger, and a span is the distance from the tip of the thumb to the tip of the little finger when the fingers are spread; it is the approximate equivalent of half a cubit. One cubit is thus approximately equal to 44.5 cm. (17.5 in.). This means that the Philistine champion was about 2.9 m. (9.5 ft.) tall (17:4). According to 2 Sam. 21:15ff., the Philistines had in their service a number of such men of unusual height. Goliath was also well protected with helmet, coat, and greaves — all fashioned in bronze — and was well armed with javelin and spear of unusual sizes. The holy war motif that the number (1 Sam. 14:6) or the size (16:7) of human beings has no significance to the LORD is what is implied here.

Goliath defied Israel, and "Saul and all Israel . . . were dismayed and greatly afraid" (17:8-11). Whereas in 11:6 Saul's anger was kindled when Nahash insulted Israel, here in contrast he is dismayed and afraid, because the Spirit of the LORD had now deserted him and the LORD was no more with him. Saul's rejection is thus indicated. His survival now depends on David, the man who does possess the Spirit of God.

17:12-16   The account in 17:11 is picked up again in v. 32. Verse 12 begins a new account where David is introduced as though for the first time. Verse 15 could thus be a gloss which tries to reconcile the contradictions by explaining how David, who according to 16:21-23 was at Saul's court as armor-bearer and musician, could also be found tending Jesse's sheep. According to the redactor David went to Saul's court at Gibeah only occasionally, only when Saul's illness necessitated it. Otherwise he remained now — as before — with his father.

David is here described as an Ephrathite (17:12). Ephrathah is a name closely associated with Bethlehem. It is either another name for Bethlehem or the name of a place in or around Bethlehem (cf. Gen. 35:19; 48:7; Ruth 1:2; 4:11; Mic. 5:2; cf. also 1 Chr. 2:24; 4:4). It is noted that Jesse "had eight sons" (1 Sam. 17:12), agreeing with what is said at 16:6ff.; but the names of only four are mentioned as if Jesse had only four sons (17:13-14). It is possible that the original tradition knew of only three sons besides David and the number eight was introduced at a later stage to resolve the tension between the traditions.

17:17-19   Jesse sends David to the army camp "in the valley of Elah" (v. 19; cf. v. 2) to take some food to his brothers and to bring back news about their well-being. This shows that Saul had a rather primitive army, one where everyone had to care for his own food. An ephah (v. 17) is about 40 l. (11 gal.). "Parched grain" was a delicacy in Israel (cf. Ruth 2:14). The purpose of bringing a "token" back to Jesse (1 Sam. 17:18) was to show that David had fulfilled his commission and to prove that the brothers were still alive.

17:20-31   On reaching the camp David leaves the things "in charge of the keeper of the baggage" (v. 22) and runs "to the ranks" to greet his brothers. There he sees how Goliath, "the Philistine of Gath," defies Israel. David's zeal for Yahweh is kindled, and he runs about to gather definite information as to what the king has announced in this connection. The news of the threefold reward seems to have stimulated David further. The rewards include great riches, marriage to the king's daughter, and the king's making his father's house "free in Israel" (v. 25). What this freedom of the father's house entails is not clear. The elder brother's annoyance at the curious behaviors of his younger brother is understandable. However, nothing could stop David from pursuing the cause of the LORD. The news of his challenge to Goliath had now been brought to Saul, and so Saul sends for David (v. 31). The Israelite forces are described here as "the armies of the living God" (v. 26). David's courage and zeal for the LORD are contrasted with the fear and cowardice of Saul and his army.

17:32-40   David takes up the challenge. His experiences of valor hitherto have been with "lions and bears." Thus he holds that this uncircumcised Philistine also "shall be like one of them," because "he has defied the armies of the living God" (v. 36). Because David was not accustomed to military armaments, Saul's weapons are of no use to him (vv. 38-39). He merely takes his shepherd's weapons — a staff, a sling, and "five smooth stones" (v. 40). The emphasis here is that it is not so much David who is going to fight, but the LORD (v. 37; cf. vv. 45-47).

17:41-54   The duel takes place. David knocks down the Philistine champion "with a sling and with a stone" and kills him. Then he cuts off Goliath's head with the enemy's own sword. The message of the whole account is contained in David's words in vv. 45-47: " . . . that all this assembly may know that the LORD saves not with sword and spear; for the battle is the LORD's." Whereas the Philistine came "with a sword and with a spear and with a javelin," David went "in the name of the LORD of hosts" (v. 45).

The "name," according to Israelite thinking, embodies the power of the person who bears that name. The "name of God" means that part of God's nature which is opened towards humanity. Behind this name is hidden God's power, which surpasses all human understanding. It is with this name that David went into the battle; naturally the Philistine did not know where this power came from. The "name of God" has an important place in Deuteronomic theology (cf. Deut. 12:5). On "the LORD of hosts," see 1 Sam. 1:3.

Seeing that their champion was killed, the Philistines fled, and "the men of Israel and Judah rose with a shout and pursued the Philistines as far as Gath and the gates of Ekron" (17:52). It was not a decisive victory, however; David is said to have "put his armor in his tent" (v. 54). At this stage David could not have had a tent of his own; it may well have been a "tent sanctuary," from which later on he receives back the sword (21:9).

17:55-58   David is introduced to Saul for the second time. According to this account David's combat with Goliath was without any prior consultation with Saul. Here is the first mention of Abner in this narrative (17:57). He is Saul's cousin, son of Ner, Saul's uncle (cf. 10:14ff.; 14:50).

The story of David and Goliath stands for all times as a paradigm for the encounter between the power of the Spirit, which is the power of God, and the power of the flesh, which is the power of this world. It is the encounter between righteousness and unrighteousness, liberation and oppression. The power of the Spirit will ultimately triumph in human history. That is the vital message of this paradigm.

DAVID, THE DARLING OF JONATHAN AND THE PEOPLE (18:1-16)

The story of Saul's fall and David's rise continues. Because "the LORD was with him" (18:12, 14), David wins the love of Saul's son Jonathan and "all Israel and Judah" (v. 16). Because the LORD "had departed from Saul" (v. 12), Saul consequently loses the loyalty and support of his own son as well as of his people.

18:1-5   David makes a "friendship covenant" with Jonathan. This section is normally taken with 17:55-58. Both are missing in the LXX. 1 Samuel 18:1 is evidently redactional, connecting the preceding and the following sections. Verse 2 picks up the account from 16:23. David is brought to Saul, and the king is refreshed by David's music. It is only natural that Saul, being impressed with David, would not let him return to his father's house but would want the young man to stay with him. While remaining in Saul's house David develops a friendship with Jonathan, and Jonathan "loved him as his own soul" (18:3; 20:17).

While Saul is portrayed as a warrior with a violent temper, David is portrayed here as a mature diplomat who builds up his political ground quite tactfully. He gets the support of the people, including that of his rival's household. As a first step, David ensures the support of Jonathan through a covenant of friendship. Jonathan could otherwise emerge as a claimant to Saul's throne, as his father wanted him to be (cf. 20:31). Because of this pact Jonathan apparently surrendered his claim to the throne and actually accepted David's supremacy (cf. 20:14-17). Jonathan, who "stripped himself of the robe that was upon him, and gave it to David" (18:4), was perhaps performing a symbolic act, that of relinquishing his right and handing it over to David.

18:6-16   Here the LXX has a shorter text. It omits vv. 6a, 8, 10-12 (except the words "Saul was afraid of David"), 17-19, 21b, and 29b, yet it gives a consistent account. These verses added in the Hebrew text must come either from a late source or are the additions of an editor.

The account continues from 17:58, where David meets Saul with Goliath's head in his hand and both return home with the army. We may assume that messengers have already brought the news of victory to the people so that "the women came out of all the cities of Israel" (18:6) to welcome their victorious men of war in a great celebration with music and dancing. They sing a song ascribing victory to David ten times more than to Saul. This act thereupon sows the seed of jealousy in Saul's mind. Thus it is the beginning of Saul's enmity to David. In the rising popularity of David among his people Saul sees a threat to his "kingdom" (v. 8). From that moment onwards Saul tries to get rid of David.

He attempts to stab him with his spear (v. 11). Then he makes David "a commander of a thousand" (v. 13) and sends him against the Philistines so that he may "fall by the hand of the Philistines" (vv. 17, 21, 25). But all these efforts fail; they even work to the advantage of David, because "he went out and came in before the people" (vv. 13, 16) and "all Israel and Judah loved David" (v. 16). This is because "the LORD was with him" (vv. 12, 14, 28) and because Saul "stood in awe of him" (v. 15). "What man proposes God disposes" becomes true in the case of Saul. Even Saul's evil designs are made to work towards the fulfilment of God's purpose.

The act of women welcoming their victorious menfolk returning from war (vv. 6-7) was widely practiced in the ancient Orient. In fact, several such instances are attested also in ancient Tamil literature in India. For such events within the OT, see Exod. 15:20-21; Judg. 11:34-35. The women's song (1 Sam. 18:7) appears to have continued to be popular throughout David's reign (cf. 21:11; 29:5).

The incident of Saul's attempting to stab David as he was playing music (18:10-11) is repeated in 19:9-10. Perhaps there were even more such attempts. Saul is presented here as well as in other places with "his spear in his hand" (18:10). It could be that at this early period of the kingship the king's spear was his scepter, his royal insignia, the symbol of his authority (cf. 19:9; 22:6; 26:7; 2 Sam. 1:6).

DAVID BECOMES SAUL'S SON-IN-LAW (18:17-30)

Different traditions arising out of genuine incidents in the life of Saul and David are merged together here. The evil intention ascribed to Saul (1 Sam. 18:17b, 21a, 25b, 28-29) may well have been a later addition.

The account of David's marriage with Saul's daughter marks an important stage in the accession narrative. To become the son-in-law of the king was a great thing, for it is stressed repeatedly (vv. 18, 23). Such a marriage probably implied a claim to the succession to Saul's throne (cf. 2 Sam. 3:13ff.). The Merab story (1 Sam. 18:17-19) runs parallel to the Michal story (vv. 20-29). Merab's story is connected with Saul's promise in 17:25. But in the Michal story the starting point is not related to an earlier promise. It was when Michal fell in love with David that David claimed Michal, not as a reward but "at the price of a hundred foreskins of the Philistines" (1 Sam. 18:25; 2 Sam. 3:14).

The account of Saul's cheating David recalls the Jacob-Laban account in Gen. 29:21ff. Nothing is mentioned as to how David reacted when he was deceived. Perhaps something is missing here.

1 Samuel 18:20-27 tries to show that all the people one after another were captivated by David's irresistible charisma and charm — Saul, his son, his army (servants of Saul), his people, and now his own daughter. According to the redactor who is responsible for vv. 17b, 21a, 25b, 28-29, Michal, whom Saul intended to become a snare to David, turned out to be a strong supporter of David. This was because "the LORD was with David" (v. 28). God overrules human plans. He appropriates even the evil intentions of mankind for the fulfilment of his ultimate plan of salvation.

Using intermediaries to negotiate marriage settlements is a practice known in Eastern countries even today. The "servants" are here preferred by Saul to serve as intermediaries because David is popular among them (v. 22). The bridegroom's bringing "marriage presents" (*mohar,* v. 25) appears to have been a common practice in ancient Israel (cf. Gen. 24:53). Saul's demand for "a hundred foreskins of the Philistines" (1 Sam. 18:25) reveals a double purpose. First he wants to ensure that David does not kill anyone from among the Israelites but from their enemies, the Philistines. Because the Philistines were uncircumcised, the production of their "foreskins" would be evidence that David had killed only Philistines. Second, the danger involved in killing all those Philistines was great. However, by bringing a double quantity of foreskins (v. 27) David proved to Saul once again "that the LORD was with David" (v. 28). Saul, who earlier stood "in awe of" David (v. 15), now becomes "still more afraid of David" (v. 29). The gradual decline of Saul is indicated here once again.

Verse 30 belongs to the original account; it stresses David's increase in "success" and "esteem."

THE WIDENING RIFT BETWEEN DAVID AND SAUL
(19:1–20:42)

This account consists of several episodes — 19:1-8, 9-10, 11-17, 18-24; 20:1-42 — all meant to show that the rift between David and Saul had become final so that David had no other option than to flee from Saul. It is possible that these episodes were circulating as independent traditions before becoming part of the literary tradition.

Saul's Attempt To Kill David (19:1-24)

19:1-8   Jonathan mediates between David and Saul. So far Saul has been trying indirect methods to get rid of David. Now he reveals his intention openly "to Jonathan his son and to all his servants, that they should kill David" (v. 1). Jonathan, remaining faithful to his friendship covenant with David (cf. 18:3), tries to protect David by mediating between him and his father. Once he is of sober mind, Saul listens to Jonathan's arguments and assures him that he would never kill David. So David returns to Saul's service as before (19:7). How sin conceived at first as simple jealousy (18:8) can develop into secret hostility and then into open hostility, leading to the self-destruction of the person involved, is depicted in the person of Saul.

The reference to Saul's being "in the field" in 19:3 causes a problem. It is not clear which field is meant here and what Saul was doing there. It is possible that this account is influenced by a similar account in ch. 20, where we have references to David's hiding "in the field" (vv. 5, 11, 24).

In Jonathan's appeal to Saul (19:4-6) we have a glimpse into the Israelite understanding of kingship. Before the LORD both Saul and David stand equal; both are bound by *tsedaqah,* by community loyalty. David has been serving Saul the king faithfully according to the behavior code prescribed by the community for an Israelite citizen, and in this sense "he has not sinned against" Saul (v. 4). If Saul, on the other hand, kills David, one of his innocent citizens, that would be against the code of conduct for Israelite kings and would therefore be regarded as "sin against his servant David" (cf. 24:11). The same argument lies behind Saul's words to David in 24:17: "You are more righteous than I."

"As the LORD lives" (19:7) is a formula used for swearing an oath (cf. Lev. 19:12). 1 Samuel 19:8 serves as a link between vv. 1-7 and vv. 9-10.

19:9-10   Here are recorded Saul's second attempt at stabbing David and David's escape. This is normally taken as another version of the incident mentioned in 18:10-11.

19:11-17   Saul makes his third attempt to kill David; this time David is saved by Michal. This narrative is perhaps influenced by the Rahab story in Josh. 2:15ff. The author assumes that "David's house" (1 Sam. 19:11) was on the city wall as in the case of Rahab's house.

Having helped David escape, Michal tricks Saul's servants with a *teraphim,* the household "image" (v. 13). *Teraphim* were probably idols in human form in varying sizes; they were in use among the Israelites until quite late (cf. Gen. 31:19ff.; Judg. 17-18). They were believed to bring blessing to the families who owned them. This would explain why Rachel stole the image and why Laban ran after it (cf. Gen. 31:19ff.), as well as why the tribes of Israel attached such importance to ownership of such images (cf. Judg. 17–18). Teraphim are often mentioned along with the ephod (Judg. 17:5; 18:14, 17ff.; Hos. 3:4). Perhaps the oracle-device ephod was used in the presence of the household-god teraphim, and thus divination and idolatry went together (cf. 1 Sam. 15:23; Ezek. 21:21). The prohibition of their use in Israel was probably the result of Josiah's centralization reform in the 7th cent. B.C. (cf. 2 Kgs. 23:24). Worship of such household gods is common among Hindus, where these gods are known as Ishta Devata, "the god of one's liking." People can choose any one of the gods of the Hindu pantheon as their Ishta Devatha; it is believed that worship of such gods ensures protection from evils and gives prosperity to all members of the family.

In Saul's efforts to kill David we see two peculiar trends. First, the words of both Saul and Michal confirm that David was to be killed not in the night but "in the morning" (1 Sam. 19:11).

Second, Saul wanted to kill David personally (vv. 11, 15). It is possible that there was a convention that blood should not be spilled in the night, possibly due to the fear that night (darkness) was the domain of gods and spirits (cf. Gen. 32:26); and since the gods had a special liking for blood, they might appropriate that time for evil against the one who spilled the blood. In Saul's intention to kill David personally, the author perhaps intends to show the sickening of Saul's heart in that he is seeking the blood of the LORD's anointed and thus plunges to his own self-destruction. Michal is telling lies both to the "messengers" and to her father (1 Sam. 19:14, 17). In early Israel hiding truth for the sake of saving life was seen more as an act of expediency and cleverness than as a morally wrong activity (21:2; cf. Gen. 12:11ff.; 20:2ff.).

19:18-24 Saul's fourth attempt to kill David is also thwarted, this time by Samuel. Fleeing from Saul, David comes straight "to Samuel at Ramah" and tells Samuel "all that Saul had done to him." Then both of them "went and dwelt at Naioth" (1 Sam. 19:18). Saul comes to know of David's whereabouts and three times sends "messengers to take David." All three times these messengers, coming into contact with the ecstatic prophets, begin themselves to prophesy, forgetting their mission from Saul (vv. 20-21). Finally Saul himself goes to Naioth personally, and he too is taken by "the Spirit of God" (v. 23).

We have here an independent tradition which probably draws from two other traditions, one connected with the etiology of the proverb "Is Saul also among the prophets?" (v. 24), and the other, a prophetic saga (similar to the one found in 2 Kgs. 1) which speaks of how God thwarted Saul's three attempts to capture David. Anyone under God's protection cannot be captured.

Naioth (1 Sam. 19:18) appears to be a place where ecstatic prophets had a guild. Samuel did not become ecstatic, but he "was standing as head over them" (v. 20). The tradition consciously attempts, however, to distinguish Samuel from the ecstatic prophets (cf. 9:9). It is not said of whom Saul inquired about Samuel and David as he came to "the great well that is in Secu" (19:22); quite probably he inquired of the young women who came to draw water from the well (cf. 9:11). It is possible that this well had some cultic significance. This is hinted at by the fact that from this point onwards "the Spirit of God came upon him" (19:23).

Stripping off one's clothes and becoming naked (v. 24) was a sign of extreme self-abasement before God (cf. 2 Sam. 6:21-22). Naked *sadhus* ("saints") are common among Hindus in India today, although in Hinduism this action is seen more as a sign of self-renunciation and of self-control.

Saul's "lying naked" before Samuel was perhaps meant to express symbolically the subordination of the king to the prophet.

David's Escape from Saul's Court (20:1-42)

This chapter contains complex material. 1 Samuel 20:1 links it with the preceding chapter; moreover, it comes from the hand of a redactor. In this chapter Jonathan confesses ignorance of Saul's intention to kill David, although this contradicts what is said in 19:1-7. Saul expects David to appear at table as usual. This shows that, according to this tradition, the open conflict between the two has not yet erupted. 1 Samuel 20:13 further indicates that the author is not yet aware of Saul's rejection by God.

There are also several internal tensions in the chapter. David and Jonathan have two conversations regarding the threat by Saul — one takes place in the city (vv. 1-10) and the other in the field (vv. 12-23). According to vv. 2ff., the plan for finding out Saul's intention comes from David; but according to vv. 18ff., the plan comes from Jonathan. Jonathan's concern for the safety of his posterity is expressed twice (vv. 14-17, 42). It is possible that different material available in the circle of Jonathan's friends has been brought together by a redactor.

The traditions deal with two main concerns. One is to show how Jonathan voluntarily relinquished his claim on the throne (see above on 18:1-5) and acknowledged David to be the legitimate successor of Saul (20:13). The other concern is the protection of Jonathan's "house" (vv. 14-17, 42). Our author is perhaps aware of the account in 2 Sam. 9, where David shows kindness to Mephibosheth, Jonathan's crippled son.

20:1-10   David confides his fears to Jonathan. David asserts his loyalty to Saul, a motif stressed again and again (cf. 1 Sam. 24:11, 17; 2 Sam. 1:14ff.; 4:10ff.), and appeals to Jonathan to show his covenant love to David and to protect him from imminent danger (1 Sam. 20:3) from Saul. "Deal kindly with your servant" in v. 8 literally means "practice *hesed* ['covenant love'] with your servant." On the theological significance of *hesed* see further at 2 Sam. 7:15. Being thus bound by his friendship covenant with David (1 Sam. 18:3), Jonathan offers to help David (20:4). David then discloses his plan to Jonathan (vv. 5ff.).

"New moon" is here celebrated in the royal household for three days (v. 5). In oriental kingship ideology the moon played an important role because it was considered to be "the giver of kingship." It is therefore not surprising to find elements of moon worship in Israelite kingship, coming out of this oriental background. Celebration of both new moon and full moon (*sabbat*, parallel to the Babylonian *shap/battu*) was part of Israelite worship (Gnana Robinson, *Sabbath*, 66ff.). The "yearly sacrifice" in v. 6 is not one of the three annual festivals which were known later. What David means here is a family festival associated with the moon, which all the members of the family were bound to attend, similar to the yearly sacrifice of Elkanah (1:3). In those days it was possible to celebrate such festivals either at home or in a temple.

The friendship covenant between David and Jonathan is here described as "a sacred covenant" (20:8). The Hebrew reads "a covenant of the LORD." All human covenants in Israel were made in the presence of God, and God was invoked as a witness to such covenants (cf. v. 12; Gen. 31:49-50). Thus all covenants became sacred. One's relationship with one's fellow humans is inseparably linked to one's relationship with God. We are here reminded of Jesus' double commandment of love to God and love to one's neighbor (Matt. 22:37, 39; Mark 12:30-31; Luke 10:27). The God of biblical revelation is the God who loves *hesed* (Hos. 6:6) and who requires that the *hesed* in human relationships be not broken, because it is "the *hesed* of the LORD" (1 Sam. 20:14).

20:11-17   The real answer to David's question in v. 10 is found in vv. 18ff., which continue the account. Verses 11-17 appear to be a secondary interpolation here. Verse 11 is from a redactor who makes the conversation between David and Jonathan continue "into the field" where David plans to hide (v. 5). The assumption is that Jonathan would explain there how he is going to communicate the news in the field where David will be hiding. However, the focus of vv. 11-17 is not so much on the disclosure of the news to David as on Jonathan's plea for the safety of his family. Jonathan pleads that when David comes to power he should show Jonathan "the loyal love *(hesed)* of the LORD" (v. 14) and should not "cut off [David's] loyalty" from Jonathan's "house for ever" (v. 15). In v. 16 the RSV reading follows the Greek versions. The Hebrew text here is broken, reading "earth, and Jonathan made a covenant with the house of David." This reflects a later situation when the house of Jonathan was dependent on "the house of David" (cf. 2 Sam. 9; 16:1-14; 19:17-21). Traditions closer to Jonathan's family could have built into the account of the friendship covenant David's pledge to protect the house of Jonathan (1 Sam. 20:17). Jonathan's love for David is thereafter repeated once again (cf. 18:1).

20:18-23   1 Samuel 20:18 picks up David's question in v. 10, but still does not provide a smooth continuation from vv. 1-10. In vv. 1-10 the plan comes from David, but here the plan comes from Jonathan. That the new moon festival went on for three days is confirmed by both passages (vv. 5, 12, 19), but that David will be missed "greatly" on the third day is here a new feature. "Then go to the place . . . in hand" (v. 19) does not make much sense. If David were already hiding, how can he be somewhere else? There is also some tension in the narration of the plan and of its implementation. Here it is said that David would hide "beside yonder stone heap" (v. 19); Jonathan, through the act of shooting three arrows and by talking to the lad, would communicate the message to David secretly (vv. 20, 22). Later, however, we see that after sending the lad both Jonathan and David meet and talk in the open (vv. 41-42). If this were possible, what then was the purpose of hiding? It is possible that originally this hiding and shooting of arrows was an act of finding the will of God in the matter of David's leaving Saul's court. This original oracle motif seems to have been lost in the course of time. The reference to "the stone Ezel" (v. 19 MT) and the use of the mystic number "three" (v. 20) are perhaps part of this original oracle motif.

Bow and arrows were as characteristic of Jonathan as the spear was characteristic of Saul (cf. 18:4; 2 Sam. 1:22).

1 Samuel 20:23 picks up Jonathan's request in vv. 14-17. This could have been secondarily introduced here from the Jonathan circle at a later period.

20:24-34   Saul's evil intention is exposed. The king's seat was "by the wall." This was perhaps the safest seat; no one could attack from behind. Saul was probably sitting with the spear in his hand (v. 33). Jonathan sat opposite to Saul at the other end of the table, and Abner the commander (cf. 14:50-51) on one side of Saul. The seat on the other side of Saul was reserved for David (20:25). This shows that David had a seat of honor in Saul's court, probably because of his status as the king's son-in-law. Because it was a cultic feast, ritual purity was expected of the participants. Saul ascribed David's absence on the first day to some uncleanness on David's part (v. 26). For ordinary uncleanness one was expected to keep away from common life until the evening of that day. Sexual intercourse was also seen as an unclean act (cf. 21:4; Lev. 15:16-18; cf. 7:20-21).

David's alleged request is elaborated here (1 Sam. 20:28-29) beyond what he said at v. 6; probably this section comes from a different tradition. The reference to David's brother commanding him to go (v. 29) might indicate that Jesse was now no longer alive. This was hinted at in 17:12, where it is said that Jesse "was already old and advanced in years." Saul's angry reference to Jonathan's mother (20:30) was meant to indicate that Jonathan's rebellious nature had been inherited right from his mother's womb.

Verse 31 shows that the notion of a dynasty was present already during the time of Saul. Jonathan, too, was aware of David's claim to the throne, but he had already voluntarily renounced his own right to succession in favor of David (cf. 18:4; 23:17). After the death of Saul and Jonathan there was an attempt to revive Saul's dynasty by making Ishbosheth, another son of Saul, king over Israel (2 Sam. 2:8ff.).

The historicity of Saul's spear-throwing incidents (1 Sam. 20:33) appears to be doubtful. In both cases, Saul is said to have thrown the spear at people who were sitting next to him and were taken unawares — David playing music and Jonathan eating at table. Both times Saul missed the mark. If this were historically accurate, then Saul should have been a poor warrior, which is not true to what we know about him. It is therefore possible that we have here exaggerated descriptions of Saul's outburst of anger and hand-gestures as he held his spear, which may be expected of persons who are emotionally upset.

20:35-42 Jonathan discloses to David Saul's evil intentions. The account is presented as happening in accordance with the arrangement agreed upon by David and Jonathan in vv. 20-22. However, there are some differences between vv. 20-22 and vv. 35-42. According to v. 20 Jonathan was to shoot three arrows, but according to vv. 36b-38 Jonathan shot just one arrow, and that beyond the lad; "arrow" in the singular is used here four times, including the *kethib* ("what is written" in the Hebrew text) in v. 38. Only in the instruction to the lad in v. 36a is "arrows" in the plural used. "The stone Ezel" behind which David should have hidden (v. 19) is missing here. In its place the Hebrew reads "from beside the south" (v. 41). It is possible that the Hebrew word for "beside," *etsel*, is a corruption for *ezel*. Thus the RSV reads "from beside the stone heap." Also the signal, in the form of instructions addressed to the lad, differs here. According to v. 22, it should be "look, the arrows are beyond you." Here it is a question: "Is not the arrow beyond you?" (v. 37), to which Jonathan responds, "Hurry, make haste, stay not" (v. 38). These differences indicate that information coming from different sources is brought together here to form this account.

In vv. 41-42 we have probably an independent account of the two bidding farewell. Falling to the ground and bowing is an oriental way of paying homage to a superior, including God (cf. 24:8; 25:23-24; 28:14). Bowing "three times" (20:41) is a sign of complete obeisance. Here Jonathan, as the king's son, is obviously the superior, and David did not fail to acknowledge that. The author is aware of the future development when Jonathan's family had to be protected by David, so he tries to make this binding on David through his friendship covenant with Jonathan. Inasmuch as Jonathan has fulfilled his "loyal love" in helping David to escape, David is now bound in turn by his "loyal love" to protect Jonathan's "descendants" (v. 42). The LORD is the witness between them forever. "Jonathan went into the city" and David "departed." It is not said here to which place David went, but from 21:1 we know that he actually went to Nob.

DAVID'S FLIGHT BEFORE SAUL (21:1–30:31)

According to the author, David's departure from Samuel's court was providential. From now on Saul pursues David, and David is always in flight. This turns out to be a period of preparation and consolidation for David, a proper preparation to become king over Israel and Judah. A number of episodes follow through which the author would like the reader to understand that all along David was guided by the Spirit of God.

David Comes to the Priest at Nob (21:1-9)

As a first stop on his long flight before Saul, David comes to the priest at Nob. According to 22:10, David found a threefold purpose in coming to Nob: the priest "inquired of the LORD for him," "gave him provisions," and "gave him the sword of Goliath the Philistine." It is possible that we have here originally two independent traditions, one dealing with the "bread of the Presence" and the other dealing with "the sword of Goliath." The purpose of bringing these two together is to show that David, the LORD's anointed, is here provided for by God. Accordingly, David participates in eating the sacred food, "the bread of the Presence," and bears the holy sword, the sword that belonged to the LORD as the spoil of God's holy war.

21:1-6 Nob (21:1) was in the territory of Benjamin, between Anathoth and Jerusalem (Neh. 11:31-32; Isa. 10:30-32). Its precise location is not known. Nob was known as "the city of the priests" (1 Sam. 22:19). There was a sanctuary in Nob where

Ahimelech was the priest. He was said to be the son of Ahitub (22:9, 11). He was also identified with Ahijah, the son of Ahitub, who was Eli's grandson born to Phinehas (14:3) and would thus be regarded as the great-grandson of Eli. Abiathar was Ahimelech's son (22:20).

David is said to have come "alone" to Nob. Perhaps David left his "young men" (21:4) in some hideout. Ahimelech "came to meet David trembling." Why this "trembling?" One reason could be that David's reputation as a hero (vv. 9, 11) and as a loyal member of the royal court and also as the king's son-in-law was known to all (cf. 22:14); so the priest was surprised to find him all alone without anyone accompanying him. The other possible reason could be that the priest, through his insight, could see in David the LORD's anointed, so that his "trembling" was an acknowledgement of the coming of the holy one into his presence. The Hebrew word *hared,* "trembling," is otherwise used six times in the OT; in all but one instance (Judg. 7:3) it indicates "trembling" because of the holiness of the object involved. "Eli was trembling for the ark of God" (1 Sam. 4:13), and people trembled at the word of God (Ezra 9:4; 10:3; Isa. 66:2, 5). The trembling of Ahimelech could have also been a holy trembling (cf. Luke 1:41).

David hides the truth from the priest and gives false reasons for his presence (1 Sam. 21:2). On the question of telling lies in early Israel, see above on 19:14, 17.

David receives all the bread that the priest had at Nob (21:6). This may be a parallel to what happened to Saul after his anointing as king — Saul receiving two of the three loaves of bread from the men going up to God at Bethel (10:3-4). Whereas Saul got only two loaves, David here receives all the loaves, an indication that — unlike Saul's kingship, which was only partial — David's kingship is going to be complete. Inasmuch as the bread of the Presence was associated with the twelve tribes of Israel, David's receiving all the bread of the Presence could have indicated his coming kingship over all twelve tribes of Israel.

The "holy bread" (21:4), the bread of the Presence (v. 6), consisted of twelve loaves set in two rows. It was presented "on behalf of the people of Israel as a covenant for ever" and was

115

changed on sabbath days. When new bread was set in place, the old bread was removed to be eaten only by the priests "in a holy place" (sanctuary); this was because it was "a most holy portion" taken from the offerings by fire to the LORD (Lev. 24:5-9).

Because it is the "holy bread," the priest says, only those who have maintained their ritual purity — particularly abstention from sexual intercourse — could eat it (1 Sam. 21:4). David claims that even on a common "expedition" or a common journey the young men abstained from women and kept "their vessels" holy (v. 5). By "vessels" male sexual organs are meant here (L. Koehler-W. Baumgartner, *Lexicon in Veteris Testamenti Libros*). Why the young men should keep themselves holy on a normal expedition is not clear. Perhaps David saw all his confrontation with Saul in the context of holy war, and so demanded they keep themselves holy (cf. 25:28; on sexual abstention during war, see 2 Sam. 11:6-13).

In the conduct here of David and his young men Jesus perceived a parallel to his mission with his disciples (Matt. 12:3-4). God's mission in which Jesus was involved was the mission of salvation for humanity. Salvation in Christ is holistic in that it concerns the total life of men and women, their physical as well as their spiritual life. Since God is equally concerned with the physical and material needs of men and women as with their spiritual needs, "human need can override the letter of the law" (S. MacLean Gilmour, *IB* 8:111).

21:7   This verse is a later interpolation intended to prepare the ground for the account found in 1 Sam. 22:9ff. Doeg the Edomite is said to be "the chief of Saul's herdsmen." This shows that at this stage of Israelite history foreign personnel were in the service of Israelite kings (e.g., Uriah the Hittite; 2 Sam. 11:6ff.). Doeg is probably retained at Nob as an act of penance for a crime committed by him or for a form of ritual purification. That may explain why he later turned against the priests in Nob and betrayed them (1 Sam. 22:9-10).

21:8-9   Regarding how the sword of Goliath could have come to Nob, see above on 17:54. The fact that it was "behind the

116

ephod" may suggest that the ephod was some sort of box. Because the sword belonged to the LORD, it was for David a unique weapon; thus he could say, "there is none like that" (21:9). Because David was the LORD's anointed one, only he was entitled to wield that particular sword.

David before Achish King of Gath (21:10-15)

This is another account of David's escape and flight independent of the preceding event located in Nob. Here also David is said to have fled "from Saul" (v. 10). In 27:1-12 we have another account of David's visit to Gath, showing no knowledge of an earlier visit. It is possible that David spent some time among the Philistines in Gath, as the title of Ps. 56 indicates. There was evidently more than one tradition current among the people about this historical episode. As 1 Sam. 27:1, 4 suggests, David's purpose in going to Gath must have been to escape from the hands of Saul.

David's intention was to enlist himself as an unknown soldier in the service of Achish king of Gath, but his identity was soon exposed and he was caught and brought to Achish. David pretends to be mad and so escapes. Gath was one of the five Philistine cities on the west coast of Palestine (cf. 1 Sam. 5:8; 6:17-18). These cities were ruled by five "lords" *(seren)*. These lords in their own eyes perhaps compared themselves to the status of the kings of the city-states of Canaan and were thus actually at times referred to as kings. Jer. 25:20 speaks of the kings of the other four Philistine cities, but Gath is not mentioned in that verse.

The author assumes that David's popularity was widespread among these enemies, in that they could immediately recognize him (though ironically, however) as "the king of the land" (1 Sam. 21:11). David was always resourceful at times of crisis, and he was known for his cunning (cf. 23:22). Perhaps he pretended to be an epileptic in convulsions, letting his spittle run over his beard (21:13). The narrative then ends rather abruptly. At the command of Achish the Philistine's servants must have cast David outside the city, and David could thus have escaped. 1 Samuel 22:1 then continues from that time.

David in Adullam and Mizpeh (22:1-5)

The author assumes that David "departed" from Gath "and escaped to the cave of Adullam" (v. 1). Verse 1 mentions only David's "brothers and all his father's house." It is assumed here that Jesse, David's father, was already dead as suggested in 20:29. But in 22:3, David pleads to the king of Moab to give shelter to his "father and mother." It is possible that vv. 1-2 and vv. 3-4 come from different circles and that v. 5 comes from the redactor who is responsible for bringing these two traditions together.

22:1-2 Here David is presented as the champion of the oppressed. "Every one who was in distress," "every one who was in debt," and "every one who was discontented" gathered to David, and David "became captain over them."

Two strands of theological thinking run through the so-called salvation history in the OT — one is the "exodus faith" and the other is the "messianic faith." It is interesting to note that both have their origin in God's liberation of the oppressed. Through Moses God delivered the slaves in Egypt from the oppression of Pharaoh; that was the origin of the exodus faith. Here, through David, God delivers the oppressed in society, so that in David there begins the messianic faith (cf. 2 Sam. 7:12-16). The God of the Bible is thus seen as the God who stands on the side of the oppressed and works for their salvation (cf. Mark 2:17; Luke 19:10).

According to Josh. 12:15, Adullam was one of the Canaanite city-states conquered by the Israelites. That Judah had close contact with Adullam is indicated by the fact that the patriarch Judah married an Adullamite woman (Gen. 38:1). Adullam was considered to be part of the heritage of Judah (Josh. 15:35). 2 Sam. 23:13-14 confirms that David was active in that region. Some scholars read "stronghold of Adullam" instead of "cave of Adullam" in 1 Sam. 22:1 in order to conform to the reference to "stronghold" in v. 4 *(BH)*. It is possible that Adullam was a rocky region with many caves (cf. 2 Sam. 23:13-14) which could serve as strongholds for rebel groups like those of David. The name Adullam is preserved in Khirbet *'Idelmiyeh,* a site about 9 km. (6 mi.) E of Beit Jibrin, a place which is characterized by a large number of caves.

22:3-4   David is presented here as a dutiful son. Like a modern guerilla leader, David was always exposed to danger so that it was unsafe to leave his parents in Bethlehem unprotected. Thus he brings them to "the king of Moab." The reader may wonder why David did not leave his parents under the care of his elder brother. The purpose of the author here seems to be rather to portray David as an ideal character, a God-fearing person who kept all the commandments of God. In caring for his parents David was fulfiling the Fifth Commandment of the Decalogue (Exod. 20:12).

The location of "Mizpeh of Moab" (1 Sam. 22:3) is not known. Mizpeh in Hebrew means "watchtower," and as such it could have designated several high places. Thus we come across Mizpeh in Benjamin (Josh. 18:26) and Ramath-mizpeh (13:26). Mizpah is probably another reading of Mizpeh (cf. Judg. 11:29; 1 Sam. 7:5-16).

The Moabites were one of the Semitic groups related by kinship to the Israelites (Gen. 19:37). David was able to win their friendship. David's ability to maintain good relationships with his neighbors was one of the reasons for his success. Whereas Saul was losing the confidence and support of all around him, including the members of his family, David was gaining the support of all around him, even some of the traditional enemies of Israel such as the Moabites. This was because "the LORD was with him."

David is presented here as one who seeks and follows the will of God. He would, like his parents, stay in Moab "till I know what God will do for me" (1 Sam. 22:3). It is important that leaders who are appointed to save God's people remain always sensitive to discern the will of God in every situation so that they may not lose sight of their original vision and turn away from obeying God's leading.

22:5   As desired by David, God's will was revealed to David through the prophet Gad: David was to leave the stronghold and go to Judah. The stronghold in Adullam was perhaps safe, but that was not the place for a leader like David. Judah was to be the setting of his kingdom, and David should be there, though it meant exposure to dangers. Likewise, true discipleship to Christ means preparedness to depart from safety shelters and move to destinations shown us by God, even though it may mean exposure to perils and dangers (e.g., the Cross).

The will of God is revealed here through the prophet. The role hitherto played by the Spirit of God will from now on gradually be taken over by the prophet in Israel. The Spirit of God now works normally through the prophet.

Gad is here mentioned as a *nabi'*. According to 2 Sam. 24:11, he was the court prophet of David. There he is described also as "David's seer" *(hozeh)*. On the relationship between "prophet" and "seer," see above on 1 Sam. 9:9. In Judah David was now staying in "the forest of Hereth." Rocky mountains and forests have often been lodging places for rebel groups.

Saul's Vengeance on the Priests at Nob (22:6-23)

This section develops further Saul's decline in prestige in contrast to David's growing popularity and strength. This passage continues the account given in 21:1-9. It narrates the consequences on the priests at Nob for their innocently assisting David in his flight. The Edomite Doeg, who appears in the previous account as a silent observer (21:7), here becomes the cause of the massacre.

22:6-8   Being rejected by God, Saul feels rejected by all around him. He complains that all have "conspired" against him (v. 8). Sin as alienation from God alienates the sinner from people around him. At such a time the sinner is expected to turn to God, his only refuge and strength (Ps. 46:1). However, when the sinner, instead of turning to God, turns to other sources of strength — as Saul does here — and tries to solve his problem in his own strength, he not only destroys himself but actually also destroys others.

Saul is said to be sitting "under 'the' tamarisk tree" (1 Sam. 22:6). Later when he was killed, his body was buried under "the" tamarisk tree in Jabesh (31:13). On the cultic significance of trees, see the Introduction. Saul is here having a meeting with his servants, holding the spear in his hand as usual (cf. 18:11). Holding meetings under the shade of trees is common in tropical countries even today.

The majority of Saul's servants appear to be Benjaminites, from his own tribe, though the presence of some foreigners among them is indicated by the presence of "Doeg the Edomite" (22:9). These Benjaminite servants may well have been workers in the royal household and so not persons who had been reduced to slavery. This is further attested by the fact that Saul hints at the possibility of their getting "fields and vineyards" and being made "commanders of thousands and commanders of hundreds" (v. 7). Saul's main complaint is that, though he is their own kinsman, his servants never disclosed to him the friendship existing between his son and "the son of Jesse." He holds that with Jonathan's support David is now lying in wait to ambush and attack him (v. 8).

22:9-19   Doeg the Edomite betrays to Saul what he had seen in Nob. Saul then summons all "the priests who were at Nob" (v. 11), and charges Ahimelech of conspiracy against him in collaborating with David (vv. 12-13). Ahimelech pleads innocence and says that he helped David because he was a "faithful" servant of Saul besides being "the king's son-in-law, and captain over your bodyguard, and honored in your house" (v. 14). He further holds that this was not the first time that David had consulted him, implying thereby that David had often come to him seeking oracles before going on Saul's various missions. But Saul was not prepared to listen to any reason; he had already made up his mind about the priests of Nob. Suspicion blinds human reason to seeing the truth. He orders his guard to kill them, "but the servants of the king would not put forth their hand to fall upon the priests of the LORD" (v. 17). Because the priests are the consecrated holy people, common people should not lay their hands on them. So Saul asks Doeg to do the job. Doeg, being a foreigner, had no hesitation in killing them — eighty-five priests with their households (vv. 18-19).

The deterioration of Saul's character is developed step by step.

Our deeper understanding of human psychology today helps us understand how this happens. Saul's deterioration can be compared to Shakespeare's shaping of the characters in his tragedies. The sinner commits one mistake after another. Though Samuel withdrew his support, the priests at Nob seem to have extended their support to Saul till now, "inquiring of God" on his behalf. Now Saul himself destroys even that one remaining source of divine help. From now on "when Saul inquired of the LORD, the LORD did not answer him, either by dreams, or by Urim, or by prophets" (28:6). The tragedy is further increased by the fact that Doeg, formerly one of his enemies, now becomes his ally, his counselor, and executioner.

1 Samuel 22:17 appears to be a later interpolation. The charge on which the priests are to be put to death is different here — "they knew that he [David] fled, and did not disclose it to me." Moreover, it is difficult to imagine that Saul tolerated such disobedience from his servants, when he was so ruthless in temper as to kill even the priests of the LORD. A later redactor, standing in either the Deuteronomic or the Priestly tradition, who thereby could not see how any Israelite could lay his hands on the priests, or why an Edomite was told to kill the priests, probably introduced this verse here. He is also responsible for vv. 20-23. The destruction of the whole village (v. 19) was not part of Saul's original order. The language of this verse has the character of the description of *herem,* meaning "total destruction." It is possible that this was subsequently added in the light of some later happenings where it was Saul who ordered the destruction of the village.

22:20-23   The priest Abiathar, one of the sons of Ahimelech, escapes from Nob and brings the news of Saul's killing of "the priests of the LORD" to David. David takes upon himself the responsibility for the death of "all the persons" of Abiathar's father's house (v. 22) and offers Abiathar asylum. According to 23:6, Abiathar "came down with an ephod in his hand."

Saul's decline and David's rise are now further developed. Not only "the Spirit of God" but also "the priest of the LORD" has moved away from Saul and joined David. God is thus establishing David's kingdom.

In Saul's decline we see the spiritual decline of any believer. One's relationship with God is fundamental in life and basic to all other relationships — one's relationships both with fellow human beings and with nature (cf. Gen. 3). Once this basic relationship to God is strained, all other relationships become strained too.

David Escapes from Keilah (23:1-13)

The author tries to show that now things move in more certain terms than before, once the priests of the LORD joined David with the "oracle-instrument ephod." David does not fail to take the counsel of God in all matters, and God guides him and protects him.

1 Samuel 23:1-5 and 6-13 seem to come from different traditions. In vv. 1-5, David inquires of the LORD twice, but the "oracle-instrument ephod" is not mentioned. Ephod is introduced only in v. 6.

23:1-5   David saves Keilah, modern Khirbet Qila, about 5 km. (3 mi.) S of Adullam. From the fear expressed by the men of David (v. 3), it appears that at this time it was not a Judean territory. Keilah may have been under the influence of Saul (vv. 7-8). It was "a town that has gates and bars" (v. 7). Perhaps it was one of the Canaanite city-states which came under Saul's influence. Later it probably came to be assigned to Judah (cf. Josh. 15:44).

The expression "Now they told David" is from the editor; it is a narrative technique to begin accounts with indefinite subjects (cf. 1 Sam. 24:1). Philistines were "robbing the threshing floors" (23:1). This confirms the fact that the Philistines were originally sea-robbers who depended on plundered goods for their living (cf. 4:1b). These "sea-robbers" harassed the coastline as far as Latakia. Recent archaeological activity has revealed that it was they who destroyed the ancient city-states of Ugarit and Ebla, whose civilization had great influence on the history of early Israel. David was thus "doing his bit," under God, in seeking to push back these invaders whom the text knows as Philistines. In fact, the very name Philistine has taken on for us today the ideas of "vulgarian," "barbarian," even though in David's day the Philistines were more advanced on iron-culture than were the Israelites. Yet the Holy Land is now called Palestine after the Philistines!

"David inquired of the LORD" as to whether he should attack the Philistines and gets a positive answer from God (23:2); but David's men express their fear (v. 3). This is perhaps to stress the fact that it is the LORD who fights and not David himself. David inquires of the LORD a second time and again gets a positive answer, and so he fights against the Philistines. He "made a great slaughter among them" and "delivered the inhabitants of Keilah" and "brought away their cattle" (v. 5). The Philistines probably had brought their cattle with them to carry home the plundered goods. The law of "total destruction" *(herem)* is not applied here. David and his men apparently depended at this stage on just such spoils of war and on the support given to them as "protectors" by people whom they protected or delivered (cf. 25:7-8).

David continues his mission as the enemy of the Philistines; in this sense he is only fulfilling the task assigned to him by Saul and is not acting against the interests of the king. The Hebrew word *yasha'* is used here twice, translated by "save" (23:2) and "deliver" (v. 5). David is thus presented here as the savior of Israel, fulfilling the task of the king in Israel, as the secretly anointed one. As the chosen one of God, David becomes the source of blessings for the people around him. This is an important election motif in the OT (cf. Gen. 12:3).

23:6-8 Abiathar is mentioned here probably just to indicate the availability of an ephod with David (cf. 1 Sam. 23:6). When Saul hears that David is in Keilah, the fortified city, he believes that David has thus made a strategic mistake and takes it as an indication that "God has given him" into Saul's hand (v. 7). In a fortified city people can withstand outside attack provided they have plenty of provisions and a strong army. David had neither of these. Saul is therefore confident of capturing David. However, Saul forgets the fact that the LORD is with David.

23:9-13 David is more clever than Saul (cf. v. 22); he has informants in Saul's court (cf. 20:9, 13). He gets prior information about Saul's plots and escapes from Keilah before Saul "comes down." In v. 11 the first question should come after the second; we find it again in v. 12, so in the first occurrence it is a duplication caused by error. That David had a small army of "six hundred" (v. 13) during his fugitive days was well established in tradition (cf. 25:13; 27:2). Of these only four hundred were in active combat; the other two hundred "remained with the baggage" (25:13; 30:10). Those who went to the battle and those who remained with the baggage shared the spoils of the battle equally (30:24; cf. Num. 31:27). This Davidic tradition appears to have influenced the Saul traditions also (cf. 1 Sam. 13:15b; 14:2).

When Saul hears that David had left Keilah, he abandons his plan of pursuing him and returns. From this event we learn that divine oracles predict only possibilities that depend upon human behavior. The latter may change as a result of a change in the human situation (cf. Jonah 4:2). This speaks clearly against any doctrine of predestination in the OT.

David in the Wilderness of Ziph and the Ziphite Betrayal (23:14-29)

23:14-15   This is an editorial introduction. 1 Samuel 23:14a redundantly describes the whereabouts of David, which is also mentioned in v. 15b. Verse 14b is an editorial summary of David's flight before Saul. David could escape because "God did not give him into [Saul's] hand" (v. 14b). "The hill country of the Wilderness of Ziph" (vv. 14a, 15b) is the rocky plateau SE of Hebron. Ziph is identified with modern Tell Zif. Horesh (v. 15) designates either a place or good pastureland in Ziph.

23:16-18   God's assurance of support comes through Jonathan, who begins his speech with the words "Fear not," which are usually the introductory words of salvation oracles (cf. 4:20; 12:20). Jonathan "strengthened his hand in God" (23:16). He further reiterates "you shall be king over Israel" (v. 17), which is the lead motif of the whole Davidic account (cf. 20:15; 24:20; 2 Sam. 3:9-10). It is said that "the two of them made a covenant before the LORD" (1 Sam. 23:18). However, according to 18:3

both of them had already bound themselves with a covenant. What is done here is thus perhaps a reiteration of the covenant noted at 20:16.

23:19-24   The Ziphites betray David to Saul; perhaps they were threatened by the presence of David in their midst. Saul, because of his experience in Keilah (23:13), exercises caution here and asks the Ziphites to make doubly sure of David's whereabouts and to come back to him "with sure information" (v. 23). Saul's words "for you have had compassion on me" (v. 21) express his feeling of utter helplessness and recall what he said at 22:8. Saul, who has lost the compassion of God, relies too much on the compassion of humans, in contrast to David who prefers to "fall into the hand of the LORD" to falling "into the hand of man" (cf. 2 Sam. 24:14).

What is meant by "among all the thousands of Judah" in 1 Sam. 23:23 is not clear. Perhaps it is a reference to the fact that Saul made David "a commander of a thousand" (cf. 18:13). However, it was not said that this thousand unit was constituted of men from Judah. Moreover, we know that only six hundred men were with David during his fugitive days (cf. 23:13). Here it is said that Saul went out searching for David (v. 23). If the Ziphites have already identified the hiding place of David, what then is the need for Saul to search for him again? Perhaps the original text is corrupt here. The Ziphites go ahead in search of David, and Saul merely follows them. In the meantime, David and his men change their station to Maon.

23:25-29   David finds his hideout among the rocks "in the wilderness of Maon" (v. 25). When Saul is about to capture David, he receives news of the Philistine "raid upon the land" (v. 27) and returns from pursuing after David. That, according to the author, gave that place the name "the Rock of Escape," an etiological explanation. Just like "Ebenezer" (cf. 7:12), this too is probably a reference to the LORD. The LORD is the rock of refuge for his people (cf. Ps. 46:1, 7, 11). Once again it is made clear that the deliverance comes from the LORD. The enemy giving up pursuing the people of God and returning because of divine intervention through news (or rumors) of enemy attack in his own land is a holy war motif (cf. Isa. 37:7). En-gedi (1 Sam. 23:29) is the modern oasis 'Ain Jidi W of the Dead Sea.

David the Righteous Spares Saul at En-gedi (24:1-22)

Scholars generally agree that behind chs. 24 and 26 are parallel traditions on a common historical event. These two chapters share several common elements (compare 24:2 and 26:2; 24:6 and 26:9; 24:8a and 26:13a; 24:12 and 26:10-11; 24:16 and 26:17; 24:14 and 26:18; 24:17 and 26:21; 24:20-21 and 26:25). The tradition has undergone considerable changes as it was handed down, causing some internal tensions. How could David converse with his servants without being overheard by Saul? As it was passed down the tradition also acquired some elements of folklore, representing Saul as an idiotic character and David as a calm, daring, and resolute hero.

The dramatic development of the two characters reaches a climax here. At Maon David had almost fallen into the hands of Saul, and God had saved him. Now at En-gedi Saul comes still closer to David, so that David could have easily killed him, but David refrains from doing any harm to Saul. Both David and Saul agree that the event was the doing of God (24:10, 18). David's innocence towards Saul is once again proved and affirmed (vv. 11, 17). Saul himself acknowledges David as more righteous than himself and declares him as king. Here the author subtly underlines the essential qualification of an Israelite king: righteousness. David proved his righteousness in all respects so that even his opponent could not but acknowledge it and declare him to be the legitimate king. The increase of David and the corresponding decrease of Saul are dramatically developed by the author (cf. Matt. 3:15; John 3:30). David is acknowledged as king by all, including his enemy — first the people (cf. 1 Sam. 18:5, 16, 18), then the crown prince (cf. 20:13ff.), and now the king himself (24:20). God, who called David to be king over Israel, leads him further still until all, including his enemies, acknowledge him as king. Now nothing stands in the way for David to assume kingship openly.

24:1-3   The account opens with an indefinite subject (cf. 23:1). As usual David and his men are hiding in one of the rock caves (24:3) "in the wilderness of En-gedi" (v. 1; cf. 23:29). The "Wildgoats' Rocks" (24:2) are not identified. "The sheepfolds" (v. 3) could have been caves with a rough wall in front where shepherds could keep their sheep overnight or during bad weather. In the Hebrew the euphemistic expression "to relieve himself" (cf. Judg. 3:24) is literally "to cover his feet." The robe of a person (1 Sam. 24:4) normally covers his feet when he sits down to relieve himself, which could have given rise to this expression. According to Deuteronomic law one is expected to go outside the camp to relieve himself (Deut. 23:12); accordingly, Saul is seeking a place away from his soldiers. In the cave where Saul goes, David and his men sit in the dark at the back. They could see Saul entering the cave, whereas Saul could not see David and his men because, coming from the bright sunlight outside, his eyes would have been blinded.

24:4-7   The order of these verses has been disarranged. 1 Samuel 24:4a, 6, 7a, 4b, 5, 7b give a proper sequence of events. The servants of David seem to be aware of an earlier oracle given to David foreboding the handing over of Saul into his hands (v. 4a). So far no such oracle has been found. Perhaps the author is here recalling some royal oracle that was current during David's reign. Saul being the LORD's anointed and thus being holy, David will not put his hands on him (v. 6; on the understanding of holiness in Israel, see above on 6:2-9). The anointed king, because he is holy, becomes sacrosanct to the people. We see here the special interest of people close to David once he became king. By showing David's respect for the LORD's anointed one, Saul — a sick, idiotic king — the author is here telling his readers how much more their fear and respect for David should be. It is possible that 24:5-7a and 10b are from this "anointment" theologian. He has a special interest in messiahship (cf. 2 Sam. 1:14).

Instead of killing Saul, David "cut off the skirt of Saul's robe" (1 Sam. 24:4b) to show that the LORD had given Saul into David's hand that day (v. 10). This shows that even when God provides us with various possibilities for action, it is left to us to decide which course of action to take, and that this decision is influenced by one's discernment of God's will in any given context. Some scholars think that this skirt-cutting was part of an ancient magical ritual to exercise control over the person whose robe is cut (Martin Noth, "Bemerkungen zum sechsten Band der Mari-Texte," *Journal of Semitic Studies* 1 [1956]: 329-330; repr. *Aufsätze zur biblischen Landes- und Altertumskunde* [Neukirchen-Vluyn: Neukirchener Verlag, 1971] 2:240-41; Fritz Stolz, *Das erste und zweite Buch Samuel,* 154). However, that was clearly not in the mind of David.

24:8-15   David comes out into the open and establishes his innocence to Saul with irrefutable evidence. David is presented here as being totally loyal to Saul by giving him full respect as king. He addresses Saul as "my lord" (v. 8) and "my father" (v. 11). David "bowed with his face to the earth, and did obeisance" (v. 8; cf. 20:41-42).

David's words in 24:10 seem to imply that the LORD delivered Saul into David's hands to be killed by him, but that David spared Saul, as though against God's will. This, however, is not the case. David, who is led by God, sees Saul's delivery into his hands also as part of God's plan. How David should then deal with Saul is still left to him to decide; it is up to David to discern the will of God here in the light of what God has already revealed to him or taught him through the community of faith of which he is a part. David's understanding of "the LORD's anointed," which he received from his faith, helps him to make the necessary decision. He is not swayed by the worldly counsel given him by his men. A believer is often placed in similar situations where he or she must make the final decision. Thereupon the person, under the guidance of the Holy Spirit and in the light of all that he has learned from the Church, has to make his own decision.

The words "I have not sinned against you . . ." (v. 11) recall Jonathan's words to Saul regarding David's innocence in 19:4-5. However, the fact that David would not inflict any harm on Saul does not mean that David does not wish any evil on Saul. Because Saul is the LORD's anointed, David is not competent to avenge himself upon Saul; therefore, David invokes the LORD to do the vengeance for him (24:12; cf. 26:10-11). We often come across such a faith among many Christians as well; they may quote Prov. 25:21-22 as the motivation for doing good to enemies (Rom. 12:20). But forgiveness in Christ is neither postponing punishment for a later time nor transferring the responsibility of punishment to someone else. It is forgetting the sin of the enemy and extending to that person the hand of love.

Pesha' is the Hebrew word used here for "treason" (1 Sam. 24:11). This word belonged originally to the political vocabulary, where it meant the treason of vassals against their kings. David presents himself here in such a position; he has been loyal to the king in all his obligations as a vassal. But Saul has not been faithful to his obligations as a king to his vassal — to protect him and to support him. David therefore invokes "the LORD" to be the judge between him and Saul (vv. 12, 15; cf. 26:10-11). On all worldly matters the king is the supreme judge, to whom a subject can appeal. But if the king himself becomes the accused, who can serve as judge? Only God.

1 Samuel 24:13 appears to be a later interpolation. A proverb from the wisdom circle is inserted here (cf. Prov. 11:3ff.). The secondary nature of the verse is attested by the fact that 1 Sam. 24:13b is a verbatim repetition of v. 12b. In a diplomatic manner David humbles himself before Saul, comparing himself to "a dead dog" and "a flea" (v. 14), both of which are contemptible and worthless creatures and are incapable of doing anyone harm.

24:16-22   Saul recognizes David's voice (v. 16; cf. 26:17) and weeps in remorse; he contrasts his sinfulness to the righteousness of David. Saul's question here, "Is this your voice, my son David?" is seen by some to be out of place in the context where the two men are standing face to face. It is taken to belong to the parallel narrative (cf. 26:17), where the two are shouting at each other in darkness across the valley. This is taken to be an indication that the second narrative is more original (Caird, *IB* 2:1010). However, if we assume that David and his men are still standing under the shade of the cave so as not to be seen by Saul's soldiers who are awaiting Saul at a distance, the question can be taken as valid.

Saul declares here, "You are more righteous than I" (24:17).

A similar declaration is made by Judah with regard to the conduct of Tamar, his daughter-in-law, who played the harlot with him: "She is more righteous than I" (Gen. 38:26). In this perhaps we have a clue to the understanding of righteousness among the Israelites at this period in their history. According to the law of the levirate marriage, when a man dies without issue all members of the family — father, brothers, and his widow — have the responsibility to see that the deceased produces a son from his widow through one of his kinsmen (blood-relations); this is in order to continue the deceased's name on earth (cf. Ruth 3:12-13; 4:5-6). However, Judah fails in his responsibility in not giving his son Shelah to Tamar; so Tamar, risking her own reputation and life, produces a child through her father-in-law and thus fulfils her responsibility to her deceased husband and to the community. In this way she becomes more righteous than Judah. Righteousness is thus being loyal to the norms and rules accepted by the community. In the Saul-David relationship, by not killing Saul, "the LORD's anointed," David remains faithful to the norms set by the community — even at the risk of his own life. Saul, on the other hand, fails in his responsibility as king. As the king he is responsible to protect the life of his innocent subject David, yet he pursues David to kill him. Thus David becomes more righteous than Saul.

In this sense righteousness in David's day was not an absolute. It was relational. It belongs to a person's relationship with God and one's fellow human beings. As such it is situational or contextual. We cannot speak of a code of justice which is universally and eternally valid. Slavery and casteism, for example, were just social orders for people living some centuries ago; today they are seen as unjust practices. Polygamy is still a just social system among many tribes in Africa, but the same is considered to be illegal in many other parts of the world. A certain community may change its norms and laws as situations change. In later centuries the great prophets introduced a whole new depth of meaning into the term "righteousness."

If we cannot speak of absolute justice, one may ask, what then is the criterion we can use to check if a given social order or political system is just or unjust? Jesus Christ saw mankind to be the only criterion to this end when he declared, "The sabbath was made for man, not man for the sabbath" (Mark 2:27). Jesus judged the whole Jewish socio-religious order with the criterion of mankind. A given system may be judged on the basis of whether or not it brings the maximum good to the maximum number of people. We consider slavery unjust today because it robs people of their God-given identity, reduces them to the level of domestic animals, and treats them as objects. Polygamy is unjust because it discriminates against women and treats them as the property of men. Casteism, apartheid practices, and so forth are unjust because they discriminate against fellow human beings and oppress and exploit the weaker elements in the community. This way every system can be judged on the basis of how it treats men and women. If "mankind" is the criterion for justice, then the question arises: what type of person are we thinking of? Are we thinking of a consumeristic, capitalistic person or of a totalitarian person as the criterion? Here we have in Jesus the right image, a "man for others" — a person who is the subject of history, one who, as the image of God, is able to enjoy all the benefits of God's creation without destroying them, a person who voluntarily lays down his life for others — he is our criterion.

David and Abigail (25:1-44)

This chapter interrupts the accession narrative. The author appears to have placed it here purposely to serve as a parallel to what had happened in Saul's life after he was acclaimed as king over Israel. "Some worthless fellows" did not recognize Saul's kingship (1 Sam. 10:27). Nabal, which means "fool" (25:25), is here presented as a parallel figure to those worthless fellows who failed to bring presents to Saul. Nabal, too, refuses to give gifts to David. The narrator, who has developed the account of David's rise to the point where Saul himself acknowledges David as king, now introduces Nabal just to show the fate of anyone who does not accept or acknowledge David's kingship. Their end will be like that of Nabal (v. 26). By contrast, all those who act wisely in acknowledging David's kingship will have the favor of David, as in the case of Abigail. The story of David and Nabal could have had an independent tradition, and it could have been passed down in the Davidic circle at court.

25:1a   Verse 1a may have come from a redactor; it appears almost verbatim in 28:3a. Perhaps the redactor saw David's total recognition as king as the right point for the disappearance of Samuel from Israel's history. From now on God works instead through his anointed one, David.

25:1b-3   Nabal and Abigail are introduced. "The wilderness of Paran" (v. 1b; cf. Gen. 21:21; Num. 10:12; 12:16) is rather far to the south, so it is not likely that David's influence at this stage reached to that extent. The LXX reads "the wilderness of Maon," which fits well in this context, but it is not clear how the MT reading came about. Most scholars therefore reject the whole sentence.

Nabal belongs to the upper class of his society. He was "very rich" and had "business" in Carmel (1 Sam. 25:2; not the Mt. Carmel farther north). His main business was sheep-rearing. Nabal and Abigail are contrasting characters; their physical appearances corresponded to their internal dispositions (v. 3). Caleb was a Kenizzite (Num. 32:12; Josh. 14:6, 14), and Kenaz was an Edomite (Gen. 36:40, 42). In some places it is suggested that this tribe was incorporated into the tribe of Judah (cf. Num. 34:19), though in other places it appears to have been independent (cf. 1 Sam. 30:14). Nabal is here described as a Calebite. Whether this is a description of his ancestry or whether it is a reference to his bad nature is not clear. Abigail's remark in 25:25, "for as his name is, so is he," might hint at a possible connection between his character and his identity as a Calebite. The consonantal text in Hebrew can be read either "like his heart" or "his dog."

25:4-8   David sends his men to Nabal to request provisions on the ground that he and his men had not only abstained from plundering Nabal's sheep but had actually protected them from various enemies "all the time they were in Carmel" (v. 7).

25:9-13   Nabal shows an uncharitable response, comparing David to a runaway slave (v. 10). David and his men become

133

provoked and prepare for an attack on Nabal. In v. 11 the LXX reads "wine" in the place of "water." Water was not so scarce that Nabal would have to provide it. On David's six hundred men, see above on 23:13.

25:14-17   "One of the young men" of Nabal apprises Abigail of all that had happened and warns her of the adverse consequences unless some remedial measure is undertaken immediately. On servants counselling their masters, see above on 9:6. The young man testifies to all that has been claimed by David (cf. 25:7-8, 21-22). Nabal is "so ill-natured that one cannot speak to him" (v. 17). This explains why the young man came to speak to Abigail.

25:18-22   Abigail, as a good-natured woman, makes haste and rushes to meet David with large quantities of foodstuff as gifts in order to pacify his anger (vv. 18-20). Much of the food mentioned here is food specially meant for feeding troops (cf. 30:11-12; 2 Sam. 16:1). 1 Samuel 25:21-22 is out of place here; it should have come after v. 12. "God do so to David and more also" is a swearing formula.

25:23-31   Abigail pays homage to David by falling at his feet (vv. 23-24; cf. 20:41-42; 2 Sam. 1:2). She takes upon herself her husband's guilt (25:24, 28) and pleads that David abstain from shedding blood (vv. 26ff.). This account clearly comes from an author closer to David's circle who wanted to present David as an ideal character — "evil shall not be found in you so long as you live" (v. 28), "the life of my lord shall be bound in the bundle of the living in the care of the LORD your God" (v. 29), "my lord shall have no cause of grief, or pangs of conscience, for having shed blood without cause or for my lord taking vengeance himself" (v. 31). Yet we know that later traditions saw David as a "man of blood" (2 Sam. 16:7), and this was seen as a reason why God did not want David to build his temple (cf. 1 Chr. 28:3). This author is perhaps not aware of that late tradition.

Abigail's meeting with David is seen here as a divine intervention to restrain David "from bloodguilt" (1 Sam. 25:26). The mention of "sure house" in v. 28 is a reference to what was spoken of David's house in 2 Sam. 7:25-29. David is said to be "fighting the battles of the LORD" (1 Sam. 25:28); he is therefore always on a holy mission (see above on 21:5).

In 25:29, the Hebrew word used for "life" is *nephesh*. Older commentators who translated *nephesh* as "soul" thought that we have here evidence for the belief in life after death in early Israel. However, the concept of mankind as consisting of body and soul which become separated at the time of death is not Hebrew, but Greek. According to Hebrew thinking, mankind as body and spirit together became a "living soul *(nephesh)*" (Gen. 2:7). In the phrase "bound in the bundle of the living" the figure is that of precious possessions being wrapped up in a bundle so they may not get lost. The life of David, the anointed one, is likewise precious, and it is "in the care of the LORD your God." That the LORD gets rid of the enemies of the LORD's anointed one is a popular motif (e.g., 1 Sam. 20:15; 2 Sam. 22:4, 18; Ps. 18:3, 17). The LORD is about to appoint David as "prince" *(nagid)* over Israel (1 Sam. 25:30; see above on 9:16).

Blood revenge is an ancient cultic institution which was practiced by the Israelites. As seen already (cf. 14:31ff.), blood in Israel was seen as being equivalent to life, and so it belonged to God. Therefore it should be handled with utmost care. The OT provides ritual prescriptions for the use of blood. Animals should not be eaten with blood (Lev. 17:10ff.; 1 Sam. 14:31ff.); the blood should either be poured on the altar as sacrifice (Lev. 17:6) or, if the animals are killed away from the temple, their blood should be poured on the earth (v. 13). If human blood is spilled, it gives rise to bloodguiltiness on the person who spilled it, and it also affects the community adversely (cf. Gen. 4:10; 9:5). Innocent blood shed this way cries to heaven (Gen. 4:10); it is restless until it is avenged and until the blood of the guilty party is spilled (Gen. 9:6). It is therefore the responsibility of the living kinsmen of the deceased to avenge the blood that has been shed. Thus there arose the institution of blood revenge in Israel.

David is here "restrained from bloodguilt" (1 Sam. 25:26) so that he may not later have any "cause of grief, or pangs of conscience, for having shed blood without cause or for . . . taking vengeance himself" (v. 31).

25:32-35   David acknowledges that it was the LORD who through Abigail restrained him "from bloodguilt and from avenging" himself with his own hand (v. 33). He receives Abigail's gifts and grants her petition not to avenge himself in person.

25:36-39   That Nabal was "very rich" (v. 2) is apparent in the feast he was celebrating; it was "like the feast of a king" (v. 36). His folly (v. 25) was coupled with addiction to alcohol (cf. Prov. 20:1; 23:29ff.); Nabal was drunk the whole night. When he sobered up, Abigail told him what had happened. Nabal was frightened to death because of possible retaliation from David. He became sick and "about ten days later" he died (1 Sam. 25:38). It was believed that "the LORD smote Nabal." According to the author the LORD, who restrained David from staining his hands with blood, executes justice by punishing Nabal himself (vv. 38-39).

According to David, "the LORD has returned the evil-doing of Nabal upon his own head" (v. 39a). Behind this lies the Israelite belief in the inseparable nature of an act and its effect. It was believed that every act, good or bad, carried with it its good or bad effect and that the LORD saw to it that every act led to its own logical outcome.

25:40-44   These verses present an account of David's wives. Further details about his wives and children are found in 2 Sam. 3:2-5; 5:13-16. David takes Abigail as his wife, along with a second woman named Ahinoam of Jezreel.

David Spares Saul at Hachilah (26:1-25)

On the question of the relationship of this chapter to 1 Sam. 24, see the introduction to ch. 24. The scene of the event and the circumstances are different in the two traditions. Various elements indicate that this was the earlier tradition, closer to the event. The tradition in ch. 24 has acquired certain folklore elements which speak for its longer circulation among people.

26:1-5   David comes to Hachilah, where Saul and his army camp. It was obviously nighttime; "Saul was lying within the encampment, while the army was encamped around him" (26:5). In both accounts the Ziphites seem to bring to David the news of Saul's whereabouts. Verse 1 assumes that the Ziphites are those mentioned in 23:19. Both accounts maintain that Saul took "three thousand chosen men of Israel" (26:2; 24:2). Whereas 23:19 locates "the hill of Hachilah" S of Jeshimon, this tradition locates it "on the east of Jeshimon" (26:3); Jeshimon means "wasteland" or "desert."

26:6-12   David and Abishai enter Saul's camp and take "the spear and the jar of water from Saul's head" (v. 12) with no one noticing. This was possible "because a deep sleep from the LORD had fallen upon them." Ahimelech the Hittite (v. 6) is not known otherwise. The account in 2 Sam. 11:6ff. attests that there were Hittites in David's army. The Hittites were an ancient people whose empire had once reached from the north of Syria throughout Asia Minor. They were probably of Cappadocian origin, and their city Boghazköy in modern Turkey has yielded considerable archaeological finds (cf. Gen. 23:3; 25:10; 26:34).

Abishai is here presented as the brother of Joab (1 Sam. 26:6). According to 1 Chr. 2:16, Zeruiah is David's sister and Abishai, Joab, and Asahel are her sons and thus David's nephews. 1 Samuel 26:8 corresponds to 24:4. 1 Samuel 26:10 is perhaps an addition. David sees a threefold possibility of Saul's death — natural death, "the LORD will smite him" with a disease, or Saul will "go down into battle and perish" with the sword. Disease and sword are parts of the curse from God, two of the various divine judgments upon sinful mankind. "A deep sleep" from God (v. 12) works for salvation (Gen. 2:21; 15:12) or for destruction (Isa. 29:10). Here it works for the deliverance of David from Saul's hands.

David asks Abishai to take the spear and the jar of water that were at the head of Saul (1 Sam. 26:11); but according to v. 12 David himself takes them. Abishai is not mentioned again in this chapter.

26:13-16   David charges Abner, Saul's commander, of negligence in keeping watch over the king, a crime which deserves the punishment of death. In David's words to Abner the author reminds the reader of the people's responsibility to protect "the LORD's anointed" — David and his successors — lest "the lamp of Israel" be quenched (2 Sam. 21:17).

26:17-20   Saul recognizes David's voice, and David offers evidence to establish his innocence. 1 Samuel 26:17 is parallel to 24:16. David could see only two reasons for Saul's chasing after him: Saul is "stirred up against" David either by God or by humans (v. 19). Neither ch. 24 nor ch. 26 seems to be aware of the tradition of the "evil spirit on Saul" (cf. 16:14; 18:10-11) which could have explained Saul's strange behavior. In David's words here are traces of early popular thinking. First, God is held responsible for human actions even when the actions are unjust (cf. Exod. 11:10; Judg. 9:23; 1 Kgs. 12:15). Second, in such a case God could be appeased by an offering (1 Sam. 26:19). The Hebrew text here literally means "let him smell an offering," which recalls Gen. 8:21, where it is said that "the LORD smelled the pleasing odor" of Noah's sacrifice. Third, Yahweh can be worshipped only in his own territory. By Saul's chasing after David, David is forced to leave Yahweh's territory so that he might have no share "in the heritage of the LORD." He is thus compelled to "go, serve other gods" (cf. 2 Kgs. 5:17; Jer. 5:19). So David prays that his blood might not "fall to the earth away from the presence of the LORD" (1 Sam. 26:20). Dying in an unclean land was considered to be a curse, for all foreign lands were considered to be unclean (cf. Amos 7:17). 1 Samuel 26:20b corresponds to 24:14.

26:21-25   Saul acknowledges his sin (26:21) and affirms David's "righteousness" (cf. v. 23). David hopes that the LORD will reward him for the good he did to Saul (vv. 23-24). The Deuteronomic principle of reward and retribution (Deut. 28) and the Israelite belief in the act-effect sequence lie behind such a belief. 1 Samuel 26:25 is parallel to 24:19-20. Saul himself blesses David: David "will do many things and will succeed in them."

Saul's readiness to acknowledge his mistake and to refrain from harming David further is an aspect of his good nature. If a sinner confesses his sin and abstains from it, his sin is forgiven and he

138

is restored to fellowship with the one against whom he had sinned. Yet here Saul's good nature appears to be but momentary, and not of a lasting nature.

David among the Philistines in Ziklag (27:1–28:2)

Here we have another version of David's stay in a Philistine city (see introduction to 21:10-15). The account here is meant to bring David's fugitive condition to an end. David secures Ziklag (27:6) as a permanent place of settlement, and he and his servants with all their households (v. 3) settle down there.

The chapter is not a literary unit in itself; there are tensions within it. According to vv. 5-7, David and his men moved to Ziklag; but vv. 8-12 still speak of events happening around Gath. It is possible that both references come from independent traditions.

27:1-4   Though Saul said that he would do no more harm to David, David cannot rely on his word because of earlier experiences. He finds refuge among the Philistines, so that Saul will refrain from seeking him; he will not find him "within the borders of Israel" (v. 1). This flight to a foreign land speaks against David's desire to worship Yahweh in his own territory as expressed in 26:19. Perhaps we have here an independent tradition which had no knowledge of the account in ch. 26. On David's "six hundred men" (27:2), see above on 23:13.

27:5-7   These verses explain etiologically how Ziklag became part of Judah. The reference to "the kings of Judah" presumes knowledge of the divided monarchy in Israel. Ziklag lies N of Beer-sheba; its exact location is disputed. It was an outpost of Gath. According to 1 Chr. 18:1, David conquered Gath; this speaks against the fact that Achish was living there still at the time of Solomon (1 Kgs. 2:39-40). According to 2 Sam. 15:18, a group of Gittities from Gath fought on the side of David. Gath could have become by then the vassal of David. Later on the whole of Gath belonged to Judah (2 Chr. 11:8). Still later it appears to have fallen once again into the hands of the Philistines

(Amos 6:2). It is possible that Ziklag was not given as a gift to David, but that David claimed it in return for the spoils he brought to Achish (1 Sam. 27:9). Abigail's blessing of a "sure house" (25:28) begins to be realized here. From this point dating formulas are used (27:7), indicating that David's kingship had already begun.

27:8-12   Now as a king David begins his conquests. He destroys the Geshurites, the Girzites, and the Amalekites, "the inhabitants of the land from of old, as far as Shur, to the land of Egypt" (v. 8). Perhaps this is seen as part of the fulfilment of God's promise to Moses and Joshua: David here destroys the people who survived the conquest by Joshua. The institution of *herem* is not implied here, though the destruction by David bears the character of a *herem* (v. 9). The cattle and the other valuable things are taken as spoils of war. The purpose of destroying men and women here is not so much to carry out a divine order as to block out news from reaching Achish (v. 11). David is here acting brutally, quite in contrast to the concern expressed in 25:26ff. yet true to his reputation as a man of blood (2 Sam. 16:8). The fact is that during the course of history David may well have been idealized in the Davidic circles as the Israelite king par excellence. The killing of foreigners was in early times not seen as sin involving bloodguilt (cf. Klaus Koch, *VT* 12 [1962]: 411): "Such was his custom" (1 Sam. 27:11).

The Geshurites are mentioned along with the Philistines (Josh. 13:2); perhaps they were one of the allies of the Philistines, settled in southwest Palestine. They are not to be confused with the people of the same name living in the northern territory E of Jordan (Josh. 13:11, 13). Girzites are mentioned only here. Perhaps the word refers to a group of people living next to the Geshurites. The Amalekites are the old enemies of Judah (1 Sam. 15:1ff.). Negeb in Hebrew means "the south country"; it is still the name for the steppelands to the south of Palestine stretching from Beer-sheba in the north of Kadesh-barnea to the edge of the desert. During the time of David there were five regions identified as Negeb, three of which are mentioned in 27:10. The other two are the Negeb of the Cherethites and the Negeb of Caleb, both mentioned in 30:14. The Jerahmeelites existed as an independent tribe in the days before the kingship (1 Chr. 2:9ff.). According to Judg. 1:16, the Kenites and the Judeans entered the Promised Land together. Still the Kenites were not finally settled. In later times they lived in the area where the Amalekites (cf. 1 Sam. 15:6) wandered as nomads.

Achish is presented here as a fool, another Nabal, in contrast to David, who is cunning and clever. He trusts David to the extent of making him his "bodyguard for life" (cf. 27:12–28:2).

Saul Consults the Witch of Endor (28:3-25)

The decline of Saul reaches its lowest ebb. Saul, who was once the chosen one of the LORD, finds himself now at the opposite extreme, in the bosom of evil seeking the guidance of a witch. In Saul we see the spiritual tragedy that can happen to a person who is no more in the fellowship of God. Such a person finds himself soon in the company of forces that are against the will of God.

The account of Saul's visit to the witch of Endor interrupts the narrative, for ch. 29 follows 28:2. This narrative forms the preparation for Saul's final tragedy, of which we learn in ch. 31. Therefore it is supposed that 28:3-25 originally stood before ch. 31 and that a Deuteronomic editor suppressed it for theological reasons. Consequently, at a later stage some other redactor could have inserted this passage at the wrong place. Perhaps we have here an originally independent tradition, a saga current in the area of Endor.

28:3 The reference to Samuel's death (28:3a) is a repetition of 25:1a. The purpose of referring to Samuel's death at this point may be to reveal that with the death of the prophet all those forces which had hitherto been forbidden under the influence of Samuel are now revived. Israelite law forbids the use of "mediums" and "wizards" (cf. Lev. 19:31; 20:6, 27; Deut. 18:10-11, 14; 2 Kgs. 17:17). During Isaiah's time also this practice was a problem (Isa. 8:19). Removal of the mediums was part of the later Josianic reform (2 Kgs. 23:24).

141

28:4-7   The context in which Saul must seek a witch is explained here. The Philistines had made ready their forces to fight against Israel. The very sight of the army of the Philistines frightens Saul, and the LORD does not answer him, "either by dreams, or by Urim, or by prophets." In utter helplessness Saul turns to the witch of Endor. Humans are not self-sufficient beings; they are dependent on God for a holistic life. So when a person moves away from God, he realizes his imperfection and insufficiency and seeks substitutes for God. But because no other person or force can substitute for God, such a person ultimately ends up in self-destruction. This is what happens in the case of Saul. The proper course of action for a sinner is repentance and return to God, who alone is able to restore that person to life in fellowship with God.

The Philistine army gathers at Shunem and Israel at Gilboa (1 Sam. 28:4). This contradicts the report at 29:1, according to which the Philistines are in Aphek. Shunem and Gilboa are places facing each other across the eastern end of the plain of Esdraelon in the area of Jezreel. On the fact that Saul "was afraid and his heart trembled greatly" (28:5), see above on 17:8-11. "A woman who is a medium" (28:7) is a witch. Endor is N of the Little Hermon and S of Mt. Tabor.

28:8-14   Saul consults the witch. The mention of Saul's taking two men with him suggests a number symbolism here; for such mystical or sacred meetings the number three is preferred (cf. Gen. 18:2). The three come to the woman "by night." Perhaps the author wants to point out that by moving away from God Saul has become a man of the night. Such symbolic language appears to have been common among the Israelites (cf. John 13:30). Since Saul had forbidden mediums and wizards, the woman has not been practicing the craft, because she knew that it meant death for her. For that reason she sees Saul's request to divine as a snare (1 Sam. 28:9). Saul assures her that no punishment shall "come upon" her. A sworn oath was binding (cf. 30:15); but how could the woman believe that an ordinary man could save her from the king? Perhaps the writer was not interested in such details! During the process of divination, in her state of trance, the woman recognizes Saul in disguise and she is afraid (28:12). Saul allays her fear (v. 13) and so she consults the dead Samuel. Saul pays the prophet homage by "bowing his face to the ground" as he did when Samuel was alive (cf. 20:41). Samuel's appearance was that of "a god *(elohim)*" (28:13).

Necromancy was part of popular religion in those days. The author questions only the acceptability of the practice in the context of the worship of Yahweh; but he never challenges its possibility. It is strange that this belief is revived in the West today as part of the New Age movements in the form of occultism, satanism, and the like.

From this account we can identify certain elements of early Israelite belief on life after death. (1) It was assumed that the spirits of the dead were in a state of rest inside the earth (cf. Isa. 29:4) and they did not want to be disturbed (1 Sam. 28:15). (2) The dead retained their professional skills as in life. The fact that Saul asked for Samuel implies that it was believed that only Samuel could reveal God's will to him, even in the state of death. (3) No notion of reward and retribution is suggested at this stage. Saul and his children would join Samuel after their death at Gilboa; in other words, both the man with the spirit of God and the man with the evil spirit would be in the same place after death. (4) Though necromancy was condemned, people believed in its efficacy. Necromancy was believed to have power over the dead, even over a sacred person such as Samuel.

28:15-19 Samuel, being a man of God, will not be able to help anyone whom God does not want to help. Thus it is foolish of Saul to have believed that Samuel would help him when God himself "has turned from" him and become his "enemy" (v. 16). However, Samuel reveals to Saul what is going to happen to him (vv. 17-19). Verses 17-18 recall what was said by Samuel in 15:26-28. The "neighbor" to whom the LORD has given the kingdom is here specified as David.

28:20-25 On hearing Samuel's words, Saul falls on the ground "full length" (28:20). Perhaps the king fainted. The author sees two reasons for this — besides the fear of death, Saul is also overtaken by exhaustion because "he had eaten nothing all day and all night." Saul thus becomes a self-defeated person before he is actually defeated by the Philistines.

Persuaded by the medium and his own servants, Saul accepts her hospitality and returns (vv. 22-25). The significance of this account is not clear. Perhaps the author here contrasts Saul's fellowship meal with Samuel at the time of his calling (cf. 9:12ff.) with his meal with the witch, and sees in it the contrast between human fellowship with God and the fellowship with evil. From another perspective, at the human level the attitude of the "witch" who forgives Saul and feeds him is a more "Christian" act.

The Philistines Oust David from Their Army (29:1-11)

The Philistine lords, as they organize their army against Israel, see David and his men among Achish's contingent. They object to David's going with them in their campaign against Israel, though Achish speaks for David's loyalty and dependability. The Philistine commanders have heard of David's reputation in Israel (29:5), and they cannot see how David could be other than loyal to "his lord" (Saul). They fear that during the course of the battle David could at any time turn out to be "an adversary" to the Philistines. Thus they demand that Achish send him back to the place to which Achish assigned him (v. 4). Achish with a sense of apology requests David to return with his men (vv. 6-7). So David and his men "return to the land of the Philistines," while the Philistines march towards Jezreel to meet Saul and his army (v. 11).

It is worth noticing that in the whole chapter the name of David's place is not mentioned. Verse 4 refers to it as "the place to which you have assigned him," and v. 11 mentions that "David set out with his men . . . to the land of the Philistines." Although 30:1 says that they came to Ziklag, that name does not appear in ch. 29. It is possible that behind ch. 29 lies an independent tradition which did not know about David's association with Ziklag.

The main purpose of this chapter seems to be keeping David out of the scene of the final combat between Saul and the Philistines, for David would have found himself in a great dilemma had he been allowed to go with Achish. To support the Philistines against Saul would have meant betrayal of Israel's cause and becoming responsible for Saul's death. This would have made David guilty in the light of the anointment theology. To turn against Achish and to fight for Israel would have meant, if Israel were successful, the non-fulfilment of the words of Samuel (cf. 15:26-28; 28:17-19). If David sided with Israel and they failed, it would have meant the denial of David's claim to be the anointed one of God, the man with the spirit of God; that would have had a demoralizing effect among David's followers. To remain quiet at a time when Saul was in danger would have meant failing in his obligations as a loyal citizen in Israel. So David is taken away from the scene to fight against another enemy of Israel (cf. ch. 30). Thus we see how much theological thinking has gone into this chapter.

In David's ousting from the Philistine army the author sees God's plan for David. God leads the pagan Philistines to rescue David from a dilemma from which he cannot save himself. The time is now ripe for David to assume his responsibility in Israel.

On Aphek (29:1), see above on 4:1b. The "fountain in Jezreel" has been identified with 'Ain Jalud at the foot of Mt. Gilboa (cf. 28:4). Achish and his men were "in the rear" of the Philistine army (29:2). Perhaps Achish was the presiding lord of the Philistines. The Philistines had no kings, only "lords" of each city-state, much like Malaysia today. It seems as if the leadership went in rotation. Achish was thus only "first among equals," *primus inter pares.* David, as his "bodyguard for life" (28:2), was with Achish. David's reputation and popularity among his own people (29:5; cf. 18:7; 21:11) speak for David's loyalty to his own people, and hence the Philistines could not trust him. When Achish asked him to leave, David again, being true to his reputation as a cunning man, pretends to be offended by Achish's mistrust and asserts his loyalty (29:8). Achish, too, testifies to David's innocence, saying, "You are as blameless . . . as an angel of God . . ." (v. 9). The Hebrew word used here for angel is *mal'ak,* which means "messenger." Angelology, which is part of apocalyptic thinking, was not known at this time. A messenger of God is blameless because he stands under the authority and protection of God.

David Redeems Israel from the Amalekites (30:1-31)

Here is repeated one of David's attacks on the southern tribes mentioned before in 27:8. Chapters 27, 29, and 30 are seen as part of one composition. Chapter 30 appears to have had its own tradition; it seems to have acquired several elements of saga over the course of time — David and his men mourning over the capture of their wives and children (v. 4), the crisis of confidence in David (v. 6), the meeting with the Egyptian (vv. 11-15), the dispute over sharing the spoils (vv. 21-25), and the sending of presents to the elders of Judah (vv. 26-31). The chapter is put in this place to save David from the charge of being disloyal to his king in not coming to Saul's rescue at a time when his life was in danger (see above on 24:17). According to the narrator, the LORD had sent David on another mission (30:8), and that is why David was not available for Saul's rescue.

30:1-6 Verse 1 is meant to link ch. 30 with the preceding chapter. Being sent away from the Philistine army, David returns to his place in Ziklag and reaches Ziklag on the third day. He discovers that the Amalekites have raided upon the Negeb and Ziklag, taken captive "the women and all who were in it," and "burned it with fire" (v. 2). The weeping of the people was an aspect of communal mourning (v. 4). David is blamed for what had happened, and "the people spoke of stoning him" (v. 6). When David killed Goliath and brought victory to Israel, the people praised him to the heavens in the exuberance of success (cf. 18:6-7). Now when a misfortune befalls them they turn against him and want to stone him to death. Such is the experience of every true leader (cf. Exod. 16:2-3). At such moments of loneliness and forsakenness, God is the only refuge and strength for his servant. Thus "David strengthened himself in the LORD his God" (1 Sam. 30:6).

On Ziklag, see above on 27:6; on the Amalekites, see the introduction to 15:1-35; and on the Negeb, see above on 27:10. The intention of burning places that have been raided may be to weaken the enemy and prevent possible retaliation, a strategy known in modern warfare as well. Here Ziklag alone is burned

(30:1, 14). This may be an act of vengeance against David because of his raids (cf. 27:8ff.).

30:7-10   David's decision to pursue after the Amalekites at a time when Saul was being attacked by the Philistines was a decision made by God.

On Ahimelech and Abiathar (30:7), see above on 21:1 and 22:20; on the ephod, see the Introduction: Beliefs and Practices. On the six hundred men who were with David (30:9), see above on 23:13. The purpose of leaving two hundred men behind was originally for keeping the "baggage" (cf. 25:13). However, since everything that belonged to David had been taken away by the Amalekites, the author gives here another reason: they were "too exhausted to cross the brook Besor" (30:10). The criterion for deciding who should stay behind could have been that those who were exhausted and weak could stay behind. "The brook of Besor" is not known.

30:11-15   Divine guidance comes to David through an Egyptian slave. On divine guidance coming through servants or slaves, see above on 9:6.

When they discovered that he was of no more use to them, the Amalekites had abandoned their sick Egyptian slave (30:13). This is the danger when human beings are reduced to the level of animals and are treated as objects. It is what is happening in our modern technocratic society where the weak, the sick, the powerless, the poor, and the marginalized are cast out of the mainstream of life. Jesus, on the other hand, came to reverse this order, "to seek and to save the lost" (cf. Luke 19:10), to make a "people" out of such "no people." He came to make mankind the subject of history and not the object of history (cf. Mark 2:27).

David and his men show kindness to this slave (1 Sam. 30:11-12), and he becomes a useful aid in their pursuit. No human being is worthless in God's eternal purpose. When properly fed and treated, such abandoned poor and sick can become effective instruments in the hand of God.

On the five types of Negeb, see above on 27:10. The Cherethites (30:14; 2 Sam. 8:18; 15:18; 20:7) seem to have had some association with the Philistines (Zeph. 2:5; Ezek. 25:16); they were one of the Canaanite peoples who occupied the country before the coming of either Israel or the Philistines. The Negeb of Caleb lay E of the Negeb of the Cherethites and S of Hebron (Josh. 14:13-14).

30:16-20   David takes the Amalekites unawares and defeats them. He not only redeems all his people and their property, but "also captured all the flocks and herds" (1 Sam. 30:20) that belonged to the Amalekites. Perhaps the Amalekites had heard about David's going with Achish and they were not expecting David's early return; so they were "eating and drinking and dancing" (v. 16) and thus fell easily into the hands of David. "Four hundred" of the Amalekites fled on camels and escaped (v. 17); the number may have some symbolic connection with that of David's forces (see above on 23:13). The Israelites did not seem to have used animals in warfare during this period. However, later in his career David seems to have captured horses and chariots from his enemies (cf. 2 Sam. 8:4). David apparently gained a lot of spoils, which gave rise to the proverbial saying "this is David's spoil" (1 Sam. 30:20). David could have taken all the spoils which the Amalekites had gathered in their raids in the Negeb and also the belongings of the Amalekites themselves.

30:21-25   Here we have the etiology of a statute on the sharing of the spoils: "As his share is who goes down into the battle, so shall his share be who stays by the baggage; they shall share alike" (v. 24). The phrase "to this day" (v. 25) is typical of etiological accounts. This is a case of a judge's decision *(mishpat)* being included later in the Law of Moses as a statute *(hoq)* that has developed from a local mishpat (cf. Num. 31:27). "To this day" is the bridge from David's day (1000 B.C.) to the formation of the Deuteronomic history. The argument behind this law of equal sharing is that the victory is Yahweh's; as such all the spoils belong to him, and no particular group has any special claim on them (1 Sam. 30:23). We who live in a competitive society have a lesson here on equal sharing of God-given resources. The rich and the strong tend to claim unequal special shares over against the poor and the weak. But God's justice demands equal justice to all — equal share for both the strong and the weak, because all that we have — health, strength, and wealth — are the gifts of God.

30:26-31   David sends part of the spoils to his "friends, the elders of Judah" (v. 26). This appears to be independent of vv. 21-25. How could the people who were against sharing the spoils with their own members have allowed David to give them to others who did not participate in their campaigns? According to Num. 31:27, 42, half of the spoils was administered by Moses at his discretion while half was given to the warriors. A similar practice could have been followed during David's time as well. David acts magnanimously to repay those who were kind to him in his desert days. By sharing the spoils with his friends and elders in Judah, David wins their confidence and support. The ground is being prepared for his anointment as king over Judah in Hebron (2 Sam. 2:4).

The name Judah is used here anachronistically as a general designation for the southern tribes. Only a few places mentioned here (1 Sam. 30:27-31) are identifiable. For "Bethel, in Ramoth of the Negeb" the LXX reads "Ramah" (cf. Josh. 19:8). Jattir and Eshtemoa are mentioned in Josh. 15:48; 21:14. Aroer (1 Sam. 30:28) is not to be mistaken for the place bearing the same name E of the Jordan Rift and the Dead Sea, which is Ararah at the southernmost limits of Judah. Hebron is the northernmost point of David's "roaming" (v. 31). Racal is unidentified; the LXX reads here "Carmel." On Jerahmeelites and Kenites, see above on 27:10. Siphmoth, Hormah, Borashan, and Athach are not as yet identified.

THE DEATH OF SAUL AND JONATHAN (31:1-13)

The account of the death of Saul and his sons takes up from the account of Saul's visit to the witch of Endor. Both accounts describe the helplessness of Saul and his tragic end, yet they seem to be independent traditions. 1 Samuel 28:4 speaks of Gilboa as the scene of the battle, whereas 31:1 places it at "Mount Gilboa." A clearer version of this event is preserved in 1 Chr. 10:1-12.

149

According to 1 Sam. 31, Saul was wounded by the archers and wanted his armor-bearer to kill him. When the armor-bearer refused to do so, Saul took his own sword, fell upon it, and died. However, a different version of Saul's death appears in 2 Sam. 1:6-10, 13-16; in that account an Amalekite saw Saul leaning on his spear, and Saul called to him and begged the Amalekite to slay him. Seeing that Saul would not survive, the Amalekite acceded to Saul's request and killed him. There seems to have been still another version of Saul's death lying behind 2 Sam. 4:9-10. According to this version, it was not the Amalekite who killed Saul — he only brought the news of Saul's death. It is probable that there circulated more than one version of the account regarding Saul's death, for no one else was there to witness it.

This chapter tries to show how the words of Yahweh pronounced through Samuel regarding Saul and his sons (1 Sam. 15:23, 26; 28:19) came at last to be fulfilled. Saul, rejected and forsaken by Yahweh, dies a tragic death, and his kingdom soon comes to an end.

31:1-3 The Philistines press upon the king and his sons, because their death could determine the course of the battle. Saul's three sons — Jonathan, Abinadab, and Malchishua — are all killed in the battle. Saul is wounded. On Saul's sons, see above on 14:49-50.

31:4-7 Saul knew that his end was near because "the chariots and the horsemen were close upon him" (2 Sam. 1:6); he knew what would happen to him if he fell alive into the hands of his enemies. Sporting with captured enemies was a common practice in the ancient Near East (e.g., Samson, Judg. 16:21-27; Zedekiah, 2 Kgs. 25:7). Moreover, falling into the hands of "the uncircumcised" was itself an inglorious thing to happen to an Israelite king. Besides, Saul was already wounded by the archers (1 Sam. 31:3). So he begs his armor-bearer to kill him; but the armor-bearer would not oblige, because Saul was the LORD's anointed and he was not supposed to lay his hands on the king in any way (see above on 24:4-7). The armor-bearer's fear was justified by what then happened to the Amalekite who killed the ailing king and brought the news to David (2 Sam. 1:14-16; 4:10). On seeing the death of Saul, his king, the armor-bearer — as a faithful servant — thereupon committed suicide. With the death of Saul and his sons, Israel lost its leadership. "The men of Israel" in that region consequently feared being plundered by the conquering Philistine army. Therefore they deserted their cities and fled, and "the Philistines came and dwelt in them" (1 Sam. 31:7).

31:8-10   The next day when the Philistines came "to strip the slain" (v. 8) they saw the dead bodies of Saul and of his three sons. They cut off Saul's head, maybe as a retaliation for David's cutting off Goliath's head. They also put Saul's armor in the temple of Ashtaroth, just as David had put Goliath's armor in the temple at Nob (21:9). The Philistines fastened Saul's body "to the wall of Beth-shan" (31:10).

31:11-13   When the people of Jabesh-gilead heard "what the Philistines had done to Saul," they traveled all night, took the bodies of Saul and his sons from the wall of Beth-shan, brought them to Jabesh, and "burnt them there." This they did probably out of their gratitude for Saul's delivering them from the Ammonite attack recorded in ch. 11. As a sign of mourning for Saul and for his sons they "fasted seven days."

Burning dead bodies was not common in Israel; this was probably a special measure to preserve the bones, with the intention of taking them back later to Israel. Such secondary burials for bones alone were certainly known in Palestine. We learn that David later on brought Saul's bones from Jabesh-gilead and buried them in the family grave of Kish at Zela in Benjamin (2 Sam. 21:12-14).

We note that the people of Jabesh buried the bones "under the tamarisk tree" (1 Sam. 31:13); but according to 1 Chr. 10:12, they buried them "under the oak" in Jabesh. The presence of the tamarisk tree in that place shows that it was well known as a spot where divinity dwelled. Such a tree was planted by Abraham in a sacred place (Gen. 21:33 J). It yielded manna. The "oak" *(elah)* mentioned in 1 Chr. 10:12 is not the European oak which is deciduous, but a special oak which is evergreen. Since it does not "die" it was believed to be the seat of divinity. Perhaps the same oak is referred to under two names. On the religious significance of trees and on the mystic number seven, see Introduction: Beliefs and Practices.

2 SAMUEL

I. DAVID BECOMES KING
OF JUDAH AND ISRAEL
2 Samuel 1:1–5:5

The history of God's salvation continues. God's plan of salvation cannot be thwarted by human failures; from time to time God raises up worthy servants who will listen to his words and carry out his eternal purposes. Such is the Deuteronomic teaching of history which lies behind this account. When Saul, the anointed one of the LORD, fails in his calling and ends in death, David succeeds him as the heir to carry out God's plan of salvation for his people.

NEWS OF SAUL'S DEATH (1:1-16)

Regarding the different versions of the account of Saul's death, see above on 1 Sam. 31:1-13. The account in 1:1-16 displays internal tensions. In v. 2 the messenger who brings the news is mentioned as "a man," but in v. 6 he is said to be "a young man." David's question to the young man ("Where do you come from?") is repeated twice (vv. 3, 13); in v. 3 the man gives a direct answer but in v. 13, instead of telling where he had come from, he talks about his personal identity. According to v. 3 the messenger appears to be a soldier who "escaped from the camp of Israel"; but according to v. 6 he came to the battlefield "by chance." According to vv. 11-12, after receiving the news David and "all the men who were with him . . . mourned and wept and fasted until evening for Saul and for Jonathan." In vv. 13-16 we seem to have another version where the messenger is first executed. It is possible that this account was in circulation for a longer period, during which it underwent changes. Perhaps an editor who wanted to show that Saul was killed by a foreigner, an Amalekite, had worked on

155

an earlier version in which the identity of the messenger was not known. The anointment theology appears to have influenced the account.

The words "after the death of Saul" in v. 1 pick up the narrative from 1 Sam. 31, and the reference to the "slaughter of the Amalekites" continues the account about David from 1 Sam. 30. The news of Saul's death reaches David only "on the third day" (2 Sam. 1:2); perhaps the number "three" here had some symbolic significance to the original readers. On rending one's clothes and putting earth upon one's head (v. 2) as a sign of mourning, see above on 1 Sam. 4:12. In pointing out that "the crown" and "the armlet" were brought to David (2 Sam. 1:10), the author is probably trying to present David as the divinely ordained successor of Saul. It was providential that the royal insignia were brought to him and were not taken away by the Philistines along with the armor of Saul. A "sojourner" (v. 13) is a protected foreigner living in Israelite territory. Israelite law took special care to protect the rights of such foreigners (cf. Exod. 20:10; 23:12; Deut. 5:14). They did not enjoy full civil rights; they possessed no land, yet belonged to a specially privileged class of needy persons along with widows and orphans (Exod. 22:21-22; Deut. 14:28-29). They were expected to respect the legal and cultic orders of the community (Lev. 16:29; 17:8). As such, the Amalekite should also have known how to deal with the LORD's anointed one. On "the LORD's anointed," see above on 1 Sam. 24:4-7; on the expression "your blood be upon your head" (2 Sam. 1:16), see above on 1 Sam. 15:32-33.

DAVID'S LAMENTATION OVER SAUL AND JONATHAN (1:17-27)

1:17-18 An editorial note introduces the song of lamentation that follows in 2 Sam. 1:19-27. The lamentation is here ascribed to David, perhaps, because of the popular tradition that David was a musician and composer of songs (cf. 1 Sam. 16:18; 18:10 and the many Psalms that are ascribed to David). According to the editor, this poem was composed for didactic purposes, to be "taught to the people of Judah" (2 Sam. 1:18). The mention of

"Judah" instead of "Israel" points to the time when David had been able to consolidate his rule over what had become the southern kingdom of Judah. "It is written in the Book of Jashar," literally "the Book of the Upright." Another poetical piece attributed to the book of this name is Josh. 10:12-14. Similar literary collections of various sorts seem to have been circulating among the people (e.g., the Book of the Wars of Yahweh, Num. 21:14); this shows that the collection of poems was made well before 2 Samuel was edited and written.

According to 2 Sam. 1:12, David mourned and fasted for Saul, Jonathan, and "the people of the LORD and for the house of Israel." However, in v. 17 David is said to have lamented only over Saul and Jonathan. This too might indicate that this lamentation comes from a different editor.

In v. 18 the Hebrew text behind "and he said it" (RSV) is unintelligible; it reads *gashet,* which means "bow." Many translators have taken this to be the title of the lamentation and, on the basis of the reference to "bow" in v. 22, read it as "the song of the bow." This is only a conjecture. Perhaps it represents the title of the music to which the song was sung, as in the headings of some of the Psalms.

1:19-27   The Hebrew word for "lamentation" is *qinah,* a word which refers to a particular rhythm suited to mourning. In Israel professional mourners could be hired to sing such mourning songs on occasions of personal and national crises (cf. Jer. 9:10; 2 Chr. 35:25). It is typical of Hebrew dirges that they often begin with the word "how," contrasting the present state of despair and suffering with the glory of the past (cf. Isa. 1:21; 14:4; Ezek. 26:17). In this dirge the word "how" appears three times (2 Sam. 1:19, 25, 27), dividing the song into three parts. Verse 19 appears to be the title of the song, where the theme of the song is given. In the death of Saul and Jonathan the "glory" of Israel has gone (cf. 1 Sam. 4:21). 2 Sam. 1:20-25 describes what this tragedy meant to Israel, and vv. 26-27 deal with what it meant to David.

"Thy glory" (v. 19) is a reference to the mighty men fallen in battle. They were slain upon "high places." That is, they were killed as they were on the offensive onward march. This news should not reach their enemies, the Philistines, "lest the daughters of the Philistines rejoice" (v. 20). When the Philistines were defeated, the daughters of Israel rejoiced with songs (cf. 1 Sam. 18:6-7). Now it must not be the turn of the Philistine women to rejoice and exult. The "mountains of Gilboa" (2 Sam. 1:21), the scene of Israel's defeat, are to be cursed. They will become barren with no vegetation, because no dew or rain will fall upon them. The Hebrew text behind "nor upsurging of the deep" (RSV) literally means "fields of offerings" (RSV mg). Scholars have found this reading doubtful and have therefore attempted to emend it. The RSV reading makes sense in the context: there will be neither the waters of the heavens (dew and rain) nor the waters of the deep under the earth to facilitate the growth of any vegetation on the mountain. Mt. Gilboa has always been a barren mountain; this may be an etiological explanation as to how it became barren. Verses 21ff. hail Saul and Jonathan as mighty warriors: the shield of Saul had not been oiled because it was always engaged in battle; the bow of Jonathan did not turn back because it was driven deep into the flesh of the enemy. Verse 23 praises the closely knit relationship between Saul and Jonathan. Jonathan, though he promised his friendship to David through a covenant, remained loyal to his father till the end of his life. The prosperity under Saul's reign showed itself in the clothes and ornaments worn by the "daughters of Israel" (v. 24); now they can only weep because they will miss all those former luxuries. How valiant and noble were the men who had now fallen in battle. Verse 25 contrasts the present tragedy with the glory of the past. The death of Jonathan was a personal loss to David, because of his friendship covenant with him (v. 26). Jonathan's love to David exceeded even the love for women. The friendship-love between Jonathan and David has become an example for all time of all true friendship relationships.

We note that there are no religious sentiments expressed in this lament, nor is there any special reference to God. It is possible that the lament originally circulated in a secular context, before it found its place in the present story.

DAVID'S ANOINTING AS KING OF JUDAH (2:1-4a)

From the earlier events we know that David avoided settling down in Judean territory because Saul had been hunting for him there (cf. 1 Sam. 22:1-2; 23:3; 27:1). Now that Saul is dead, David is bold enough to return to Judah, perhaps along with those who were with him (cf. 1 Sam. 22:1-2). The people of Judah had only loose contact with the northern tribes, and so with the death of Saul they try to make their own arrangements for administration by anointing their own man of the south, David.

David is again presented as following the guidance of God. He consults Yahweh as to whether and whither he should enter any of the cities of Judah (2 Sam. 2:1). The ephod was probably the device used here to know God's will. If this were a lot device such as the Urim and Thummim evidently were, David could have received a straightforward answer to his first question; but it is not clear how a lot device could have answered the question "To which shall I go up?" Perhaps the priest who performed the divination had some means of interpreting the result of the fall of the dice. Outside the books of Samuel Hebron is mentioned as a city belonging to Caleb (cf. Josh. 15:13; Judg. 1:10, 20). Its former name was Kiriath-arba. We may assume that Caleb was by the time of David officially incorporated in the tribe of Judah, but with a certain amount of independence (cf. 1 Sam. 25:3). Hebron is modern el-Khalil, about 32 km. (20 mi.) from Jerusalem. "Go up" appears to be a religious expression. The modern Jew still "goes up" to Jerusalem from the ends of the earth. Jesus, too, went up to meet his death in Jerusalem. David here goes up to Hebron on God's mission.

DAVID'S MESSAGE TO THE PEOPLE OF JABESH-GILEAD (2:4b-7)

After becoming king of Judah, David probably wants to win the support of the tribes of the north. A message of gratitude to the people of Jabesh-gilead for what they did for Saul and his sons when they fell in the battle would be an appropriate act in that context. It would illustrate David's loyalty to Saul and win the goodwill of the northern tribes, which were closer to Saul than those in the south.

The scene now picks up the account in 1 Sam. 31:11-12. Saul had earlier delivered the Gileadites from the attack of the Ammonites (cf. 1 Sam. 11:1ff.). The Gileadites in turn had shown their loyalty to the house of Saul by giving Saul and his sons a decent burial. Yahweh will now keep his "steadfast love and faithfulness," and David, as Yahweh's anointed, will see to its fulfilment (2 Sam. 2:6). *Hessed* is the Hebrew word translated "steadfast love" here; for its theological significance, see below at 7:15. David assures the Gileadites of his continued support, thereby indirectly presenting himself as Saul's legitimate successor as the LORD's anointed and inviting their loyal support (2:7). However, according to vv. 8-10, Abner has sought to claim the Gileadites for the northern kingdom by placing Saul's son Ish-bosheth over Gilead.

WAR BETWEEN THE FORCES OF DAVID AND ISH-BOSHETH (2:8-32)

2:8-11   Abner, the commander of Saul's army, tries to secure Saul's kingdom by making Ish-bosheth, the only surviving son of Saul, king over the northern tribes. Abner had already encountered David when he was insulted by David (cf. 1 Sam. 26:13ff.). It is therefore understandable why Abner wanted not to join David but to establish Saul's kingdom through Ish-bosheth (2 Sam. 2:8-9). His intention probably was to rule himself by keeping the weak Ish-bosheth as his puppet. This is confirmed later when Ish-bosheth objected to Abner's taking Saul's concubine, for such was the legitimate right only of Saul's successor (cf. 3:6ff.).

The name Ish-bosheth means "man of shame." Originally it was Ish-baal, "man of Baal" or "man of the lord." Because Baal was the name of the Canaanite fertility-god, who in later times became unpopular among the Israelites, it was removed as an element of names; in its place was substituted the word *bosheth*, meaning "shame" (cf. Mephibosheth, 4:4). Ish-bosheth is not mentioned previously among the sons of Saul; perhaps he is the same as Ishvi in 1 Sam. 14:49.

At Mahanaim Abner makes Ish-bosheth king over "all Israel," not including "the house of Judah" (2:8-10). Israel is mentioned for the first time as a name for the northern tribes, as different from Judah. Mahanaim is a place N of the brook Jabbok; it was the capital of Gilead (cf. Gen. 32:2; 1 Kgs. 4:14) E of Jordan. In spite of David's promise of support (cf. 2 Sam. 2:4b-7), the Gileadites seem to have yielded to pressure from Abner. Perhaps the Philistines were still occupying the west of Jordan. "Ashurites" (v. 9) is thought to be a corrupt form of "Asherites" (Judg. 1:32), a dominant tribe in the north. It is doubtful whether Ish-bosheth was really "forty years" old (2 Sam. 2:10); from the way Abner treats him, it would appear that Ish-bosheth was still a minor. That would have been reason enough why he did not go with Saul into battle. "Forty years" is a round number indicating human maturity (cf. Gen. 25:20; 26:34). The reference to Ish-bosheth's reign over Israel as "two years" (2 Sam. 2:10) and David's reign over Judah as "seven years and six months" (v. 11; cf. 5:5) is probably historically reliable.

2:12-16   The war between Ish-bosheth and David begins with a series of combats between individuals (see above on 1 Sam. 17:1-11). The picture of each catching his opponent by the head and thrusting his sword in his opponent's side is attested by ancient Mesopotamian paintings. The outcome of such single combats would normally decide the course of a war (cf. 1 Sam. 17:9).

Gibeon is modern ej-Jib, 10 km. (6 mi.) NW of Jerusalem. The Gibeonites were allowed to live in the midst of the Israelites because of a covenant which Joshua had made with them earlier (cf. Josh. 9:3). Joab was one of David's nephews (see above on 1 Sam. 26:6); he appears here for the first time as the head of David's slave-soldiers. He was an able commander who played a major role in David's military campaigns. David was even afraid of Joab at one point (cf. 2 Sam. 3:39). In the place of "one man-single combat" as in 1 Sam. 17, here twelve men are chosen (2 Sam. 2:15), perhaps with some symbolic significance about which we do not know. Verse 16b gives an etiological explanation for the origin of the name Helkath-hazzurim, which means "the

field of sword-edges" (RSV mg), "the field of adversaries," or
"the field of sides."

2:17 Here is a summary of the course of the battle. Abner and
his men are defeated by "the servants of David."

2:18-23 Asahel, one of Joab's brothers, chases Abner and is
killed himself. This appears to be an independent tradition. The
following account in vv. 24-28 reveals no knowledge of Asahel's
death at the hand of Abner. All three sons of Zeruiah, "Joab,
Abishai, and Asahel," are presented as valiant soldiers (cf. 3:39).
Asahel, who was a fast runner, relentlessly chases the retreating
Abner. Abner, though slow in running, was a veteran in warfare,
and Asahel was no match for him. Abner warned Asahel to stop
from following him, but Asahel would not listen and therefore
Abner had to kill him. Abner is said to have hit Asahel with the
"butt of his spear" (2:23). In that case it is difficult to see how
the spear could come out at Asahel's back. Accordingly, the KJV
translates "with the hinder end of the spear." A. R. S. Kennedy
suggests a small change in the text to read "Abner smote him with
a backward stroke," which makes sense. Without slackening his
speed in running, Abner delivers a powerful thrust backwards
with his long, sharp-pointed spear, piercing his pursuer through
and through (Kennedy, *Samuel*, 201).

2:24-28 This too is an independent tradition. According to
v. 28, there was no more fighting between Israel and Judah. But
according to 3:1, "There was a long war between the house of
Saul and the house of David." The chase of Abner is here continued by the other two brothers, Joab and Abishai. They come
to "the hill of Ammah" (2:24) where Abner and his men have
taken their position. The scene is set for a second round of battle.
But Abner appeals to Joab's reason, drawing his attention to their
kinship relation and pointing out that further fighting would only
mean loss of more innocent lives. Joab responds positively, and
the fighting stops. Neither Abner's appeal nor Joab's response
reveals any knowledge of Asahel's death. Abner's question in v. 26,
"Shall the sword devour for ever? Do you not know that the end

will be bitter?" echoes wisdom sayings. It is possible that this tradition could have come from wisdom circles.

The whole conflict is presented here as a political struggle; killing each other is not the motive. We see here a respect for human life and human relations even in the face of political hostilities. Ammah and Giah (v. 24) are not identified.

2:29-32 This section continues the account from v. 23. According to the latter, the chase of Abner stopped with the fall of Asahel. Now Joab and his men take Asahel's body and return to Hebron. On their way they bury Asahel "in the tomb of his father, which was at Bethlehem" (v. 32). Arabah (v. 29) is the name given to the broad floor of the great valley S of the Dead Sea, around 4,265 m. (1,300 ft.) below sea level. The loss on Abner's side was very heavy compared to that on Joab's (vv. 30-31), an indication of how Saul's house was losing ground and David's growing ever stronger (cf. 3:1).

DAVID GROWS STRONGER AND STRONGER (3:1-39)

3:1 This verse is an editorial introduction to what follows. "David grew stronger and stronger, while the house of Saul became weaker and weaker" has been the theme on which the history of David's accession to kingship over Judah and Israel has been gradually developed.

3:2-5 Here are listed the names of sons born to David in Hebron through his six wives, Ahinoam, Abigail, Maacah, Haggith, Abital, and Eglah. The names agree with those listed at 1 Chr. 3:1-4, except for the name of the son of Abigail, Chileab, which in 1 Chr. 3 is given as Daniel. Obviously the list at hand speaks only of children born to David while he reigned in Hebron; more children were certainly born to him later on. We know, for example, that Absalom had a sister, Tamar (cf. 2 Sam. 13:1). Of the six sons mentioned here, Amnon, Absalom, and Adonijah figure again later in the account (cf. 13:1ff.; 1 Kgs. 1:5ff.). With this list, then, the author prepares the ground for the succession account. Geshur (2 Sam. 3:3) was a small Aramaean kingdom NE of the Sea of Galilee.

3:6-11   Abner falls into dispute with Ish-bosheth on the question of taking Saul's wife, and resolves to change sides and join David. This is another move towards making David's house stronger.

Verse 11 is an editorial note introducing the following account. As already seen, Abner was obviously intending to rule by himself, using Ish-bosheth as a mere puppet (see above on 2:8-11). In Abner's act of having sexual relations with Rizpah, Saul's concubine, Ish-bosheth sees Abner's veiled claim to the royal authority. To take possession of the harem of a deceased king was to stake a claim to the throne (John Bright, *A History of Israel,* 197; cf. 12:8; 16:20-23; 1 Kgs. 2:22). Abner feels insulted by Ish-bosheth's questioning of his act and uses this as a pretext to change his loyalty to David. As 2 Sam. 3:9-10 suggests, Abner may already have been convinced that God was establishing David's kingdom. Here Abner refers to an oracle given to David, to which we have no access. Abner would now join David and help in the process of the transferring the kingdom from the house of Saul to David, in accordance with the oracle of God. That God establishes the kingdom of David is the leading motif of the accession account (cf. 1 Sam. 18:12ff.; 20:15ff.; 23:17; 24:20).

In Abner we have a typical example of persons who have vested interests, who are after power and personal privileges. Such people attach themselves to a party or a government, not because they are committed to their policies or principles, but because of their vested interests. When they realize that those interests are in danger, they change their loyalty to some other party or government which seems to promise better privileges.

Abner asks, "Am I a dog's head of Judah?" (2 Sam. 3:8); "a dog's head" may have been a common saying referring to something worthless. "Dog" in the OT is used metaphorically in such a way as to show that it was an object of contempt. The LXX omits "of Judah." Perhaps this was added later by a scribe who saw in "Caleb," which means "dog," a reference to the tribe of that name, which was later incorporated into the tribe of Judah. "From Dan to Beer-sheba" (v. 10) indicates approximately the northern and southern boundaries of David's kingdom, which become the ideal limits of Israel (17:11; 24:2). When Abner left,

Ish-bosheth was afraid, because he knew he could rule as king only with Abner's support (cf. 4:1). Army commanders often become a threat to kings and governments; the policies of many governments are thus influenced by the heads of their armies. David, too, later found himself in just such an embarrassing situation when Joab was chief of his army (cf. 3:39).

3:12-16   Abner acts quickly. He sends messengers to David offering his support to David and "to bring over all Israel" to him, provided David makes a covenant with him. We are only left to conjecture what Abner would have expected to achieve through such a covenant. Quite likely he would have bargained for a top position in the army. This possibility is confirmed by the fact that Joab later kills Abner, in spite of David's goodwill towards him. It is possible that Joab saw in Abner a threat to his own position.

David, who was probably waiting for just such an opportunity, readily accepts Abner's offer, but on condition that Abner should be certain to bring Michal when he comes to meet David. We recall that Saul gave Michal to Paltiel in marriage (1 Sam. 25:44). There is some tension between 2 Sam. 3:12-13 and vv. 14-16. In vv. 12-13 Abner is commanded to bring Michal; but in vv. 14-15 David sends messengers to Ish-bosheth to send Michal back to him, and Ish-bosheth readily obliges. Later we see that Michal returns with Abner (v. 16). It is possible that David, after making this condition to Abner, could have sent messengers to Ish-bosheth to facilitate the process for Abner. To separate Michal from her husband Paltiel arbitrarily was not a normal procedure, and Ish-bosheth's royal authority would have been needed to accomplish it (v. 15). By operating with the knowledge and sanctioning of the king it also would appear as though nothing were out of the ordinary, and the matter of Abner's secret dealing with David would still be hidden from Ish-bosheth.

The Michal episode ends abruptly. There is no further mention of Michal's being brought back to David. The episode involving Michal is here introduced purposely, perhaps as part of legitimizing David's claim to Saul's kingdom.

Later law forbade taking back a wife who had been given to

another man (Deut. 24:1-4). We see here that the rights and feelings of neither Michal nor her husband Paltiel are respected. The fact that Paltiel ran after Michal weeping indicates that the marriage was based on love and that Michal was taken away by force. This is another example of a woman being treated as an object. We also see here the arbitrary rights exercised by Israelite kings following Canaanite practices (cf. 2 Sam. 11; 1 Kgs. 21).

Bahurim (2 Sam. 3:16) is a village NE of the Mount of Olives (cf. 16:5; 19:16).

3:17-19   Abner confers with the elders of Israel. He apparently knew that the popular mind in Israel was in favor of David (3:17), but it was because of his own selfish interests that he ignored the people's opinion and continued Saul's dynasty. Whether in v. 17 Abner is referring to some secret efforts by the northern tribes to reach an understanding with David is not certain. Now that he has difficulty with Ish-bosheth, Abner fans the suppressed aspirations of the people (v. 17) by proclaiming the divine sanction legitimizing David as the next deliverer rather than Ish-bosheth (v. 18).

David's calling as king is not because of any special virtue on his part but for the purpose of saving God's people: "By the hand of my servant David I will save my people Israel . . ." (v. 18). The same motif is found throughout the Deuteronomic history of Israelite kingship (cf. 1 Sam. 9:16; 2 Kgs. 8). Abner first confides with his own people, the Benjaminites, and then goes to speak to David in the name of "Israel" and "the whole house of Benjamin."

3:20-21   Abner meets David at Hebron with twenty men and conveys the happy news of Israel's willingness to accept him as king. David accords them a grand feast. The next move is the making of the covenant between David and the people of Israel. Abner will now prepare the people for that important event.

Covenant-making has an important place in David's reign (cf. 1 Sam. 18:3-4; 23:18; 2 Sam. 5:3). It was expected that the Israelite kings, unlike their neighbors, should rule with their people's concurrence, that is, by making covenants with them.

Such covenants are obviously "between the LORD and the king and people" and also "between the king and the people" (2 Kgs. 11:17). David, as a clever diplomat, knows how to rule people by winning them to his side, rather than by exercising his arbitrary authority and power over them — a policy which every administrator, if he or she is wise, must learn.

3:22-30   Joab kills Abner. As noted above (cf. 2 Sam. 3:12-13), Joab perhaps recognized in Abner a potential threat to his own position as commander in chief. That could have been the reason why Joab killed him. The words "for the blood of Asahel his brother" in v. 27 and all of v. 30 appear to be later additions. The two verses are at variance with each other. According to v. 27 Joab alone smites Abner; but according to v. 30 "Joab and Abishai his brother slew Abner." Neither David's reaction to Joab's act nor his lamentation on Abner shows any knowledge of the deed as blood revenge. Nevertheless, David holds Joab responsible for Abner's blood (v. 29). Verse 30 appears to come from a later hand.

That Joab kills Abner stealthily by deceit and not in open combat might indicate that Abner was stronger than Joab and that Joab was afraid of such an encounter. This might also explain why Joab wanted Abner out of his way once David reigned over all Israel.

Bloodguilt means misfortune for the total life of the guilty one. Sickness, drought (hunger), and sword are the three divinely ordained calamities that fall on people who stand under the judgment of God. All three fall on Joab. Joab's end is detailed in 1 Kgs. 2:28-33.

3:31-39   David mourns over Abner's death. Here again we see David's wisdom or cunning in dealing with crucial situations. Since Abner was the cousin of Saul and the strongest statesman in Israel, his assassination was of great national significance. It could easily arouse the suspicion in Israel that David was behind the killing. Therefore David's intense mourning over the death of Abner, even overdoing it, may have served to convince the Israelites "that it had not been the king's will to slay Abner the son of Ner" (2 Sam. 3:37). Further, David's condemnation of Joab's act as an act of "wickedness" and the invocation of the LORD's requital on him could have so satisfied the Israelites that "everything that the king did pleased all the people" (v. 36). Abner was given a royal burial, and a public mourning was declared (vv. 31ff.), including weeping at the grave and fasting.

Just as for Saul (cf. 1:19ff.), David sings a lamentation for Abner (3:33-34). Abner has had a shameful death "as one falling before the wicked" (v. 34). Here the guilt for Abner's shameful death is put on the "wicked," thus indicating Joab. That David was counting on the services of Abner, probably to counter the threat from Joab and his brother, is hinted at by v. 39; with the death of Abner David feels "weak." Why was not Abner's body sent to Ish-bosheth for burial? Taking that responsibility upon himself, David perhaps intends to make it clear to Ish-bosheth and the people in Israel that he has already assumed his kingship over Israel. That may be why Ish-bosheth and all Israel "was dismayed" (4:1) at the news of Abner's death.

ISH-BOSHETH IS MURDERED (4:1-12)

The tragedy of Ish-bosheth's death is narrated parallel to the tragedy of Saul's death. In both accounts the persons who brought the news to David are put to death. In this way David shows to Israel that he is their "bone and flesh" (5:1) and that it was not his intention to wipe out the house of Saul from the earth. The story of Mephibosheth is purposely inserted here (4:4) in order to show the Israelites on the one hand that the seed of Saul is not cut off from the earth, and on the other hand that it is David who cares for the protection and continuation of Saul's line.

Baanah and Rechab, sons of Rimmon, were "captains of raiding bands" (v. 2). The purpose of the bands was to raid enemy territories and to bring spoils for the royal household (cf. 1 Sam. 23:5; 2 Sam. 3:22). 2 Samuel 4:2-3, given in parenthesis, is an editorial gloss which explains how Benjaminites were living in Beeroth, a Canaanite city which had maintained its independence through a treaty with Joshua (cf. Josh. 9:17; Neh. 11:33). As per Joshua's territorial assignment, Beeroth fell within the area assigned to Benjamin (Josh. 18:25); it has been identified with modern el-Bireh, 14 km. (9 mi.) N of Jerusalem on the road to Bethel. Gittaim is not identified. Mephibosheth is introduced here because he plays a role in later history (cf. 2 Sam. 9:1-13; 16:1, 4; 19:24-30). His original name was Meribaal, as is attested in 1 Chr. 8:34; 9:40. On its change to Mephibosheth, see above on 2 Sam. 2:8. Meribaal means "loved by Baal," and Mephibosheth means "he who scatters shame" or "from the mouth of shame" (Edward R. Dalglish, "Mephibosheth," *IDB* 3:350).

4:5-12   Rechab and Baanah stealthily murder Ish-bosheth and bring his head to David, thinking that David would be pleased by their act. But David disappoints them. He holds that Yahweh, who so far has redeemed him from all adversities (cf. 1 Sam. 23:14-29; 25:29; 26:12-22), would protect him further, and that he has no wish to have it done by unjust means (cf. 24:12-13). David does not hold Ish-bosheth responsible for the injustice done to him by his father Saul; Ish-bosheth was a "righteous" man (2 Sam. 4:11). By killing him Rechab and Baanah had acted wickedly, and they deserved death. Verse 10 alludes to the event in 1:14-16. On the discrepancy between the two accounts, see the commentary above.

The above account exposes the primitive nature of a royal household in early Israel: no guards, and the doorkeeper is a woman who has also other household responsibilities such as cleaning wheat.

"Require his blood at your hand" (4:11) is a blood revenge formula. By executing Rechab and Baanah, David acquits himself of having had any hand in the murder of Ish-bosheth and thus convinces the northern tribes that he is not against the house of Saul. The groundwork for the future events in David's life is thus prepared.

DAVID'S ANOINTING AS KING OF ISRAEL (5:1-5)

According to 5:1-2, "all the tribes of Israel came to David," whereas according to v. 3 "all the elders of Israel came to the king." In vv. 1-2, we have an independent tradition which was later added to v. 3. Verses 3-4 refer to the length of David's reign, the verses coming from the hand of the editor. 2 Sam. 5:1-3 is found almost verbatim in 1 Chr. 11:1-3. In 1 Chr. 11:3 the Chronicler adds "according to the word of the LORD by Samuel," implying that the prophecy in v. 2b was from Samuel. However, we do not meet with such a prophecy in the earlier accounts of Samuel. 2 Samuel 5:2a alludes to the events in 1 Sam. 18:5, 13-15.

According to 2 Sam. 5:2b, the LORD wants David to be the "shepherd of my people Israel" and "prince over Israel." Both "shepherd" and "prince" are used as titles for David in Ezek. 34:23-24. On "prince" *(nagid),* see above on 1 Sam. 9:16. "Shepherd" as a title for king is known throughout the ancient Near East. The Sumerian kings were known as "shepherds." In the OT this title is primarily used for Yahweh (cf. Ps. 23:1; 28:9; 80:1). In a few places it is also used for Israelite kings: Ps. 78:71 (of David), Jer. 23:1-4 (of shepherds who scatter the flock and those who care for the flock). A good king is a shepherd who cares for the flock. The king in Israel thus becomes the shepherd of the (master) shepherd, who is God, and his authority to rule over the people is a delegated authority. When kings use their authority arbitrarily according to their whims and fancies, they become oppressive, shepherds "who destroy and scatter the sheep" (Jer. 23:1). I have seen for myself how in Palestine a shepherd walks in front of his flock, and the sheep follow him in a line one after another with a dog at the rear. This image of the shepherd "as one who walks in front" was probably seen as parallel to the king as *nagid* ("prince," literally, "the one who walks in front"). The Israelite king is expected "to walk before the LORD" faithfully so that the people too may follow him and thus themselves walk before the LORD. When the king does not walk in accordance with the will of God the people go astray, and for this the king is held responsible.

On David's making a covenant with the people (2 Sam. 5:3), see above on 3:20-21. The covenant making and the anointing both take place "before the LORD," that is, in a sanctuary (cf. 2 Kgs. 11:12-17). We are not told who anoints David as king here. It could have been Abiathar, David's priest, or perhaps

Nathan the prophet. During the early period in Israel, priests as well as prophets could anoint people as kings.

David ruled over Judah with Hebron as capital for "seven years and six months" (cf. 2 Sam. 2:11) and over "all Israel and Judah" for "thirty-three years." Therefore altogether he was king for forty years and six months. 2 Samuel 5:4 describes his reign in round figures as "forty years."

II. DAVIDIC DYNASTY ESTABLISHED
2 Samuel 5:6–8:18

This section gives a series of events which show how David's dynasty is established step by step with the help of God. 2 Samuel 5:6-25 shows how David became established as king over Israel; 6:1-23 shows how the ark of God was brought to Jerusalem to ensure to David the abiding presence of Yahweh in the midst of the people during his reign; 7:1-29 shows how through the covenant God establishes the Davidic kingdom forever; 8:1-18 shows how God gives David rest from all his enemies.

DAVID MADE KING OVER ISRAEL (5:6-25)

The theme of the whole chapter is given in the following two sentences: "David became greater and greater" (5:10); "the LORD had established him king over Israel" (v. 12). In order to illustrate this main theme, a number of events are now cited: David conquers Jerusalem (vv. 6-8), builds the City of David (v. 9), builds his royal house (v. 11), takes more concubines and wives and begets more children (vv. 13-16), and finally defeats the Philistines (vv. 17-25; cf. 7:1). The whole chapter is from one hand; of course, the author could have used material deriving from different sources.

David Conquers Jerusalem (5:6-16)

David conquers the Jebusite city of Jerusalem and names its stronghold "the City of David." He builds the city, constructs his house in it, and establishes the city as his royal capital.

Jerusalem (5:6) remained a Canaanite city-state until late (cf. Josh. 15:63; Judg. 1:21; 19:10-12), perhaps because of its "stronghold," the fortress. Jebus was another name for the city (Judg. 19:10). The name Jerusalem appears first in Egyptian Execration Texts of the 19th and 18th cents. B.C. in a form equivalent to Urshalim. In the Amarna Letters of the 14th cent. it is written U-ru-sa-lim. Later Assyrian texts have the form Urusi-limmu. In the Hebrew Scriptures the Masoretic vowel pointing indicates the pronunciation Yerusalayim; in the Aramaic parts of the OT, however, the pronunciation indicated is Yerusalem. Its meaning is "foundation of Shalem" (Millar Burrows, "Jerusalem," *IDB* 2:843). According to Burrows, "the traditional interpretation, 'city of peace' is as inaccurate etymologically as it is inappropriate historically." "Shalem" was originally the name of the deity worshipped there. In the Amarna Letters the city is apparently called Beth-shalem, "the house of Shalem." The first name under which the city appears in the Bible is Salem, or more exactly Shalem (Gen. 14:18). The word Salem has the same letters as Shalom in Hebrew, and thus the meaning "city of peace" was associated with Jerusalem. The name Jerusalem is applied to the territory of which it is the capital.

The meeting of Melchizedek and Abraham in Gen. 14 is probably an indication of the close affinity of Yahweh worship and Zedek worship. The fact that the law of *herem,* the law of total destruction (see above on 1 Sam. 15:3), was not applied on the city but that David simply took the city and dwelt in it as king, might further confirm that affinity. Archaeological research also shows no evidence of any serious attack on Jerusalem in that period. David seems to have taken over the social and political structures as they were found in Jerusalem. Nathan the prophet and Zadok the priest of David's court also apparently come from the cultic background of Jerusalem. As we shall see later, David seems to have adapted the priestly kingship of Jerusalem for his own self-understanding. David also takes wives and concubines from among the Jebusites (2 Sam. 5:13).

Since Jerusalem did not come under the claim of any of the tribes in the north or the south, it was an ideal place for David to make the capital of his kingdom — a place common to all the

tribes. Being neutral, it was free of association with either north
or south.

5:6b-8   Here we have an etiological explanation of the saying
"the blind and the lame shall not come into the house" (v. 8).
The fact that the Chronicler's parallel history does not include this
account might indicate that here we have an independent tradition. Lev. 21:16-23 prevents the physically disabled, including the
lame and the blind, from performing any priestly duties. The
physically handicapped are included among the unclean, just as
are lepers (cf. 2 Sam. 3:29). Accordingly, this saying could have
had its origin in a cultic context. "The house" here is probably a
reference to the temple (cf. Mic. 3:12). The Jebusites taunt David,
saying that the blind and the lame were sufficient to ward off
David from entering into the stronghold of Zion, because the
stronghold in their opinion was impregnable.

The Hebrew text of 2 Sam. 5:8 is corrupt; the meaning is not
quite clear. Hebrew *tsinnor* is here translated as "water shaft," and
probably refers to "a system providing access for water from a
spring into a city" (William L. Reed, "Water Shaft," *IDB* 4:811).
It is believed that the Jebusite inhabitants of the city had dug a
tunnel "to bring the waters of Gihon toward the foot of a vertical
shaft sunk to water level from above" (R. W. Hamilton, "Water
Works," *IDB* 4:815). This was later used by King Hezekiah for
the start of his conduit (cf. 2 Chr. 32:30). How David succeeded
in taking "the stronghold of Zion" (2 Sam. 5:7) is not reported.
The reference to the "water shaft" (v. 8) might suggest that David
used a water tunnel to enter into the stronghold of Zion without
being noticed by the soldiers, who would probably be waiting on
the fortress walls ready for the attack. According to 1 Chr. 11:5-6,
Joab entered the stronghold, and that qualified him to become
commander in chief. Joab could have gone first through this tunnel
and others could have followed him. Another possibility is to take
2 Sam. 5:8 as describing what happened after the capture of
Jerusalem (as mentioned in v. 7), and to take "whoever would
smite the Jebusites" as the beginning of a general amnesty proclaimed on the Jebusites and the rest of the verse as a corruption
of some curse invoked as punishment on those who might do

harm to the Jebusites (cf. 3:29). That such an amnesty could have been proclaimed on Zion is indicated by the fact that "the Jebusites dwell with the children of Judah at Jerusalem to this day" (Josh. 15:63; cf. Judg. 1:21).

The name Zion appears here for the first time (2 Sam. 5:7). The etymology of the name is uncertain. It may be related to Hebrew *tsayon*, "dry place," "parched ground" (and so a rocky hill with no vegetation; cf. Isa. 25:5; 32:2). It is the name of the fortified hill of pre-Israelite Jerusalem, between the Tyropoeon Valley and the Kidron Valley, south of the temple area or the Haram esh-Sharif, as it is known today. This account explains how "city of David" came to be substituted for the name Zion, and to apply to the whole area within the fortified part of the city as it was restored and eventually modified and extended by David. 2 Samuel 6 tells how the ark of God was later brought into the "city of David." Later when Solomon built the temple, he brought the ark from the city of David and kept it in the inner sanctuary of the temple (cf. 1 Kgs. 8:1ff.; 2 Chr. 5:2ff.). This transfer of the ark seems to have extended the name Zion to the temple area itself, as evidenced by numerous passages in the Psalms. Yahweh is said to dwell on the mountain of Zion. Throngs of pilgrims long to go to Zion and present themselves before God (Ps. 84:5). In the poetic books and the prophetic writings, Zion becomes an equivalent of Jerusalem considered as the religious capital, or as the object of God's favor or punishment (Isa. 28:16; cf. Rom. 9:33; 1 Pet. 2:6; G. A. Barrois, "Zion," *IDB* 4:959). The expression "city of David" is used as a synonym for the stronghold of Zion. The expression in 2 Sam. 5:7 is a marginal gloss anticipating its occurrence in v. 9.

5:9-12 The Millo (v. 9) is apparently some part of the fortification of the citadel of Jerusalem (cf. 1 Kgs. 9:15). There was a Beth-millo at Shechem (Judg. 9:6). The word may originate from the verb "to fill," and so describe a "filling" of a ravine in the original hilltop.

According to the author, with the capital being established in Jerusalem the kingship of David approaches its consummation: "David became greater and greater" (2 Sam. 5:10a). However, the reason for David's greatness is neither his might nor the might of his men, but the fact that "the LORD, the God of hosts, was with him" (v. 10b). Building a house for the king is an important aspect of the process of establishing a kingdom. It was noted how primitive the household of Saul was (cf. 4:6); but David planned to build a palace for himself in the manner common among oriental kings. The fact that Hiram king of Tyre came forward to extend his support in building a house for David was a proof for David that God has "established him king over Israel" and has "exalted his kingdom" (5:12a). The objective phrase "for the sake of his people Israel" (v. 12b) is very important here. The establishment and exaltation of David's kingdom is for the sake of God's people, not for the personal enjoyment of the king. That kingship in Israel is meant for the service of God's people is once again stressed here (cf. 7:8). God's plan to use Israel as his servant to bring all nations to him (Isa. 49:6) is developing here from its beginning in creation: "[While I was] stretching out the heavens and laying the foundations of the earth, [I was] saying to Zion, 'You are my people'" (Isa. 51:16b). This election idea is further developed in the NT; the new community in Jesus Christ becomes the chosen community for the salvation of the whole world (Eph. 1:4).

Tyre (2 Sam. 5:11) was a leading harbor city in Lebanon from ancient times. The forests of Lebanon were known for their magnificent cedar trees, and their cedar wood was exported to neighboring countries like Egypt and Babylon. The Israelites, being newcomers to settled culture among the countries in the ancient Near East, were not familiar with the Phoenicians' advanced techniques in building construction. David therefore uses foreign material and experts to build a palace for himself matching the palaces of other kings in the region.

5:13-16   In. vv. 14-15 we have the list of children born to David through his "concubines and wives from Jerusalem" (v. 13). For the Hebron list see 3:2ff. Not only in terms of territory and in the administrative infrastructure required by such a fortified capital city and a palace, but also in terms of his family with wives, concubines, and children, David is now established as king on a par with the kings of other nations of his time. As with the others, David too had a large harem. On concubines and harem, see above on 3:6ff. Here we are reminded of the people's desire to be "like all the nations" in having a king (cf. 1 Sam. 8:5; Ezek. 20:32). In establishing his kingdom step by step, David is slowly conforming to the pattern of kingship that was known in the ancient Orient. That conforming too much to the world, without reference to God, can allow us to drift away from following God is evident from what happens in David's life (cf. 2 Sam. 11–12). Thus we are shown two aspects of David's kingship. He builds it up as God establishes his rule "for the sake of God's people," and he is disloyal to God's lead when he seeks to make his kingship a merely worldly throne.

David Defeats the Philistines (5:17-25)

Here is yet further evidence to show that David's kingdom has been truly established. That David is free from all his enemies is a leading motif in this context (cf. 7:9). Among Israel's enemies, the Philistines come first and foremost (cf. 3:18; 1 Sam. 23:1ff.); their defeat is very vital for the peace and stability of the newly established kingdom of Israel.

The author is apparently not reproducing an exact historical account here. The Philistines are said to have gone "in search of David" (2 Sam. 5:17), which is perhaps a reference to David's fugitive days when he was in flight from Saul. The author is not sure of his historical data; he is probably writing from memory.

It is understandable that the Philistines saw in David's acclamation as king over Israel and Judah a threat to their own existence, and that they therefore wanted to curtail David's power before it was too late. It is said that, when David heard of the Philistine preparation for war, he "went down to the stronghold" (v. 17). We may assume that, on hearing about the Philistine threat, David returns from a campaign outside Jerusalem and takes up his position in the stronghold for the defense. "David inquired of the LORD" (v. 19), probably through the Urim and Thummim. The author wants to show that at every step David acted according to the will of Yahweh, and that was the secret of the success of

177

his reign. "The valley of Rephaim" (v. 18) was located S of the plain of Rephaim, which is identified with modern el-Baqa', SW of Jerusalem.

In vv. 20-21 we have an etiological account concerning the origin of the name Baal-perazim. Verse 24 was originally part of this account. Both v. 20 and v. 24 deal with the LORD's "breaking through" the enemy force before David; "the sound of marching in the tops of balsam trees" (v. 24) was probably "like a bursting flood" (v. 20). (A similar etiological explanation of the place name Perez-uzzah is found in 6:8.) 2 Samuel 5:22-25 speaks of yet another attack by the Philistines. It is possible that it is a duplication of the account in vv. 19-21. The OT contains several evidences of plants and trees becoming places of a theophany and of divine oracles (cf. Gen. 12:6; Exod. 3:2). Here we have a relic of ancient animistic belief (see Introduction). Baal-perazim could originally have been the name of a local god. The tension between Baal and Yahweh at this stage was not great; both could be worshipped side by side. Baal-perazim could mean "the lord of breaking through," and it is here associated with the LORD's breaking through the Philistine army. This seems to have been a decisive victory for Israel; even after two centuries the prophet Isaiah could refer back to it (Mount Perazim, Isa. 28:21).

The holy war motif is found here. The victory is Yahweh's: "the LORD has gone out before you to smite the army of the Philistines" (2 Sam. 5:24). It also meant the victory of Yahweh over the gods of the Philistines. As they retreated in defeat before the Israelites the Philistines abandoned "their idols," and "David and his men carried them away" (v. 21). The writer is here hinting at the futility of other gods, or idols. Idols cannot save people (cf. Isa. 45:20; 46:7; Jer. 2:27-28); Yahweh alone is the God who saves his people (cf. 1 Sam. 14:6, 23, 39; 2 Sam. 3:18). The idols of the Philistines, which were meant to protect them, were themselves abandoned and lay unprotected. Similar cynical accounts are typical of OT writers, e.g., Dagon falling down before the ark of the LORD (1 Sam. 5:3) and the Israelites carrying their idols into exile so that those very idols which were meant to deliver the Israelites themselves became a burden to the people of God (Amos 5:26).

David chases the retreating Philistines "from Geba to Gezer" (2 Sam. 5:25). Geba lies about 10 km. (6 mi.) N of Jerusalem on an important trade route. Saul was active here militarily (1 Sam. 13–14). Gezer is a Canaanite city in the west.

THE ARK BROUGHT TO THE CITY OF DAVID (6:1-23)

The motif that David's kingdom is firmly established is now continued — a capital city with its stronghold, a permanent royal house, more wives and children, rest from all enemies, and now the assurance of God's abiding presence guaranteed through the presence of the ark of God.

The history of the ark in 1 Sam. 4–6 is continued here. The account is concerned with the establishment of the ark cult in Jerusalem. David brings it from Kiriath-jearim (1 Sam. 7:2), where it rested after it was returned by the Philistines. During David's reign it remained in a tent in the City of David (2 Sam. 7:2). Later when Solomon built the temple in Jerusalem, he brought the ark from the City of David and placed it in the inner sanctuary of the temple (1 Kgs. 8:1-8). Apart from this, we have no other information about the role the ark played during the reign of David and afterward. What later happened to the ark is not known; it is not mentioned among the objects Nebuchadnezzar took away to Babylon (cf. 2 Kgs. 24:13; 25:13-17). As noted above, the ark account comes from a special tradition. In this particular account of David's bringing the ark to Jerusalem no mention is made of Abiathar the priest. David himself performs the duties of the priest. This shows that the ark account here did not know of the presence of a priest in the city. This raises the question as to when in David's reign Abiathar actually joined him.

In Israelite belief, the ark symbolically represented the presence of Yahweh. Thus the people's attitude to the ark reflected their attitude to Yahweh. Those who feared Yahweh and walked in his ways were blessed when the ark was in their midst. However, those who acted against the will of Yahweh were actually punished when they sought to retain the ark in their midst. On the "holiness" of the ark, see above on 1 Sam. 6:7ff.

179

David Brings the Ark from Baale-judah (6:1-5)

Baale-judah (2 Sam. 6:2) is probably another name for Kiriath-jearim. In Josh. 15:9 a place called Baalah is identified with Kiriath-jearim. In Josh. 18:14 Kiriath-jearim is identified with Kiriath-baal. Kiriath simply means "city" in the OT sense of "settlement" or even "village." Baalah is the feminine form of Baal. A Baal sanctuary was probably located in Kiriath-jearim, and the ark was kept in it and not in any common place. In early times the Israelites had no hesitation about using Canaanite cultic places and altars such as high places for their worship of Yahweh (cf. 1 Sam. 9:14; 1 Kgs. 18:19ff.).

"The LORD of hosts who sits enthroned on the cherubim" (2 Sam. 6:2) appears to be the name of God in the ark cult (cf. 1 Sam. 4:4). On "the LORD of hosts," see above on 1 Sam. 1:3. The "cherubim" are mixed beings made up of eagle, lion, and human. Images of such mixed beings were known in the ancient Orient. Yahweh was envisaged as seated upon them; he also rode on them whenever he appeared in a storm theophany (cf. 2 Sam. 22:11).

By bringing the ark (which earlier had been kept in the "temple" at Shiloh) to Jerusalem, David displays his reverence for the traditions connected with Shiloh and at the same time asserts his claim over the cult in Jerusalem. Thus the northern tribes are made to move towards Jerusalem, not only politically but also cultically. David thus initiates a movement of political and religious concentration in Jerusalem which continues for several centuries, culminating in the Deuteronomic reform of King Josiah (cf. 2 Kgs. 23) ca. 621.

"They carried the ark of God upon a new cart" (2 Sam. 6:3); the oxen which pulled the cart also were not to have been used before. These stipulations were because of the Torah's rules regarding holiness (see above on 1 Sam. 6:7ff.). On Abinadab (2 Sam. 6:3), see 1 Sam. 7:1. Eleazar was Abinadab's son who had charge of the ark. Here Eleazar is not mentioned; two other sons, however, Uzzah and Ahio, are driving the cart carrying the ark of God, with Ahio in the front and Uzzah behind. "David and all the house of Israel were making merry before the LORD with all their might" (2 Sam. 6:5); perhaps people saw the event as being Yahweh's royal entry into Jerusalem, rather than David's. Several Psalms refer to such occasions (cf. Pss. 24; 47; 132; 146:10; 149:2). Ecstatic elements in worship with dancing, singing, and so forth, hitherto strange in Israel but typical of Canaanite worship, are now brought into Jerusalem worship. Perhaps these should be seen as positive syncretistic elements that now infiltrated into Israelite religion. This is something which Christians living in non-Christian contexts should note. "Lyres and harps and tambourines and castanets and cymbals" (2 Sam. 6:5) were musical instruments known in Israel (cf. Ps. 150:3-5). In Israelite tradition David was known as a great musician. David and his men were making merry before the LORD "with all their might," which may mean, in accordance with the law: "You shall love the LORD your God with all your heart, and with all your soul, and with all your might" (Deut. 6:4). When one worships God with the heart, soul, and might it is natural that one forgets the self and becomes fully immersed in the ecstasy in the presence of God. This is probably what happened to David when he stripped himself and danced (2 Sam. 6:14, 16, 20).

The Ark in the House of Obed-edom (6:6-11)

Before coming to its place in Jerusalem, the ark appears to have stayed in the house of a person called Obed-edom (vv. 10-11). This section explains how the ark came to his house. Verses 6-8 offer an etiological explanation of the place name Perez-uzzah; a similar explanation is found in 5:20-21. On Uzzah's death, see above on 1 Sam. 6:7, 19. The oxen "stumbled" as they came to "the threshing floor of Nacon" (2 Sam. 6:6). Perhaps that was a cultic place, and the stumbling of the oxen was the sign of the presence of some spirit there, a relic of some primitive animistic belief (see above on 1 Sam. 6:14; cf. 2 Sam. 24:16). Perez was probably the name of the deity in that place. Uzzah obviously was following the ark. Because of the stumbling of the oxen, the cart could have moved backward and the ark could have fallen on Uzzah, causing his death. People could have given a cultic interpretation to his death — that Yahweh's anger was kindled because Uzzah put his hand on the holy ark. Uzzah and Ahio, as the sons of a priest and also responsible for driving the new cart with the ark of God on it, should have been consecrated for that special task. Still, Uzzah is killed. This is probably one reason why David was angry and why he was afraid to bring the ark to his capital city. Accordingly, the ark was brought to "the house of Obed-edom the Gittite" (6:10), and it was there for "three months" (v. 11). The Gittites were the inhabitants of the Philistine territory Gath (cf. 15:18). Why Obed-edom is chosen is not known. Because Gath was a Philistine town, David probably wanted the LORD's "breaking forth" to happen on the Philistines! It is quite unlikely that Obed-edom had any freedom to say no against David's decision to keep the ark in his house.

David the king uses here one of his less privileged subjects to test the effect of the dangerous ark. We are reminded of a similar phenomenon followed by the superpowers of our time in using their weaker neighbors, the Caribbean and Pacific Islands for example, for testing their dangerous chemicals, drugs, arms, and so forth.

The Ark Finally Brought to Zion (6:12-19)

David hears that the household of Obed-edom is blessed because of the ark of God; he immediately arranges for the ark to be moved to his own place (6:12). We hear no more about the cart and the oxen; interest is now centered on "those who bore the ark of the LORD" (v. 13). According to Exod. 25:13-15 the ark was carried by people on two poles with four rings (cf. 1 Kgs. 8:7-8). To avert any outburst of anger by Yahweh, as a precautionary measure David "sacrificed an ox and a fatling" (2 Sam. 6:13) after every "six paces," i.e, on every seventh pace. Here the symbolic number seven probably had some cultic significance (see Gnana Robinson, *Sabbath,* 109ff.).

That David was "girded with a linen ephod" suggests that he was performing a priestly function (cf. 1 Sam. 2:18). This shows that the cultic priesthood in Israel was not as yet firmly established. This account also suggests that David is here performing the role of a priest-king. The conception of a priest-king appears to have come from pre-Israelite Jerusalem. This is indicated by Ps. 110, a piece of old enthronement liturgy in which the Davidic king is spoken of as "a priest for ever after the order of Melchizedek" (v. 4). Melchizedek was a Canaanite king in Jerusalem (Gen. 14:18). Not only in Jerusalem, but also in other ancient Near Eastern countries, the king was the head of the cult and the presiding priest. David is thus performing the priestly functions of such a king, as in the pattern of his predecessor in Jerusalem.

"Shouting" and the blowing of the "horn" or the trumpet are elements characteristic of the celebration of the enthronement of kings (cf. 1 Kgs. 1:34, 39-41; 2 Kgs. 11:12-14). The entry of the ark into the capital city would therefore have symbolized for David and the people Yahweh's triumphal entry into Jerusalem as its king. In the Psalms Yahweh's kingship is often associated with Zion: "The LORD will reign for ever, thy God, O Zion, to all generations" (Ps. 146:10; cf. 132:13-14; 149:2).

Michal is displeased at David's behavior as if he were a common man on the street (2 Sam. 6:16). David was not dancing naked, as some derive from Michal's reaction; he was wearing a linen ephod which probably did not cover his whole body. The fact that David's behavior appeared strange to Michal could also attest that here are recorded cultic practices which were hitherto foreign to the Israelites. How could the author have thus read Michal's mind? He was probably preparing the ground for his etiological explanation for Michal's barrenness (v. 23). After performing his priestly duties before Yahweh, David now turns to the people to bless them "in the name of the LORD of hosts" and to distribute to them his gifts (vv. 18-19). He distributes to each "a cake of bread, a portion of meat, and a cake of raisins." These were probably first offered to God, so that the people now received them from the priest-king as a sacrament, as *prasada* in Indian religions. It appears to have been common practice in Israel for the priest first to worship God, and then to turn to the people and bless them (cf. 1 Kgs. 8:14; 2 Kgs. 11:14).

Michal's Barrenness (6:20-23)

After blessing the people, David returns "to bless his household." But Michal's response was unfriendly. Michal's complaint was about David's "uncovering himself . . . before the eyes of his sevants' maids" (2 Sam. 6:20). Perhaps during his frenzied movements in the dance the linen ephod which he was wearing slipped from his body so that his nakedness could be seen. In a state of ecstasy such happenings were not uncommon (cf. 1 Sam. 19:24). Israelite law forbids priests to expose their nakedness in holy places (Exod. 20:26). Exposing one's nakedness openly was taboo in Israel (cf. Gen. 9:22ff.; Lev. 18:6ff.). David's ecstatic behavior was typical of Canaanite practice, and that could have been one reason why Michal could not appreciate it. David justified his behavior as self-abasement before the LORD, as an expression of his gratitude to God for all that God had done for him (2 Sam. 6:21-22).

By referring to Michal's barrenness (v. 23) the author is preparing the ground for ch. 7, which announces the establishment of the Davidic kingdom "for ever." If Michal were to have a son, being the grandson of Saul the child could have staked a claim to be David's successor. In that way some remembrance of Saul could have still continued. However, with Michal's barrenness Saul's lineage is finally cut off. The ground is now ready for a new kingship in David alone to be established "for ever."

DAVID'S THRONE ESTABLISHED FOREVER (7:1-29)

Yahweh binds himself through his covenant with David to establish David's throne forever (7:13-16). This is an important but difficult chapter. Just as with the origin of kingship, the establishment of the Davidic dynasty was also most important for the faith of Israel; just as in the case of 1 Sam. 7–12, this chapter too has been worked over and over again by various hands, and it is now difficult to identify and separate the various layers of material.

The motif of house-building is used in a twofold way. Yahweh will build the house of David (2 Sam. 7:16), and David in turn will build the house of Yahweh (vv. 2-3, 5, 13). Here two trends can be identified. In vv. 2-3 Nathan encourages David to go ahead with his plan to build a house. However, in vv. 4-7 Nathan questions the whole idea of building a permanent house for Yahweh, basing the argument on the desert ideology that Yahweh has always been "moving about in a tent" (v. 6). This argument does not appear in v. 13, where Yahweh says that David's son "shall build a house" for Yahweh's name. Some scholars tend to ascribe the account which questions the necessity of a permanent house for God to a much later spiritual development, such as that in the time of Trito-Isaiah when such an earthly temple was considered to be unnecessary (cf. Fritz Stolz, *Das erste und zweite Buch Samuel,* 121). However, what we have here is not the total rejection of an earthly temple, but only a preference for the movable sanctuary of the desert to a fixed temple as was common among Israel's neighbors — the preference of the sanctuary of the nomads to the temple of the settler. The expression "since the day I brought up the people of Israel from Egypt to this day" (v. 6) recalls 1 Sam. 8:8. It goes with the anti-kingship tradition found in 1 Sam. 12–15. This could have been part of a prophetic tradition which saw the desert wanderings as the ideal period of Israel's religious pilgrimage with Yahweh, and always longed to return to it (cf. Hos. 2:14-23).

Another fact is that Yahweh's promises are directed on the one hand to David (2 Sam. 7:9-11, 16-17) and on the other hand to his son (vv. 12-15). However, no reference is made to his son in the whole of the thanksgiving prayer of David (vv. 18-20). It is possible that this is material coming from Davidic traditions as well as from Solomonic traditions. Verse 10 recalls the ideal state of the messianic kingdom prophesied in Mic. 5:4 (cf. 1 Kgs. 4:25); 2 Sam. 7:1, 11 reflects the "rest" *(menuha)* theology of the Deuteronomist; and v. 14 recalls Ps. 2:7. In 2 Sam. 7:15-16 we have the covenant theology again. Possibly, then, we have here elements coming from different streams.

The author rightly sees this establishment of the Davidic dynasty as part of God's saving act in history, as a logical sequence of the Exodus from Egypt and the settlement in Canaan (vv. 23-24). The theme of the establishment of the Davidic dynasty is thus further brought to its focus at this point; David's kingdom is established not just for the present only, but forever (vv. 12, 14, 16, 26, 29).

This, in my opinion, is the most important chapter in the OT, in that it has played a very decisive role in the future history of

Israel. In God's covenant with David we have the seed of the belief in the Messiah, the anointed one of Yahweh. This belief kept the lamp of Israel's hope burning even during days of stormy darkness, the hope of their continuing as a nation and as a people. This was so even when the kings were removed, and the kingdom was destroyed, and the possibility of any restoration of the kingdom was utterly remote. The Hebrew concept of *hesed* (translated "steadfast love" in the RSV) plays an important role here. *Hesed* indicates all that is involved in God's covenant with mankind. It "reveals the on-going, creative, consistent, unswerving, suffering, loyal love of God for his chosen people" (G. A. F. Knight, "Is 'Righteous' Right?", *SJT* 41 [1988]: 2). In his covenant with David Yahweh binds himself with *hesed*, which means that Yahweh will not fail in fulfilling his covenant obligations, irrespective of how the king sitting on the Davidic throne behaves — whether he remains faithful to his covenant obligations or not (vv. 14-15). As the Psalmist puts it, "his steadfast love *(hesed)* endures for ever" (Ps. 136).

It is to this covenant-binding by Yahweh that Israel attached its hope even in the midst of hopeless conditions and thereby was enabled to survive all kinds of crises in its history. Members of future generations invoked God to fulfil the *hesed* he promised to David (cf. 1 Kgs. 8:23; Ps. 89:24; 130:7; 132:11-12; 136). According to this belief, it is therefore impossible for the Davidic kingship to be destroyed forever. Accordingly, even when there was no king and all the infrastructure for the kingship — the palace, the temple and the cult, the ark, the capital city — was totally destroyed, people could still hope for the restoration of the Davidic kingdom through the coming of the Messiah, the LORD's anointed one. This expectation, according to the NT, has been fulfilled in Jesus of Nazareth, born within the family of David (cf. Matt. 2:2; 3:3; Luke 3:22; 4:18-19).

David's Concern for a House for the Ark (7:1-3)

The LORD gives David "rest from all his enemies round about" (2 Sam. 7:1). This is a common expression used by the Deuteronomist to indicate an ideal state of life, characteristic of a just rule where the threat from one's enemies has been removed (cf. 1 Kgs. 4:25; Mic. 4:4; Zech. 3:10). Hebrew *menuhah* is the word translated here as "rest." The term does not mean physical rest in the sense of relaxation, but signifies persons or objects on the move coming to a settled position (cf. Gnana Robinson, *ZAW* 92 [1980]: 32-42). *Menuhah* from enemies thus means the condition of being safely settled in a place, and thus different from fleeing away as fugitives before the enemy. David, who has been fleeing as a fugitive for a long time, has now been brought to a "safe settlement," and this has been the doing of God. As long as he was fleeing as a fugitive before his enemies, David could not think of building a permanent house for the LORD. Now that he is safe and has built for himself a permanent house, he can think of building a house for the LORD. Nathan the prophet gives general approval to David's plan. "All that is in your heart" (2 Sam. 7:3) is a common expression to indicate the total inclination of a person. The heart in Hebrew psychology was regarded as the seat of human thinking and decision. If the wishes of a person, in whose heart God abides, are in full harmony with the will of God, then the wishes of such a person can be carried out without hesitation. David is here represented as a person whose wishes are in harmony with the will of God.

Nathan (v. 3) appears here suddenly. He plays no role in David's reign before the settlement in Jerusalem. It is therefore possible to assume that Nathan derives from pre-Israelite Jerusalem. David conquered Jerusalem intact, taking over not only its stronghold and buildings, but also its social and religious institutions. Nathan was probably already an important leader of the Jerusalem royal court and temple prophecy. The role he played in the succession to David speaks for such an origin (12:25; 1 Kgs. 1:11ff.). After coming into contact with the Israelites, Nathan must have studied the Mosaic traditions of Israel and learned from them about the nature of Yahweh. Evidently God accepts a heathen prophet as his mouthpiece. Nathan takes sides with Bathsheba, a Jerusalemite woman, in support of her son Solomon and his party, the Zadokite priesthood (cf. 2 Sam. 8:17; 1 Kgs. 1:32ff.), whose origin is also to be seen in Jerusalem. The Jerusalemite origin of this prophet is further supported by the fact that one of the sons born to David in Jerusalem was given the name Nathan (2 Sam. 5:14). As a prophet born in Jerusalem, Nathan knows the will of the God who sits enthroned in Jerusalem and is now worshipped by the name Yahweh.

Yahweh's Preference for Tent-dwelling (7:4-7)

In its content this section has no connection with the preceding verses. The account that follows tends to idealize the period of desert wandering when the ark was housed in a tent (7:6). As seen above, there appears here a tendency to object to the settled culture of Canaan. The reference to the "night" (v. 4) might suggest that Nathan received this revelation through a night "vision" (cf. v. 17). No mention is made here of the ephod and Urim and Thummim. With the shift of the cult to Jerusalem the mode of revelation also seems to have changed. The prophet and the priest of the Jerusalem cult were probably not familiar with the cultic devices of the Shiloh tradition.

"The word of the LORD came to Nathan" (v. 4) is an oracle introduction formula, common in OT prophetic writings. It occurs more than two hundred times in the OT, mostly in the prophetic and Deuteronomic writings. The Hebrew translated "came to" is *hayah le,* and it describes the word of God as alive. Since God is the living God, his word too is alive, and so "comes" (cf. John 1:14; cf. also Hos. 1:1; Jonah 1:1). In the books of Samuel this formula occurs in this sense elsewhere only in 1 Sam. 15:10; 2 Sam. 24:11. This might indicate that we have here a tradition which was closer to classical prophecy. This tradition holds that Yahweh was always contented with dwelling in a tent and that he never demanded of the leaders of Israel to build for him "a house of cedar" (7:7). The statement "since the day I brought up the people of Israel from Egypt" (v. 6; cf. 1 Sam. 8:8) shows that the Exodus event is understood here as the beginning of the history of Yahweh's movement with his people. Israel's distinctness among the peoples lay in the reality that their God Yahweh went with them always. Thus Moses says, "If thy presence will not go with me, do not carry us up from here. . . . Is it not in thy going with us, so that we are distinct, I and thy people, from all other people that are upon the face of the earth?" (Exod. 33:15ff.). So the LORD moved about with them all through their journeys (cf. Exod. 40:34ff.). "Tent" (2 Sam. 7:6) means "the tent of meeting" (Exod. 33:7-11). The ark was kept in this tent (cf. Exod. 26:33ff.).

God's Covenant with David (7:8-17)

The messenger formula "thus says the LORD" in 2 Sam. 7:8 indicates that here a new oracle begins. David was called "from the pasture, from following the sheep," that is, from a condition of insignificance. This is an important election motif in the OT. People of little significance are chosen to be God's instruments of salvation — Abraham the shepherd (Gen. 12:1-3); Jacob, "a wandering Aramean" (Deut. 26:5); a stammering Moses (Exod. 4:10); a dresser of sycamore trees, Amos (Amos 7:14); a young Jeremiah (Jer. 1:6). From being "no people" Israel was called by God to become "a people" (cf. Deut. 7:6-8; 32:10; Hos. 1:10; 2:1). Election in the OT is not for privilege, but for responsibility. David was called by God from going in front of *(neged)* the sheep to go in front of (as *nagid,* "prince") God's people (2 Sam. 7:8; cf. 1 Sam. 10:1; 2 Sam. 2:4; 5:3, 12).

"And I have been with you wherever you went, and have cut off all your enemies" (7:9): this of course had been the secret of David's success. Yahweh has been with him wherever he went and has "cut off" all his enemies from before him (1 Sam. 16:18; 18:12, 14, 28; 23:14; 25:29; 26:12; 2 Sam. 4:9; 5:10). 2 Samuel 7:9b gives God's real intention for David; he aims at making David "a great name, like the name of the great ones of the earth." All David's efforts therefore are meant to realize this goal. Verse 9a may thus be understood as an attempt to legitimize David's aim and his efforts. The anti-kingship tradition underlying much of the books of Samuel condemned the temptation to become "like all the nations." However, here the author, who is sympathetic to David, legitimizes David's efforts to conform to and excel his neighbors by providing a divine sanction for his actions. "I will give you rest from all your enemies" (v. 11): What is given in v. 1 as the present reality is now repeated here as a promise for the future (cf. vv. 10-11). This shows the secondary nature of this section in its present context. "That they may dwell in their own place, and be disturbed no more; and violent men shall afflict them no more" (v. 10) is exactly the condition of *menuhah* ("rest"). According to the Deuteronomic historians, this promise was fulfilled in the reign of Solomon (1 Kgs. 4:25). The phrase "as formerly" (2 Sam. 7:10) points to the earlier days of David, which were characterized by continued threats from enemies. "House" (v. 11b) refers to the Davidic dynasty. What is implied in vv. 10-11 is explained in v. 12: "I will raise up your offspring after you . . . and I will establish his kingdom." It was probably the Jerusalemite tradition which pressed for Solomon's succession, expressed accordingly in terms of the Jerusalemite royal ideology. "The king, as the son of God, ruling for ever" is a royal ideology which was widely spread in the ancient Near East.

It is maintained that Solomon, David's son, would build a "house" for Yahweh's name and Yahweh would in return establish his kingdom forever (v. 13). The author here employs a pun: the word "house" can mean both the house of David — sons and daughters — and also the temple, the house of the LORD. The Hebrew word for "house" *(bayit)* comes from the root *banah*. The words for "son" *(ben)* and "daughter" *(bat)* also come from the same root. Thus "he shall build a house" can also mean "he shall build a house by having sons and daughters." However, biblical tradition understood this more in terms of Solomon's building the temple (cf. 1 Kgs. 8:17-20). The Deuteronomic idea of reward and retribution is implied here. It has been a popular oriental view that acts of service to the cult such as building temples, supporting festivals, and so forth are rewarded by God with peace and prosperity in the kingdom. In this same vein, most of the temples in India were built by kings.

In 2 Sam. 7:14-15 the climax of the chapter is reached: Yahweh's "steadfast love" *(hesed)* will remain with the heirs of the Davidic kingdom "for ever." Originally God's promise in vv. 14-15 may have been unconditional; but later writers, who saw the possibility of kings going astray from following Yahweh, appear to have added v. 14b. That is, when a king goes wrong, Yahweh will discipline him and correct him by human hands; yet Yahweh will keep the king on the throne of David, and Yahweh's steadfast love will remain with the king forever. Later writers were apparently not satisfied with that; they made the promise conditional (cf. 1 Kgs. 6:12ff.; 8:25).

The noun *hesed* occurs 245 times in the OT, 63 times in secular contexts dealing with interpersonal relationships. More than half of the references (127) occur in the Psalms, mostly in the Psalms ascribed to David. In the books of Samuel it occurs 16 times, translated differently by the RSV in different contexts: "steadfast love" (2 Sam. 2:6; 7:15; 15:20; 22:51), "kindness" (1 Sam. 15:6; 20:8, "deal kindly"; 2 Sam. 9:1, 3, 7), and "loyalty" (1 Sam. 20:15; 2 Sam. 2:5; 3:8; 10:2, "deal loyally"; 16:17). The etymology of this word is uncertain. There is no consensus among OT scholars as to whether covenant *(berit)* was constitutive for *hesed,* but all agree more or less on its meaning and theological significance. *Hesed* is basically a relational concept; it has to do with the relationships of persons — interpersonal relationships as well as God's relationship with his people. *Hesed* indicates one's benevolent dealings with another person or group of persons, one's fellowship with them and the steadfastness or stability of that fellowship. "Doing *hesed*" always implies doing good to the other person or persons at a time of their need. As such "doing *hesed*" presupposes readiness to face risk and accept suffering for the sake of others.

No single word in English expresses its meaning adequately. John Wycliffe invented the English word "lovingkindness" to translate *hesed,* and the KJV made use of it (mostly in the Psalms). Modern English translations have tried about sixteen words including "mercy," "love," "kindness," "loyalty," and "steadfast love."

Whether covenant was constitutive for *hesed* in its origin or not, it becomes constitutive in God's relationship with David. The future generations in Israel (as is evident from repeated references in the Davidic Psalms) fixed their hope on the *hesed* promised to David, because of God's everlasting covenant with David. This becomes quite evident from the following verses in Ps. 89 —

I will sing of thy *steadfast love,* O Lord, for ever;
with my mouth I will proclaim thy faithfulness to all
  generations.

191

For thy *steadfast love* was established for ever,
thy faithfulness is firm as the heavens.

Thou hast said, "I have made a *covenant* with my chosen one,
I have sworn to David my servant:

'I will establish your descendants for ever,
and build your throne for all generations.'"
. . . .
Mψ *steadfast love* I will keep for him for ever,
and my *covenant* will stand firm for him.

I will establish his line for ever
and his throne as the days of the heavens.

If his children forsake my law
and do not walk according to my ordinances,

if they violate my statutes
and do not keep my commandments,

then I will punish their transgression with the rod
and their iniquity with scourges;

but I will not remove from him my *steadfast love,*
or be false to my faithfulness.

I will not violate my *covenant,*
or alter the word that went forth from my lips.

Once for all I have sworn by my holiness;
I will not lie to David.

His line shall endure for ever,
his throne as long as the sun before me.

Like the moon it shall be established for ever;
it shall stand firm while the skies endure. Ps. 89:1-4, 28-37

Hesed becomes thus God's binding of himself through covenant
to love, to discipline, and to continue the Davidic heirs on his
throne forever. It is thus God's covenant love to his people.

Unfortunately, *hesed* is often translated in the LXX by *eleos,* showing in the Magnificat (Luke 1:50, 54) a wrong understanding of covenant love for Greek readers, and so in English. One hundred years ago George Adam Smith of Aberdeen suggested "leal-love" for *hesed,* but not everyone understood his Scottish word "leal," which means "loyal." Indeed, that is what covenant love entails — the idea of "love that will not let me go."

The Church presents this concept in the service for Christian marriage. There each party *covenants* with the other to take the other for good or ill. At the same time the idea of love is included with the stipulation "for better or for worse, for richer or for poorer, in sickness and in health, to love and to cherish, till death us do part." That promise can be upheld only if each partner covenants to keep hold of the other at the cost of taking up their own cross. Covenant has been likened to a coconut shell: it lasts forever, but inside is the fruit, the loving and caring.

The NT interpreter misleads the Church with the words: "This cup is the *new* covenant in my blood," if "new" is presented in terms of the Greek word *neos. Neos* means something totally new that renders the old obsolete. The word used here is actually *kainos,* which means "renovated," "refurbished," "reconditioned." Thus it builds upon the Mosaic covenant, which is God's (Exod. 19) and which is to last forever, and God does not change. Thus the content of the Mosaic covenant is that of the cross, of suffering love.

David's Prayer of Thanksgiving (7:18-29)

This is a hymn based on David's covenant with the LORD. It apparently comes from a later period. The hand of the Deuteronomic theologian is evident here. The Deuteronomic scheme of salvation history is evident in 2 Sam. 7:22-24 (cf. Deut. 26:5-9). By means of a covenant Yahweh established himself as the God of Israel and Israel as his "people for ever" (2 Sam. 7:24). It follows logically, David argues, that the LORD established his house "that it may continue for ever" (v. 29): a people of God forever and a "servant" (v. 25) of God forever, to rule over them on behalf of God.

"Who am I . . . that thou hast brought me thus far?" (v. 18) is a self-abasement formula (cf. 9:8; Ps. 8:4). Indeed, "there is none like thee, and there is no God besides thee" (2 Sam. 7:22). A strictly monotheistic faith, such as that found in Deutero-Isaiah, was hardly to be expected during David's time. The "word" of God to which David refers in v. 25 and the "revelation" of God of which he speaks in v. 27 are references to the promise God made to David in v. 16. David takes courage to pray as he does only because God has spoken first in his prevenient grace. That God's name will be magnified among his devotees for his wonderful deeds among them (v. 26) is an element characteristic of many hymns in the OT in all periods of its development.

DAVID'S VICTORY OVER HIS ENEMIES (8:1-18)

The same motif of David's kingdom being established forever is continued even further. "The LORD gave victory to David wherever he went" (8:6b, 14b) is the theme of the whole chapter. The author tries to show how God fulfilled his covenant promise to David to give him "rest from all his enemies round about" (7:1, 11) and to establish his house forever (7:25ff.). As promised (7:9), the LORD now cuts off all the enemies of David from before him — the Philistines (8:1), the Moabites (v. 2), the Zobahites (vv. 3-4), the Syrians (vv. 5-6), the Edomites (vv. 12-14), the Amalekites, and the Ammonites (v. 12). Through these military victories David gained control over the whole of Palestine, and the kings of the neighboring countries became his vassals, paying him tribute. David was also able to amass great wealth — gold (vv. 7, 10-11), silver (vv. 10-11), and bronze (vv. 8, 10) — rare metals which now became available to the Israelites. David also obtained horses and chariots (v. 4), which hitherto had contributed to the superiority of some of the enemy armies. The Israelites during their early days appear to have used no animals for fighting. Now, however, like all the other nations, David has built up a full-fledged army with an infantry, a cavalry, slave-soldiers, bronze weapons, and so forth. He is now economically established as well, with much gold and silver; added to that the vassal people now bring him regular tribute.

According to 5:17-25, David had already attained a final victory over the Philistines. 2 Samuel 7:9 maintains that David's victory over his enemies was an accomplished fact. The account in ch. 8, therefore, could have come from an independent tradition. It intended to give a summary of all the victories of David in order to show how "the LORD gave victory to David wherever he went" (8:6b, 14b). We have here perhaps information gathered from various sources. Information regarding the conquests over the Philistines (v. 1), Moab (v. 2), and the Aramean king Hadadezer (v. 3) are introduced by the words "David/he defeated." However, the victory over Edom (v. 13) is not introduced in this way. Edom was the "cousin" people who had rejected the birthright (through Esau) and thus separated themselves away from God. For that reason they were special. Along with the above-mentioned enemies, vv. 11-14a mention other enemies conquered by David — the Ammonites, the Edomites, and the Amalekites. This could have been a final summary of the overall victory of David.

In spite of the fact that the empire of David now resembled the empires of other nations, the author holds that the uniqueness of David's kingdom depended more on the fact that "David administered justice *(mishpat)* and equity *(tsedaqah)* to all his people" (v. 15). This is the keynote of the Deuteronomic theologian, who sees Israel's uniqueness not so much in its worldly wealth and power as the fact that David dealt justly both with Israel's own people and with others. The greatness of a nation is to be measured not so much by its strength and wealth as by its just treatment of all its people (cf. Deut. 4:7-8).

8:1 The victory over the Philistines is mentioned first, because they were the first and the foremost threat to the Israelites. According to one tradition, David was called to save God's people "from the hand of the Philistines, and from the hand of all their enemies" (cf. 2 Sam. 3:18). It is possible that 8:1 is a reference to the defeat of the Philistines recorded in 5:17ff. The meaning of Metheg-ammah is not clear. *Metheg* in Hebrew means "bridle." Perhaps the term refers to some sort of demarcation fence laid by the Philistines which David removed.

8:2 Moab is defeated. The Moabites shared a common ethnic heritage with both the Israelites and the Ammonites (cf. Gen. 19:37), but they continued to be unfriendly to the Israelites (cf. Num. 21:28-29). Two-thirds of the Moabites were put to death by David; only one-third were spared. The reason for such a serious punishment is not known. The separation of people with "lines" is also new here.

8:3-8 David gains control along the trade route toward the north. The same events may be reported again in 2 Sam. 10:6ff. A number of small kingdoms seem to have been situated in the region of Syria, one of which was Zobah. The meaning of the statement, "as he went to restore his power at the river Euphrates" (8:3), is not clear. Some manuscripts mention only "Euphrates," but the words "the river" by themselves can also refer to the river Euphrates. It is quite unlikely that David's political control extended as far as the Euphrates. Ps. 72:8; 89:25 seem to imply that the Davidic empire extended "from the sea to the river." This poetic vision could have been given a literal sense here.

Hadadezer seems to have had a strong cavalry corps. It is difficult to imagine how David's infantry corps was able to defeat the army of Hadadezer, with his infantry and cavalry. The figures here are perhaps exaggerated. It is not clear why David killed so many horses, sparing only enough for one hundred chariots. This reflects the first use of horses in the Israelite army. Aram (2 Sam. 8:6) is the name of the whole Syrian territory, the capital of which was Damascus. David's victory does not appear to have lasted long. According to 1 Kgs. 11:23-24 Rezon, a former vassal of Hadadezer, redeemed Damascus and ruled over Syria.

Gold, silver, bronze — valuables of enemy spoils (2 Sam. 8:7-8, 10) — are dedicated to the LORD (v. 11). This seems to be a later development from the *herem* institution, where usable and valuable goods of the spoils of war are preserved. Earlier tradition demanded the total destruction of all the spoil (cf. Deut. 7:2, 5, 16, 25: 1 Sam. 15:3).

8:9-10 Hamath (2 Sam. 8:9) is another Syrian kingdom. Its king Toi, being an enemy of Hadadezer, congratulates David on his victory, sending through his son "Joram" (v. 10) tributes of silver, gold, and bronze to David. Thus Toi avoids an open clash with David by accepting David's suzerainty. The gifts from Toi and other tributes were perhaps stored for the future for the purpose of building a temple. Solomon could have made use of them.

8:11-13a David's conquests are given in summary. The statement "and David won a name for himself" (v. 13a) could have been part of the original account. It does not fit into the present context where David's victories are ascribed to Yahweh (vv. 6b, 14b).

8:13b-14 The Edomites are conquered. They too were a people ethnically related to Israel (Gen. 36:1ff.), but they always lived in hostility with the Israelites. Edom, too, appears to have been later reclaimed by Hadad "of the royal house in Edom," during Solomon's reign (1 Kgs. 11:14-22). "Valley of Salt" (2 Sam. 8:13b) was probably a place S of the Dead Sea.

8:15-18 David is established as an emperor, as one among all the emperors in the ancient Near East. The extent of an ideal kingdom in Israel was often seen to stretch "from the river of Egypt to the great river, the river Euphrates" (Gen. 15:18) or "from the entrance of Hamath as far as the Sea of the Arabah" (2 Kgs. 14:25). Internally David's reign was marked by "justice and equity to all his people" (2 Sam. 8:15). David thus became the ideal king, as that generation understood the term.

For such an ideal rule David required a proper administrative structure. Verses 16-18 give some information about that structure — Joab as army commander, Jehoshaphat as "recorder," Zadok and Ahimelech as priests, Seraiah as "secretary," and Benaiah the son of Jehoiada "over the Cherethites and the Pelethites." The mention of Zadok and Ahimelech as priests points to the existence of two priestly traditions at this time, Ahimelech representing the old Siloahic priestly tradition and Zadok coming from the Jerusalemite tradition. There may well have been tensions between the representatives of these two traditions; in the end the Zadokite

tradition appears to have gained the upper hand. Already in
15:24-29 attempts are being made to put Zadok above Abiathar.
Later on Abiathar was removed from office, and Zadok replaced
him (1 Kgs. 2:26-27, 35). 1 Samuel 23:6; 30:7 speak of "Abiathar
the son of Ahimelech" (rather than "Ahimelech the son of Abiathar"). It is suggested that we follow that reading here, with the
Syriac (*Biblia Hebraica* mg), but according to 1 Kgs. 4:4 "Zadok
and Abiathar [not Ahimelech] were priests."

Benaiah the son of Jehoiada (2 Sam. 8:18) is the commander
of the guards here; later he succeeds Joab as the commander of
the whole army. Cherethites probably refers to the people from
Crete (Caphtor, Amos 9:7), the same as Carites (2 Kgs. 11:4, 9;
cf. 1 Sam. 30:14; 2 Sam. 15:18; 20:7). Pelethites were a sea
people like the Philistines (see above on 1 Sam. 4:1b; cf. 2 Sam.
15:18; 20:7).

"And David's sons were priests" (8:18b) appears to be an
addition. If original, it should have been mentioned along with
Zadok and Ahimelech/Abiathar. Perhaps this tradition about
David's sons was one which saw kingship in Jerusalem as a priestly
kingship after the order of Melchizedek, and as such recognized
the Davidic kingship also as a priestly kingship (cf. 6:14). According to 1 Chr. 18:17, "David's sons were the chief officials in
the service of the king."

III. DAVID'S DESIRE TO
PRACTICE "HESED"
2 Samuel 9:1–10:19

The idea of *hesed* (on the translation of this word and its meaning, see above on 2 Sam. 7:14-15) is the central theme of both of these chapters. David is here presented as one who "loves *hesed*" (cf. Mic. 6:8). David, who received the *hesed* of God, now desires to practice *hesed* towards others (cf. 2 Sam. 9:3), specifically to all those to whom he had bound himself with a covenant before God. 2 Samuel 9 provides a positive example of David's successfully practicing *hesed* (the word occurs here three times — vv. 1, 3, 7). Chapter 10 gives an example of David's offer of *hesed* being rejected, with the result that a war breaks out. The chapter also continues one of the author's main themes: "David administered justice *(mishpat)* and equity *(tsedaqah)*" (8:15) to all. David is not at fault for the outbreak of wars. It is those who reject the offer of *hesed* who are responsible.

DAVID SHOWS HESED TO THE HOUSE OF SAUL
(9:1-13)

9:1 David wants to show *hesed* to those who are left in the house of Saul "for Jonathan's sake." He is obviously trying here to fulfil his covenant obligations to Jonathan (1 Sam. 18:3-4; 20:15-16, 42; 23:18). Because of that covenant David was bound to show to the house of Jonathan "the loyal love *(hesed)* of the LORD" (1 Sam. 20:14). By his swearing to Saul (1 Sam. 24:21-22) David is also committed not to "cut off" Saul's descendants after him. Now that the LORD has cut off David's enemies from the face of the earth (cf. 1 Sam. 20:15), David proceeds to protect

199

Jonathan's house from being "cut off from the house of David" (v. 16).

9:2-8 David shows *hesed* to Mephibosheth the son of Jonathan (2 Sam. 9:6). We meet Ziba (v. 2) here for the first time; perhaps he stayed in Benjaminite Gibeah where Saul once lived and managed Saul's properties. Mephibosheth was already introduced in 4:4. Machir the son of Ammiel from Lo-debar (9:4) appears again in 17:27, where he is listed among those who brought gifts to David in Mahanaim. Machir appears to be a man of sufficient resources that he could accommodate and support Mephibosheth. When summoned by David, Mephibosheth is perhaps frightened, but David allays his fears. David promises to restore to him "all the land of Saul" (9:7), probably meaning Saul's personal property. Mephibosheth is also given the special privilege of eating at the king's table as one of his sons (v. 11), the same privilege which David enjoyed in Saul's house (cf. 1 Sam. 20:18ff.). It could also be that David wanted to have Mephibosheth under his personal supervision, lest there be any revolt from his side. 2 Samuel 16:1ff. supports such a fear. "A dead dog" (9:8) is an expression of self-abasement (see above on 3:8).

9:9-13 David returns Saul's properties to Mephibosheth. He commissions Ziba, Mephibosheth's servant, to work on that land and to "bring in the produce" (9:10) to Mephibosheth's family for their maintenance. However, Mephibosheth himself will have the privileged position of eating at the king's table (vv. 10-11, 13). The status of Ziba and his family here is that of landless agricultural laborers. The emergence of such a dependent class in society is the result of Israel's introduction to the agrarian culture in Canaan.

That "he was lame in both his feet" (v. 13) may have been why Mephibosheth always remained in Jerusalem. David's sympathy and special concern to a lame person like Mephibosheth speaks against the veracity of 5:8. Nothing more is mentioned about Mephibosheth's son Mica (9:12) in Samuel. Saul's genealogy in 1 Chr. 8:34ff.; 9:40ff. does mention Mica and further shows that the house of Saul continued for several generations through the lineage of Jonathan.

AMMONITE REJECTION OF "HESED" (10:1-19)

In 2 Sam. 8:3ff. the account of David's victory over his enemies was given in summary form. Here that account of war in the east is given in detail. According to the author, David, reigning with justice and equity (8:15), was only interested in practicing *hesed* (10:2), but it was the enemies (here the Ammonites) who dragged him into war. David was thus drawn to fight not only the Ammonites, but also the whole of the area summed up in the name Aram.

Verses 1-5 explain the background of the confrontation. Here the Ammonite king Hanun is mentioned by name (v. 1), but this name does not appear again in vv. 6-19. In vv. 6-14 Joab leads the war, but in vv. 15-19 Joab no longer appears. Rather, it is David who leads the war. The motif of "insult" which is dominant in vv. 1-5 does not appear in vv. 6-19. It is possible that these three sections originally came from different circles. The author who placed vv. 15-19 after vv. 6-14 probably wanted to give the credit for victory to David, as in the case of the event mentioned in 12:26-30.

10:1-5   As in 1 Sam. 11, the Ammonites are here presented as an arrogant people (on the Ammonites, see the introduction to 1 Sam. 11:1-15). They reject David's offer of *hesed* and humiliate the Israelites by shaving off "half the beard of each" of David's messengers and cutting off their garments "in the middle, at their hips" (2 Sam. 10:4). Such an attitude is typical of dictators, whose policies are always tinted with pride and arrogance. However, "pride goes before a fall" is a truth confirmed repeatedly in history. The Ammonite king who died (v. 1) was Nahash, against whom Saul had fought (1 Sam. 11:1-2; 1 Chr. 19:1). Hanun is the son of Nahash, and David desires to render *hesed* to Hanun because of the *hesed* Nahash had shown to him. We do not know of any such incident where Nahash showed kindness to David. For that reason, scholars wonder whether this could be a reference rather to Moab, which gave shelter to David's parents. On the death of Nahash David sends a message of condolence to his son Hanun; but Hanun and "the princes of the Ammonites" take them to be spies and insult them (2 Sam. 10:3-4). Shaving off "half the beard" and cutting off the garments "in the middle" were signs of mourning, and to do this to the messengers of an emperor was perhaps the worst form of humiliation. The messengers of a conqueror are here turned into messengers of defeat, messengers of mourning. In Israel a man's beard was regarded as a sign of his manhood. Only as a sign of intense mourning are the beard and the hair on the head shaved and the clothes rent (cf. Jer. 41:5; 48:37). When others do these things by force, they become acts of serious insult and shame. By insulting the messengers the Ammonites are in effect insulting the person who sent them, and are thus challenging his authority and power. It is therefore the legitimate duty of a king to establish his authority and power over his enemies. Thus war becomes inevitable.

10:6-14   The Ammonites knew what the consequences of their action would be. They were afraid of an attack from David, and so they seek the support of the Syrians. David delegates the command to Joab. Ammon appears to have been a fortified city. The Ammonite army organizes itself at the entrance to the fort, while the Syrian forces take their position in the open area outside. The idea is to launch a double frontal attack on Israel, both in the front and in the rear. Joab, as a veteran of war, sees what that would entail (2 Sam. 10:9). He divides his army into two divisions, one under his own command to attack the Syrian forces outside, and the other under the command of his brother Abishai to attack the Ammonite forces at the gate (vv. 10-12). Both the Syrians and the Ammonites lose their separate battles and flee (v. 14). The Ammonites are said to have "entered the city"; perhaps they even closed the door of the city gate. Taking over "the royal city" is yet to be accomplished by David at a later stage (cf. 12:26-31). The author sees the victory of the Israelites as a victory given by the LORD (10:12).

Beth-rehob, Zobah (cf. 8:5), Maacah, and Tob are places in Syrian territory. Zobah lies in the Anti-Lebanon range. Beth-rehob and Tob could have been places near Ammon, NE of Damascus. Maacah is in southern Hermon. The expression "the cities of our God" in 10:12 is unique in the OT; it is probably a scribal error for "city of God" referring to Jerusalem (cf. Ps. 46:4; 48:1, 8; 101:8).

10:15-19 While going to the assistance of the Ammonites, the Syrians seem to have underestimated the strength of David. By their defeat their prestige and repute would appear damaged; they could not accept such defeat. So "they gathered themselves together" (2 Sam. 10:15). Hadadezer sends messengers and brings out "the Syrians who were beyond the Euphrates" (possibly on another military campaign) in order to strengthen his attack on David. The battle takes place in Helam (v. 17), and the Syrians are defeated badly, though not finally. This victory of David over Hadadezer, a strong power in that region, creates fear among his vassals. Consequently "they made peace with Israel, and became subject to them" (v. 19). Thus David is relieved from the threat of any enemies in the northeast, in fulfilment of the "rest from all his enemies" (cf. 7:1) promised by God.

On Hadadezer, see 8:3ff. Helam (10:17) is a place in Gilead. The statement that "the Syrians feared to help the Ammonites any more" (v. 19) indicates that the Ammonite menace still continues (cf. 12:26ff.).

IV. DAVID'S SIN AND NATHAN'S WORDS TO DAVID

2 Samuel 11:1–12:31

The account of David's sin and Nathan's encounter with him (11:2–12:25) is placed in the context of the Ammonite war. 2 Samuel 11:1 says that Joab and his men went to fight against the Ammonites and that David stayed in Jerusalem. That gave the occasion for David's sin. 2 Samuel 12:26-31 concludes with the account of David's final onslaught and victory over the Ammonites. The account of David's affair with Bathsheba is given here as the preparation for the Succession narrative that follows. The Bathsheba account records the birth of Solomon, David's successor. It also gives a theological reason for the hostilities and wars that take place within David's royal household: they are in fulfilment of Nathan's word against David for killing Uriah the Hittite — "Now therefore the sword shall never depart from your house, because you have despised me" (12:10).

The succession theme is systematically developed by the historian. It is indirectly hinted at in 6:23, which mentions the barrenness of Michal. Yahweh's guarantee for the Davidic throne is proclaimed in 7:13-14. Ch. 9 reports the final subordination of Saul's family to David. Now the successor is born.

It is the greatness of the Bible that it speaks not only about the glorious side of its characters, but also about their darker side. It speaks both about the good and the bad in its characters, yet of course, often with a certain amount of theological bias. The Deuteronomic historian, who step by step builds up the image of David as an ideal king, is not guilty of covering up David's weaker side; this certainly adds to the credibility of the account. Here are the bare facts of an account without any toning down or touching up. There is so much realism in the report which exposes the basic nature of David — an ordinary man, vulnerable to human temptations, unscrupulous and crafty in removing any barriers that block his plans and in getting things done in his own way. This certainly does not add to the positive image of David which the narrator is interested in building up. It only speaks for the historicity of the account, which the narrator could not simply ignore. This account is also meant to affirm God's promise to David regarding his throne, that the LORD will not take his "steadfast love *(hesed)* from him (the king)," but will chasten the king "with the stripes of the sons of men" when he "commits iniquity" (7:14-15). This promise is now illustrated in David's life itself: David, the guilty one, is chastened with the death of his son born of Bathsheba (12:14ff.). Nevertheless, God's steadfast love continues, and the continuation of the Davidic throne is ensured through the birth of Solomon, David's successor (vv. 24-25). Clearly the ages have accounted David "great." This has not been for anything in himself, but because of God's *hesed,* God's "loyal love" that never lets his children go. As the ancestor of Jesus, David received forgiveness and renewal because of God's loyalty to God's own plan for the redemption of the world.

DAVID'S SIN (11:1-27)

In 12:13 David confesses, "I have sinned against the LORD." This chapter explains how David committed the sin. The story appears as an object lesson on what was taught about sin in Gen. 3 — its conception, its concretization, and its consequences. Sin is conceived in the heart and is concretized in actions in one's life. It then actually affects the sinner's relationship to himself, to his neighbors, and to his God. This chapter speaks of the conception and concretization of David's sin.

The Conception of Sin (11:1-3)

Sin is conceived in the heart by temptation. Genesis 3 explains vividly how a person normally is tempted. All temptations have three aspects: the object or the person who tempts the sinner appeals to the sinner as being highly desirable; the sinner finds this object easily obtainable; his action leads to undesirable consequences. In the story of the fall Eve saw that the fruit of the tree was desirable in all respects — it "was good for food [physical interest], . . . a delight to the eyes [aesthetic interest], and . . . was to be desired to make one wise [intellectural interest]" (Gen. 3:6). Here too David finds Bathsheba desirable: "the woman was very beautiful" (2 Sam. 11:2). The story of the fall says that Eve "took of its fruit and ate," which shows that the fruit was within reach of her hand; it was easily obtainable by her. Here too David finds the circumstances very advantageous for him to get Bathsheba. His servants and "all Israel" are away in the battle against the Ammonites (v. 1); Bathsheba's husband is also away. Moreover, David's royal authority is to his advantage; when David sends messengers to fetch Bathsheba, she goes with them without any protest because the men have come with the authority of the king. Had they been ordinary civilians she would have certainly protested. David thus finds Bathsheba both desirable and obtainable. A sinner is often taken unawares by the impulsive nature of temptation so that it blinds his or her eyes from its consequences. It is for this reason that Jesus warned his disciples to "watch and pray that you may not enter into temptation" (Matt. 26:41) and also taught them to pray, saying "lead us not into temptation" (Matt. 6:13).

Kings in Palestine seem to have gone out for battle during the spring (1 Sam. 11:1). The rainy season (end of October to late May) in Palestine is characterized by strong winds and rains, and so is unsuitable for war. David is not prepared to stop without taking revenge on the Ammonites for the insult they inflicted on his messengers. He sends an army who "ravaged the Ammonites, and besieged Rabbah" (v. 1). Rabbah, the capital of Ammon, appears to have been a fortified city. Defeated by Joab and his brother Abishai, the Ammonites retreated and took shelter in their fort (10:14). The Israelite army is now besieging the city. This account continues in 12:26. In between lies the story of David's sin.

David walks on the roof of his house, from where he could

see Bathsheba bathing (11:2). Most of the houses in Palestine were built with a flat mud roof, with a staircase leading to it from outside (cf. 1 Sam. 9:25). It is possible that some houses had walled quadrangles behind the house where roofless toilets and bathrooms were located, as in many houses in Third World countries today. Because it was the palace of the king, the roof of David's house would probably have been the highest in that area, so that from there he could look down into the open bathroom in the quadrangle of the neighboring house.

On "the Hittite" (2 Sam. 11:3), see above on 1 Sam. 26:6. Ezekiel describes Jerusalem as the daughter of an Amorite and a Hittite (Ezek. 16:3). It is possible that some Hittites lived in Jerusalem during the Jebusite period and that Uriah could have been born there.

The Concretization of Sin (11:4-27)

11:4-5   The temptation conceived as sin now begins to take shape. Through his messengers David orders Bathsheba to come to his house, and there he has sexual intercourse with her. Bathsheba was "purifying herself from her uncleanness" (2 Sam. 11:4) in David's house, probably because she had her menstrual period while she was there. It is not said how long her cleansing should take; perhaps it was for seven days, as required by the law regarding menstruation (Lev. 15:19ff.). When Bathsheba realizes that she has conceived, she informs David (2 Sam. 11:5). She knows what would happen to her if the public came to know that she had conceived outside her marital relationship. Moreover, David, as the supreme judge, should know that it was he who was responsible for her sin. According to the law, those who are involved in adultery — both the man and the woman — must be stoned to death (Lev. 20:10). David must act quickly. In taking another man's wife, David had used his royal authority arbitrarily. This trait is characteristic of Canaanite kingship (1 Kgs. 21:5ff.), and therefore it comes under severe prophetic condemnation.

Sin leads on to undesirable consequences. Sin breeds further sins; in order to hide one sin, the sinner commits more sins. This is what is illustrated in David's life.

11:6-13 David makes cunning efforts to absolve himself of responsibility for his act. He first attempts to cover up Bathsheba's conception by making it appear as normal through her marital relations with her husband Uriah. Perhaps in those days people were not so conscious about the time factor involved as they are in modern times. David orders a compulsory holiday for Uriah and tries to persuade him to go to his house and sleep with his wife. However, Uriah as a loyal citizen cannot enjoy life for himself when the nation is in an emergency, with "the ark and Israel and Judah" dwelling "in booths" and his "lord Joab" and other fellow servants "camping in the open field" (2 Sam. 11:11). David then makes a second attempt to send Uriah to his wife. This time he tries to make Uriah drunk, in the hope that in the state of drunkenness Uriah might go and have sex with his wife. Here again Uriah disappoints David: "he did not go down to his house" (v. 13).

11:14-25 David plunges still deeper into the darkness of sin. Having failed in his attempt to make Uriah appear responsible for the child in Bathsheba's womb, he now conceives a heinous plot to eliminate the innocent Uriah, so that there will not be anyone to refute the claim that the child is Uriah's. As a crafty warrior, David knows every move made by the army (cf. v. 20). Thus he devises the plan to have Uriah killed on the battlefield, and orders Joab to execute it. Uriah is to be set "in the forefront of the hardest fighting." His fellow soldiers are to "draw back from him, that he may be struck down, and die" (v. 15). Joab thus becomes the accomplice in David's crime. The sinner does not stop with sinning himself, but implicates others also in his sin. In this way David sold himself to Joab; this may be one reason why David was afraid of Joab (3:39).

David writes down his secret plan for Joab and has Uriah deliver it. Note the irony of the tragedy! Uriah carries his own death sentence (11:14). Joab must have been a very loyal and committed commander of David if David could trust him even on such delicate matters. Joab does not question the plan; he simply executes the order of his superior, the king (vv. 16-17). In order to have Uriah killed without arousing the suspicion of people, Joab must put him in the front along with other "servants of David." As the account indicates, they were killed along with Uriah (v. 17). Thus David becomes responsible for a mass murder. This is again a phenomenon known in modern times: an entire aircraft with all its passengers is made to crash in order to kill a political figure or some other important person traveling in that plane.

Joab communicates the news of Uriah's death to David in a veiled manner through a messenger, under the cover of general news from the battlefront (vv. 18-21). Verses 20-21 are probably an independent tradition that was originally part of the military instructions which every soldier should know. But vv. 23-24 do not indicate that the messenger was aware of vv. 20-21. Here he merely conveys the message of the death of Uriah along with the general news. Verses 20-21 could have been secondary, except for the last sentence: "then you shall say, 'Your servant Uriah the Hittite is dead also.'" This goes well with v. 19. "Abimelech the son of Jerubbesheth" (v. 21) refers to Judg. 9:50-55. What is said in 2 Sam. 11:24 is not included above where the actual events of the war are narrated. Perhaps v. 24 is part of the original text. Getting near the city wall where the enemy can attack from above could appear as a tactical mistake in warfare; therefore a redactor could have inserted vv. 20-21 in its present context to show that Joab was aware of the danger, yet purposely acted as he did to get Uriah killed. David now pretends the attack had been a more casual happening and so sends a message of encouragement back to Joab. "The sword devours now one and now another" (v. 25) could have been a proverbial saying current in military circles.

11:26-27   Now that Uriah is dead, David could take Uriah's widow Bathsheba as one of his legal wives, as he did in the case of Abigail (1 Sam. 25:39-42). In 2 Sam. 11:27b the whole act of David is brought under prophetic condemnation: "But the thing that David had done displeased the LORD." The Bible, both the OT and the NT, holds love to God and love to mankind together; one without the other is not possible. As such, David's loyal love *(hesed)* to God, if real, should have been reflected in his relationships to his fellow humans, and most especially to his subjects. In this then David failed. Instead of protecting the life of his subjects, he himself becomes the cause of their destruction. Living in the fellowship of God, one becomes the source of blessing to others; living in sin, one becomes the source of suffering to others.

We note here that God's covenant-love for David remains unaffected by what David has done. God's commitment to us can either make use of our loyalty in return for his, or just as much God can use our disloyalty by weaving it into his projected pattern and plan. God does so by himself, carrying David's disloyalty on his heart. He does not break covenant with David and so "divorce" him, wiping his hands of David, as a man does when he divorces his wife. This story then recalls how God can say in Mal. 2:16, "I hate divorce," for it is the rejection of the covenant. In Christian marriage the couple are not just united by "love." Secular marriage brokers, who in the West are government agents, only put the question to the couple: "Will you remain together so long as you love each other?" They do not understand the word *hesed,* which means "loyalty" through sickness, abandonment, or even mental breakdown, which is the content of the promises made in Christian marriage ceremonies.

We should also take note of another fact here. Very often when a person dies prematurely — especially if innocent people ask, "why did this happen?" — some try to put the blame on the person himself; others try to find the answer in the mystery of God. We ought to realize that very often we ourselves are the cause of the death of others. Abel had to die because of Cain's sin; Uriah and his fellow soldiers must die because of David's sin. Likewise in today's world, we become responsible for the deaths of many millions of people who die from hunger in Third World countries, of people who die in traffic accidents, of people who die because of taking wrong drugs, of people who die in man-made wars, of people who die from the pollution of water or atmosphere.

NATHAN'S WORDS TO DAVID (12:1-25)

2 Samuel 11:27b spoke of Yahweh's displeasure over David's act. This chapter expounds upon it. God intervenes and encounters

David. That God intervenes in human history whenever injustice is done to his people — the poor, the weak, the orphan, the widow, and the like — is a theme which runs throughout the whole OT (cf. Gen. 4:10; 1 Kgs. 21:17ff.), leading to the incarnation of God in Jesus Christ in the NT (cf. John 3:16). This God of the poor and the oppressed is still the hope of millions of people all over the world whose lives are threatened by the forces of death.

Since this is a theologically and religio-historically important chapter, more hands have probably worked on it, though we cannot identify them today. 2 Samuel 12:15b-25, which talks about Bathsheba's first and second children, could belong to an independent tradition.

The Parable of the Poor Man's Ewe Lamb (12:1-6)

Nathan uses a beautiful parable to drive home the message to David. Speaking in parables was an effective didactic method used by many prophets, e.g., Jotham's parable of the bramble (Judg. 9:7-15) and Isaiah's parable of the vineyard (Isa. 5:1-7). This parable exposes so vividly the injustice involved that it could not escape the attention of David. David pronounces the judgment immediately (2 Sam. 12:5-6), which in fact is a judgment on himself.

The contrast between the poor and the rich here is most realistic (vv. 2-3). The description of the poor man ("The poor man had nothing but one little ewe lamb") fits very well with the condition of the homes of the poor in Third World countries. In India, for example, most of the poor are landless and roofless. They squat on roadsides or on properties that do not belong to them. For many of them a lamb, or a goat, or a calf is their only property in this world. Such poor folk are always the victims of exploitation by the rich, as in the case of the poor man of the parable. The rich man "was unwilling to take one of his own flock or herd" (v. 4). This is again typical of the rich. They are very reluctant to part with even a small portion of their riches. Their tendency is frequently to exploit the poor and the weak, and to accumulate more. The more one has, the greater is one's greed. This parable wakens David's dormant sense of justice. He pronounces the death sentence on the rich man who has done this wrong to the poor man, "because he had no pity" (v. 6). There seems to be some tension between v. 5 and v. 6. Verse 5 pronounces the death sentence on the guilty one, but v. 6 says that "he shall restore the lamb fourfold." How can one restore after being killed? Perhaps the restoration would precede the death.

David's judgment recalls Jesus' words: ". . . you see the speck that is in your brother's eye, but do not notice the log that is in your own eye" (Matt. 7:3). Passing judgment on others and preaching to others is always easy, but practicing what we preach is difficult. The comparison between the rich man in the parable and David is clear. David's sin is of a much greater nature both in quality and quantity.

Nathan's Oracle and David's Repentance (12:7-15a)

2 Samuel 12:7-10 and 11-12 record two prophetic oracles, each introduced by the messenger formula "thus says the LORD." The seriousness of David's sin is stressed repeatedly: David has "despised the word of the LORD, to do what is evil in his sight" (v. 9); he has "despised" Yahweh (v. 10); he has "utterly scorned the LORD" (v. 14). David's sin is twofold — taking Uriah's wife Bathsheba and killing Uriah by the sword. The retribution announced is related to both these acts of David's sin. For David's having taken Uriah's wife, David's own wives will be taken by his "neighbor," who will deal with them in a similar way, bringing shame to David (v. 11). It will be worse: "For you did it secretly; but I will do this thing before all Israel, and before the sun." The author is here perhaps thinking of what Absalom did to his father's concubines: he lay with them "upon the roof" of the house "in the sight of all Israel" (16:21-22). For killing Uriah with the sword, "the sword shall never depart from your house" (12:10). Here the author is probably thinking of the continued struggle in David's family as the fulfilment of this prophetic oracle — the violent deaths of Amnon, Absalom, and Adonijah (13:28-29; 18:14; 1 Kgs. 2:25).

That God shows no partiality, but deals justly with all his people — the strong and the weak, the rich and the poor — becomes evident here. God's favor to David does not condone his evil deeds. Here again we see that election is not for privilege, but for responsibility. We are here reminded of Amos's words: "You only have I known of all the families of the earth; therefore I will punish you for all your iniquities" (Amos 3:2). One other question that can be raised here is, why did God not prevent David from sin and save Uriah from dying? One should remember that the Bible does not deal with the issue of theodicy, where God is believed to dictate and control every human action. The freedom of mankind is the most important aspect of the biblical doctrine of creation. Mankind always possesses the freedom to choose between the good and the evil, between life and death, between God and mammon; yet God intervenes out of his love and grace when mankind opts for death.

The forthrightness of OT prophecy is evident here: "You are the man," says Nathan to the king (2 Sam. 12:7). The prophet, as the messenger of God, comes with the authority of God. It does not matter for the prophet whether the man to whom he prophesies is big or small, rich or poor. Before God all are alike to the prophet (cf. 1 Kgs. 21:20). This kind of prophetic ministry is becoming weak in the Church today. Very few people are prepared to stand and speak for justice in cases where the persons involved are powerful and influential. When a "speck" is found in the eyes of the poor and the weak, people make a hue and cry of it and demand justice. However, even when a "log" is found in the eyes of the rich and the powerful, many tend to keep quiet and nod their heads in passive acceptance. This situation should change. The Church must regain its prophetic ministry as we see it expressed in Nathan and Elijah.

12:12-15a The account of David's repentance and forgiveness is given very briefly. David's confession is confined to just one sentence: "I have sinned against the LORD" (2 Sam. 12:13). Nathan's proclamation of absolution also comes quickly: "The LORD also has put away your sin; you shall not die." This forgiveness saves David from premature death, but not from the consequences of his act. As the psalmist says, Yahweh is a forgiving God, but "an avenger" of the sinner's wrongdoings (Ps. 99:8).

213

All that Nathan pronounced earlier (2 Sam. 12:7-11) is to take its course in fulfilment. The child illegitimately born to "the wife of Uriah" is also to die (v. 14). Behind this may lie the Israelite belief in the connection between an act and its effect. Every act brings forth with it its effect, and God sees to its happening (cf. Gen. 4:7). That is to say, every human act has eschatological significance (Matt. 25:31-46).

We have something to learn from David's confession here. Every sin against our neighbor is a sin against God. This thought runs throughout the Bible. Our love to God and our love to mankind should always go together (cf. Deut. 6:5; Lev. 19:18; Matt. 22:37-39). One without the other is not true and is not possible (cf. 1 John 4:20).

David and the Dying Child (12:15b-23)

As announced by Nathan (2 Sam. 12:14), the child that is born to David through Uriah's wife falls sick and dies. David's behavior before and after the death of the child is narrated vividly with much realism. The main theme around which the story is developed appears to be the finality of death. David fasts and prays while the child is sick; but when the child is dead he washes himself, worships, and eats. He also questions the practice of mourning after a death. This is not typical of the David whom we know in history. That David is one who is intensely sentimental and emotional. He weeps and mourns over the death of Saul and Jonathan, of Abner, and of Absalom. The whole account here appears to have developed in wisdom circles for didactic purposes. This account shows no knowledge of Nathan's words to David. The reference to the "house of the LORD" in v. 20 also points to a later period (cf. 7:2).

Behind this acccount we are able to identify a number of religious beliefs that were current among the people. (1) Sickness is often caused by God as his punishment on people. "The LORD struck" is a common expression, which introduces sicknesses that are believed to have been caused by God. (2) God grants prayers. Fasting and self-abasement can help in this regard. (3) Sin is hereditary. Children die because of their parents' sin. This belief was later questioned by Jeremiah and Ezekiel (Jer. 31:29-30; Ezek. 18:2ff.). (4) Death is seen as the final destiny of mankind; there is no hope of resurrection. David says, "I shall go to him, but he will not return to me" (2 Sam. 12:23). Behind this lies the belief in Sheol, a place thought to be at the center of the earth. A dying patient was believed to be descending slowly to Sheol. When one recovered from illness through the fasting and prayer of the people, it was believed that God had lifted up the dying one by his hand (cf. Ps. 18:4-5; 30:2-3; 49:15; 86:13).

The Birth of Solomon (12:24-25)

The main purpose of the whole narrative is now reached: the successor to the throne of David, the one promised by the LORD (2 Sam. 7:12), is now born in the person of Solomon, and "the LORD loved him" (12:24). Thereby the author wishes to tell his readers that Solomon was chosen to be the successor to the throne of David right from his birth. Verses 24 and 25 appear to come from different sources. According to v. 24 David "called his name Solomon." However, according to v. 25 the LORD sent a message by Nathan the prophet, and on the basis of that message David "called his name Jedidiah," which means "beloved of the LORD."

VICTORY OVER THE AMMONITES (12:26-31)

The military account that was interrupted by the David-Bathsheba story is resumed here. The Ammonites are decisively defeated (vv. 26-29). Joab fights against Rabbah, the "royal city" of the Ammonites, and brings its inhabitants to the level of surrender (v. 26). In addition, he has taken "the city of waters" (v. 27), which means that the water supply to the royal city can be stopped at any moment. Having thus prepared the conditions for the Ammonite surrender, Joab as a loyal servant calls David to harvest the victory over the Ammonites (v. 28). So David fights against Rabbah and takes it. Joab defers to David, "lest I take the city, and it be called by my name" (v. 29). The person who conquers a city appears to have been entitled to call that city by his name. We recall that David called the stronghold Zion, which he conquered, by his name as "the city of David" (5:7, 9). Recorded here is an ancient practice according to which, though the army fights, the king must personally command the army at the final onslaught in order to own the victory for himself.

The Ammonite king had a crown of gold and precious stones, as common among oriental kings. "A talent of gold" is about 30 to 40 kg. (66 to 88 lbs.) of gold. The amount is probably exaggerated. David takes this ornamental crown for himself. In terms of the nature of the crown, David thus becomes a king like the kings of the other nations.

David brings "the spoil of the city, a very great amount" and also "the people who were in it" (12:30b-31). The captives brought forth are subjected to forced labor. This is not the first time we hear of forced labor under David's rule; it has already been mentioned in association with the capture of people from a conquered country (cf. 8:6, 14). During Solomon's reign forced labor was at its height (1 Kgs. 9:15ff.). The Ammonites appear to have been well versed in working with iron implements ("saws and iron picks and iron axes") and also in working "at the brick-kilns." Till then the Israelites had built houses with mud and mud bricks made with straw; it appears that under David they begin construction with kiln-burned (baked) bricks. As a king aiming to become one like the kings of the other nations, David may well have undertaken construction programs on a large scale, and for this purpose he seems to have used war captives.

The system of forced labor was even then seen as part of the negative heritage of kingship in Israel. Samuel had already warned the Israelites of the danger of the king's using their own sons and daughters under forced labor (1 Sam. 8:11). The Israelites could therefore have felt happy when foreigners were reduced to such labor (cf. Lev. 25:44-45). But the Exodus faith called on the Israelites to remember the days when they themselves had been subjected to forced labor in Egypt, and to be kind to others (cf. Exod. 22:21; 23:9). Ancient kingdoms all over the world have left historic monuments such as the pyramids of Egypt, the Great Wall of China, and the Taj Mahal of India, and we rejoice today to look at them as tourists. However, seldom do we realize that such monuments stand as witness not to the glory of such kings, but to the sweat and blood of millions of men and women who were reduced to the level of construction machines, parallel to the cranes and bulldozers of our times, thereby being denied their God-given freedom and human dignity.

V. DAVID'S CHILDREN
AND THE QUESTION
OF SUCCESSION
2 Samuel 13:1–20:26

That Solomon was Yahweh's choice for David's successor has
already been indicated at 2 Sam. 12:24. The Jerusalemite forces
— Bathsheba, Zadok the priest, and Nathan the prophet — were
obviously behind such a move. However, David still had older
sons (3:2-5) who also had a claim to the throne. Of these Amnon,
Absalom, and Adonijah appear to have staked their claims for the
throne. The accounts that follow in 13:1–20:26 are therefore
meant to show why these persons were disqualified from being
the successor to David.

ABSALOM AVENGES TAMAR (13:1-39)

This account has legendary character. The name Tamar was associated with a sex scandal even earlier (Gen. 38). The story here
is narrated vividly in folklore style. It could have circulated among
people as an independent tradition.

Amnon's Temptation (13:1-6)

Absalom and Tamar (2 Sam. 13:1) are directly brother and sister,
born to David through the Aramaic princess from Geshur, whereas
Amnon had a different mother (cf. 3:2). Amnon loves his half-
sister Tamar because she is "beautiful." Here we are reminded of
the first element of temptation in the Fall account in Gen. 3:
things or persons that tempt us are always desirable physically,
esthetically, or intellectually (cf. Gen. 3:6; see also 2 Sam. 11:2).
According to Lev. 20:17 marriage between a half brother and a
half sister is discouraged, though that law comes from a later

period. Tamar's confidence that the king would agree to her marriage with Amnon, if Amnon approached David in a proper way, shows that at this period marriage between a half brother and a half sister might be allowed, though not encouraged. Abraham and Sarah were half brother and half sister (Gen. 20:12).

The virgin Tamar lives in a different place from Amnon, so it is not possible for Amnon to meet her in private. The desirable person is unattainable for him, and so he is "so tormented" (2 Sam. 13:2) that he becomes ill. Amnon's intense sexual feelings and his later behavior in hating Tamar (v. 15) clearly show that his desire for Tamar was not motivated by true love; rather, it was the mere lust of the flesh. Jonadab, Amnon's cousin and friend (v. 3), leads Amnon into the temptation by showing him a stealthy plan to make Tamar attainable to him. (Jonadab is said to be the son of Shimeah, David's brother, but such a brother of David is not mentioned earlier.) Amnon should pretend to be sick and when his father the king visits him, he should request from the king the services of Tamar at his sick bed. Amnon follows Jonadab's advice, and David apparently grants his request (v. 6). Behind Amnon's request for the service of the person of his choice and the kings' sanctioning of the same, there appears to be some ancient custom, of which we know little. Did the princes live on their own at this time? Why did not Amnon's mother attend to him, and why did not David suggest that to Amnon? Why did not David find something strange in Amnon's request to have Tamar in particular at his side, and why should the king oblige such a request? Was there such a custom that a sick person's wish had to be honored, as is the custom today with dying patients in many communites? These are questions for which as yet we have no answer.

Amnon Rapes Tamar (13:7-14)

The account of Amnon's rape of Tamar is given in vivid detail with much realism. David orders Tamar to attend to Amnon. In this way Tamar, the object of Amnon's temptation, becomes reachable to him, thus fulfilling the second condition of temptation. The innocent Tamar is caught as a lamb in the mouth of a wolf. Her human reasoning (vv. 12-13) does not appeal to Amnon, because his human faculties are overpowered by his animal instincts. Tamar is not against having Amnon as her husband; but she objects to being used as an object of his lust, to being raped, for this is a "wanton folly" (*nebalah,* v. 12), done only by "wanton fools (*nebalim*) in Israel" (v. 13; cf. 1 Sam. 25:25).

Tamar, living ca. 1000 B.C., recalls the stipulation of the covenant (*berit*), "Thou shalt not commit adultery." She responds, "Such a thing is not done in Israel," although the contemporary Canaanites did it aplenty. The basic elements of the Mosaic code had been passed on to her generation, following Moses' demand that parents teach their children. Children were to ask their parents about the covenant and what it meant for God's dealings with Israel.

Virginity is still a pre-condition for marriage for women in most Asian countries. Any premarital sexual relations can seriously damage any prospects for a woman's being married. This seems to have been the case also in Israel. The Israelites appear to have had a strange custom to prove the virginity of a woman. Deuteronomy 22:13-21 refers to "the tokens of virginity." These seem to be those clothes that show blood from the first intercourse after a proper marriage, which are then preserved by the girl's parents as proof of their daughter's virginity at the time of marriage. In Deuteronomy a girl playing the harlot in her father's house is also seen as committing a "folly" (*nebalah,* Deut. 22:21) punishable by stoning to death. Moreover, the child which Tamar might conceive through intercourse with Amnon would become a "shame" for her (2 Sam. 13:13). Tamar not only appeals to Amnon's reason, but also protests at his physical act. Nevertheless, Amnon, "being stronger than she," forces her (v. 14). His muscular power overpowers her. Very often sin involves the abuse of strength and power given to us by God. God bestows these qualities to be used for redemptive purposes. When we use them to exercise control over others for our own ends, they become destructive and therefore sinful.

The Consequences (13:15-39)

The third characteristic of a temptation which leads to sin is that a desirable and reachable object can lead to terrible ends.

The immediate consequence of sin is shame, which is in fact the result of the disturbance of the harmonious relationship within one's own self. Moreover, it affects one's relationship with God and his world — fellow men and women, animals, and nature (cf. Gen. 3–4). This is seen to be true in the case of Amnon as well. "Then Amnon hated her with very great hatred" (2 Sam. 13:15), and "Absalom hated Amnon" (v. 22). The folly that Amnon committed induced this internal change within him, resulting in the hatred of the one whom he had liked the most. Further it strained his relationship with his brothers and his father; David "was very angry" (v. 21). The sinful act actually ends in the death of Amnon (vv. 28-29). When sex takes place within marriage in an atmosphere of love, each partner respects and honors the other, and thus through sexual intercourse the love between the two is deepened. Here sex becomes the expression of passion, not of true love. When sexual passion is aroused as a result of lust, the one person treats the other as a mere object and not as a person. Thereupon that one "spews out" the other in distaste.

The shame and the sense of guilt in Amnon turns his lust into hatred, and he says to Tamar, "Arise, be gone" (v. 15). This is even worse than what Amnon had done first. "For this wrong in sending me away is greater than the other which you did to me," says Tamar (v. 16). Israelite law pardoned a person who raped a virgin, if he agreed to remain with her as husband (Deut. 22:28-29). In the case of David and Bathsheba, Bathsheba waited in David's house until her uncleanness was gone. Here Amnon orders his servants to force Tamar out of his house immediately "and bolt the door after her" (2 Sam. 13:17). Verse 18a, the description of Tamar's virginal dress, interrupts between vv. 17 and 18b. It probably comes from a redactor. Being thrown out of Amnon's house, Tamar resorts to a public mourning so that others may know what happened to her (v. 19). Otherwise, if she were discovered later to be pregnant, she would have to die on the charge of fornication. Putting ashes on the head, rending clothes, laying the hand on the head, and crying aloud all are elements in mourning rituals (cf. 1 Sam. 4:12).

221

13:20-22   Tamar runs to her brother Absalom. Perhaps her mother is no longer alive and Absalom plays the role of guardian. In a family with many wives and concubines, David apparently had no direct control over his children. Absalom as a good elder brother consoles Tamar and asks her to remain quiet. 2 Samuel 13:20 indicates that Absalom was already aware of Tamar's being with Amnon. Verse 32 makes us suspect that Jonadab actually betrayed it to Absalom. Jonadab, while helping Amnon, perhaps expected that Amnon would approach Absalom and ask him for Tamar in marriage. When Amnon acted to the contrary and treated Tamar badly, Jonadab could have turned against Amnon. In spite of Absalom's consolation, Tamar dwelt in Absalom's house as a "desolate woman" (v. 20). A woman who can have no more sex and so could not bear children was considered to be desolate. For Tamar marriage with another man has now become an impossibility; nor can she return to the house of the virgins. Thus her life becomes "desolate." Verse 21 notes that the king was aware of this incident and was angry. It does not say what the king did to render justice to Tamar and to defuse the tension between Absalom and Amnon. Since this is probably a later gloss, it is perhaps intended to show that Nathan's oracle on David has already begun to take effect: "I will raise up evil against you out of your own house" (12:11).

Absalom's hatred against Amnon is internalized (13:22) in that he is now devising secret plans to take revenge. Quiet persons, who do not react openly, can be much more dangerous than persons who do react openly. This is true of Absalom. He seems to have already made up his mind; but he does not want to create any suspicion in the minds of Amnon and the other sons of the kings lest his secret plot should be crushed.

13:23-29   Absalom waits for two whole years to execute his plans. At the end of that period he celebrates a sheepshearing festival and invites all the sons of the king to be present. At the opportune moment during the festival his servants strike and kill Amnon (vv. 23-29). Sheepshearing was a happy festival in Israel (cf. 1 Sam. 25:2-8), to which close friends and relatives were invited.

Absalom first invites David the king as a formality. He probably knew well that the king would not go. When the king excuses himself, Absalom makes a special request to David to order Amnon to go (2 Sam. 13:26). Perhaps Absalom thought that Amnon would not go if he invited him personally, because of what he had done to Tamar. There is some tension here between v. 26 and v. 27. According to v. 26 Absalom requests the king to send Amnon only; but in v. 27 Absalom's request appears to have been to send Amnon and all the sons of the king. This could have been a wise thing to do on the part of Absalom in order to avoid the king's suspicion. Yet Amnon, as David's firstborn, could have been regarded as the legitimate heir to the throne. Thus when the king was not able to go, it was only natural to request the next in authority to represent the king. This might explain why Amnon is mentioned specifically. It is possible that since Amnon was a strong man (cf. v. 14) Absalom avoids direct confrontation with him. Absalom orders his servants to wait until his brother gets drunk, and when Amnon reaches that state they kill him (vv. 28-29). When the other princes see that Absalom is killed, each mounts his mule (cf. 18:9) and flees. Note that even as late as this horses were not used in royal circles in Israel.

13:30-33 The panic created by Amnon's murder spreads the rumor that all the sons of the king are slain. That would have meant a conscious attempt on the part of Absalom to usurp the throne. As this rumor reaches King David, he and his people begin to mourn (13:31). Jonadab, as an insider (see above on v. 20), allays the king's fear by giving him the correct news.

13:34-36 The words "but Absalom fled" appear here by mistake, because it is a duplication of what is said in v. 37. The rest of the section confirms the news given by Jonadab. The king's sons who fled from Absalom's feast arrive, and they and the king weep bitterly (v. 36), obviously for the death of Amnon.

13:37-39 Verse 38 repeats almost exactly what is said in v. 37. It is possible that each of these verses comes from a different hand. Absalom, being the son of a Geshurite princess, escapes to his mother's people for protection. Apparently his grandfather Talmai the son of Ammihud is still the king of Geshur (cf. 3:3). 2 Samuel 13:38 adds the information that he remained there for "three years." Verse 39 prepares the ground for future developments in which Absalom plays the key role. Now that the king is comforted about Amnon, "seeing that he was dead," David's spirit longs "to go forth to Absalom." The thought that death is final and once a person is dead nothing can be done, seen in 12:23a, is again found here.

CONFLICT BETWEEN DAVID AND ABSALOM (14:1–20:26)

Absalom's Reconciliation with David (14:1-33)

This chapter explains how Absalom, whose relationship with the king was strained, was restored to normal fellowship with David.

The Wise Woman from Tekoa (14:1-20)

The account of the wise woman, who with a story makes the king pass judgment on his own case (14:13), recalls Nathan's parable in 12:1ff.

14:1-3 2 Samuel 14:1 picks up the narrative from 13:39. Joab, having sensed the change in the king's mood in favor of Absalom, realizes that the opportune moment has come to bring Absalom back to Jerusalem. We are not told why Joab was particularly concerned with the return of Absalom. 2 Samuel 14:25-26 seems to suggest that among the king's sons Absalom was the most popular and that the public probably expected him to succeed David. Therefore Joab felt sympathy for and gave support to Absalom.

Joab engages "a wise woman" from Tekoa (v. 2) to pretend to be a mourner and to bring a message to David. Tekoa, a village about 3 km. (5 mi.) S of Bethlehem, was the birthplace of the prophet Amos (Amos 1:1). Apparently it had a reputation as a place where wise men and women could be found. Some OT scholars believe that eighth-century prophecy came out of a wisdom school, the roots of which are perhaps seen here. Jer. 9:17 indicates that there were in Israel professional mourners who could be hired. These women were endowed with the special gifts of acting (mourning), talking in parables and stories, and arguing logically (cf. 2 Sam. 20:16ff., where another "wise woman" negotiates for a besieged city). The wise woman of Tekoa shows all such talents. Joab puts his words in her mouth and sends her to the king. What Joab told her can be assumed only from what the woman does and says.

14:4-7 As instructed by Joab the woman comes to the king and pretends to be a widow whose only heir, her son, is threatened by the law of bloodguiltiness. Her two sons "quarrelled with one another in the field; there was no one to part them, and one struck the other and killed him" (14:6). She argues that this was a domestic fight such as happens in every family; but here because no one mediated between the brothers, the one struck the other and he died. The woman is subtly turning the blame on David, who failed to intervene between Absalom and Amnon. Had he intervened to avenge Tamar, he could have prevented the killing of Amnon. Now the kinsmen within the family demand blood revenge and seek to kill the woman's only surviving son. In so doing they will actually violate another Israelite law which demands that kinsmen ensure that a deceased man has an heir to bear his "name" and to continue his "remnant" on this earth. David as the supreme judge in Israel is here asked to give his verdict in a difficult case. He must decide between two laws, the law of blood revenge and the law of succession.

14:8-11 David is in a dilemma; he needs time to think. So he asks the woman to go to her "house," assuring her that he would let her know his verdict later (v. 8). But the woman is persuasive; she wants a decision immediately. She senses the king's dilemma and prompts him further to make up his mind. She is prepared to take upon herself the guilt, if the king's verdict should be wrong (v. 9). That the king and the king's throne are "guiltless" is a theme which the author wants to stress. By this time David has made up his mind, and he gives his verdict: "he [the adversary] shall never touch you again" (v. 10). This means that the adversary will not act against her. The woman is not satisfied with such a vague verdict to protect her. She wants clear assurance that her son will be protected from "the avenger of blood" (v. 11a), so David finally pledges to that effect (v. 11b). "Not one hair of your son shall fall to the ground" is a common expression in Hebrew to assure safety to the person concerned. "As the LORD lives" is a formula used in an oath (cf. 4:9).

14:12-17   As one who pleads professionally, the woman appears to be well versed with the formalities of speaking to a king. One should have prior permission to speak to the king (14:12). Through her clever argument, David is trapped into passing a verdict on his own conduct (v. 13), as in the case of Nathan's earlier encounter with him (cf. 12:5). The woman seems to imply that by keeping Absalom away, the king is acting "against the people of God." Here "the people of God" means Israel. The analogy seems to regard Absalom as the heir to the throne. Because the firstborn son Amnon (3:2) is dead now, the next eldest surviving son should be the natural heir to the throne. According to 3:3 Chileab, the son of Abigail, is in fact the second son of David, and Absalom only the third. But we hear of Chileab no more. Perhaps he is already dead. Thus Absalom is here presented as the heir, and David seems to have had nothing against it. However, the analogy of the woman's story fails, in that Absalom is not the only surviving son of David. 2 Samuel 14:14a appears to be a wisdom saying on the finality of death (cf. 12:23; 13:39); but premature death is a curse. The woman seems to imply that if David would only bring back his banished son God will grant the king long life. God will not take away David's life before the appointed time (14:14b). In vv. 15-17 the woman's personal story is continued, though it is out of place at this stage of the narrative. Originally it may have come after v. 7. It is interesting that here the concepts "settlement" (*menuhah,* RSV "rest") and "the heritage" (*nahalah*) are used together (vv. 16-17). *Menuhah* is the condition of being brought back from one's fugitive condition to one's own *nahalah,* to one's peaceful "settlement." David is here compared to "the angel of God" because of his wisdom in discerning between good and evil (vv. 17, 20; cf. 18:13; 19:27).

14:18-20   The moment David realizes that the woman was pleading the case of Absalom, he could see Joab's hand behind the whole thing, perhaps because Joab was known to be a supporter of Absalom. Like the angels, David was able "to know all things that are on earth" (v. 20). Angels, being the messengers of God, were believed to know everything in the world, and David's wisdom is compared to the wisdom of the angels (cf. 18:13; 19:27).

Joab Brings Back Absalom (14:21-33)

14:21-24   Joab now appears on the scene, and the woman is mentioned no more. David grants Joab's request. Joab can now bring back Absalom from Geshur. However, as a punishment for his crime, Absalom must "dwell apart in his own house" and not come into the king's presence (14:24). Joab sees this as a personal favor done to him and as an evidence of David's trust in him. Perhaps Joab was afraid of David's displeasure toward him because of his killing Abner against David's will (cf. 3:28-29).

14:25-27   Here is supplied information about Absalom's personality and children. He was most handsome, with long hair, and he had three sons and one daughter. His daughter is named Tamar, and she too is described as "a beautiful woman" (14:27), just as his sister Tamar had been described (13:1). It is possible that both names refer to the same person, for we do not hear again about Absalom's daughter Tamar. Absalom's hair is said to have weighed 200 shekels. One shekel is about 10 gm. (.3 oz). The "king's weight" was probably the standard weight, meant to be employed in all the kingdom.

14:28-33   Absalom lives in isolation for "two full years" without coming into the presence of the king (14:28). After those two years, he decides to speak to Joab, probably his benefactor and well wisher; but Joab does not come (v. 29). Perhaps Joab was afraid of being charged with conspiracy against the king, or of suspicion on the part of the king's other sons. They are already angry with Absalom because of Amnon's murder. Absalom, as a resourceful young man, knows how to bring pressure on Joab. He sets fire to Joab's barley field. Joab immediately comes to meet Absalom (cf. vv. 30-31). Absalom explains the reason for his act and asks Joab to take a message to the king. He wants a clear verdict from the king, because his ambiguous position is painful for him. He is prepared to face even death if the king should declare him guilty. Otherwise, Absalom wants to enjoy the full privilege of being the king's son (v. 32). Joab sees the fairness of Absalom's request and communicates the message to the king. David, who was longing to meet Absalom (13:39), was probably waiting for just such an opportunity. He responds readily to the words of Joab and sends for Absalom. As Absalom enters the presence of the king, David receives him as an affectionate father (v. 33). In David we have the typical example of a just ruler who is at the same time an affectionate father. As a just ruler he should not let his personal likes and dislikes influence his judgments. He should treat his son as any other subject before the law and discipline him. However, as an affectionate father David's love impels him: "the king kissed Absalom" (v. 33). Kissing in Israel was a sign of welcome (cf. Gen. 29:13; Luke 15:20). David welcomes Absalom back into his presence and favor.

Absalom's Conspiracy (15:1-12)

15:1-6 It is the tactic of all aspirants to political power to appeal to all who are discontented with the existing regime and to try to win their confidence and support by promising a better government and by offering special favors. Absalom adopts this very tactic. Israel during its formative stage as a nation has undergone administrative difficulties (Exod. 18:13ff.). Now with the expansion of the kingdom, the nation seems to have faced a similar crisis. The demands of a growing government could have kept David apart from the common people, and there was probably no proper machinery to listen to their grievances. Absalom exploits this situation by fanning the discontent of such people (2 Sam. 15:3) and by offering them a better government (v. 4). Also, by showing his respect for common people (v. 4) he steals their hearts to himself (v. 6).

The fact that no particular tribe is mentioned in v. 2 might suggest that Absalom from the beginning intended his rebellion to include all Israel (cf. vv. 6, 10, 13). Perhaps as a matter of tactics, Absalom concentrates first upon the northern tribes among whom he is better known (cf. 13:23) and whose discontent with David's regime could be quite real. 2 Samuel 15:1 comes here as a fulfilment of what was earlier warned regarding kings in Israel: "He will take your sons and appoint them to his chariots and to be his horsemen, and to run before his chariots" (1 Sam. 8:11). Absalom probably got his own "chariots and horses" from those that David captured from the Syrians (2 Sam. 8:4). Perhaps David had entrusted to him his cavalry unit in the army. This action of David would later serve to Absalom's advantage during his revolt against the king.

David lives in the stronghold of Jerusalem, the city of David (5:9). Therefore all who want to see the king have to pass through the gate of the fortress. This gives Absalom the opportunity to meet all such people individually (15:2). The exceptional affection and concern which Absalom shows to the people are not genuine. He only pretends to show concern for them, as many politicians do today. This way he "stole the hearts of the men of Israel" (v. 6). He did not *win* them! Absalom's promises and tactics resemble the pre-election promises and practices of many of our modern politicians, who pretend to show special affection for poor people. This becomes dramatic at times — embracing an old woman from a village and kissing her; lifting in his arms a dirty, naked child from a slum; and shedding tears on hearing about the sufferings of the poor — all before a movie or television camera or before a large public audience. However, only a few aspirants to office remember the poor common people once they come to power. Absalom forgets that the God of Israel reveals himself as the God of the poor.

15:7-12 Absalom takes four years to prepare the ground for his revolt. After four years (v. 7), Absalom gets permission from the king to go to Hebron under the pretext of fulfilling a vow he made while in exile in Geshur (vv. 7-8). Instead, Absalom sends "secret messengers throughout all the tribes of Israel" to proclaim him as "king at Hebron" as soon as they hear "the sound of the trumpet" (v. 10). Absalom keeps his conspiracy away from the people who are close to David. Still, he needs their support. Accordingly, he takes two hundred of them, who "went in their simplicity, and knew nothing" (v. 11). In Hebron Absalom offers sacrifices, perhaps following the traditions of the priestly kingship in Jerusalem (see above on 6:12-19), evidently as a preparation for his enthronement. It is said that while he was sacrificing Absalom sent for Ahithophel the Gilonite, David's counselor. Perhaps the sacrificial rituals went on for more than one day, and it was in this time before the actual enthronement took place that Absalom sent for Ahithophel.

Absalom was born in Hebron (3:2ff.). The Hebronites could have been dissatisfied with David for changing the capital from Hebron to Jerusalem. (Hebron had been David's capital for seven years and six months; cf. 2:11.) In 15:8 some versions read "Yahweh in Hebron"; this may reflect early Israelite practice where Yahweh was worshiped in different localities, just as Baal was worshiped in different places. This kind of vow-making in religious centers and in special places is a common practice today among all groups — including Christians — in India. It is not clear how the sound of the trumpet could be heard in all places in Israel at the same time (v. 10). There may have been a chain of trumpeters placed within hearing distance of each other starting from Hebron. Perhaps Absalom sent messengers inviting representatives from all tribes of Israel to come to Hebron for the enthronement ceremony. Blowing the trumpet was part of the enthronement rituals (cf. 20:1; 1 Kgs. 1:34; 2 Kgs. 9:13; 11:14).

David's counselor Ahithophel (2 Sam. 15:12; cf. 16:23; 23:34) was from Giloh, a place in the hill country of Judah. It has been identified with Khirbet Jala, 10 km. (6.5 mi.) W of Hebron. The title "counselor" for Ahithophel occurs only here in the books of Samuel; he is so designated also in 1 Chr. 27:33. According to 2 Sam. 11:3; 23:34 Bathsheba is the granddaughter of Ahithophel, so according to some scholars Ahithophel's desertion of David was an act of revenge for what David had done to his granddaughter. From later narratives (15:31, 34; 16:15-23; 17:1-4) we learn that Ahithophel was behind the whole conspiracy.

David's Flight before Absalom (15:13–16:14)

David's Flight (15:13-18). A message telling of Absalom's conspiracy reaches David. David, fearing an immediate takeover of Jerusalem by Absalom's rebel army, flees from the city with "all his household after him," leaving behind just "ten concubines to keep the house" (15:16). The "messenger" (v. 13) who brought the news could have been a David-loyalist from Hebron or one of the two hundred men whom Absalom had taken with him from Jerusalem. The speed with which David flees indicates that he could recognize the imminence of the danger, perhaps because of the large number of chariots and horses which Absalom possessed. With a chariot, the enemy could set fire to and destroy a city so quickly that no time would be left for the inhabitants to escape (v. 14). Apparently David did not possess chariots or horses at this time; for his flight he depended on the asses later given to him by Ziba (16:2).

Another reason for the flight was that "the hearts of the men of Israel have gone after Absalom" (v. 13), so that David was not sure even of local support. Only the foreigners, his hired servants, seem to have stayed by him and assured him of their loyalty (vv. 15, 18). On the Cherethites and the Pelethites, see 1 Sam. 30:14; 2 Sam. 8:18; on the Gittites, see 6:10-11. David, however, does not give up his claim over the city. As a sign of his sovereignty over Jerusalem he leaves part of his harem, ten of his concubines (15:16), behind in the city. It is strange that here no mention is made of the commander of the army, Joab, or of the national militia. Perhaps this account of David's flight comes from another tradition. David's retreat from before Absalom once again shows his wisdom as a leader. The greatness of a leader lies in his ability to discern the strength and weakness of his enemy and to plan his strategy accordingly.

David and Ittai the Gittite (15:19-23). Ittai the Gittite and his men
want to follow David in his flight. As a sign of his concern for
Ittai, a foreigner who had arrived only the day before (vv. 19-20),
David tries to persuade him and his men to return from following
him. Ittai was probably the leader of the "six hundred Gittites"
mentioned in v. 18. David's reference to "the king" (v. 19) raises
the question whether David had actually recognized Absalom as
the legitimate king. Yet this is very unlikely. Peter R. Ackroyd
wonders whether this is "an allusion to a rite in which for a limited
period some person is appointed to take over the royal duties
while the real king is humiliated or in flight" (*The Second Book of
Samuel,* 144).

David acknowledges his fugitive condition (v. 20). His self-
humiliation here could well have been due to his awareness that
he had sinned before God. Nathan's words, "Now therefore the
sword shall never depart from your house . . ." (12:10), are clearly
beginning to be fulfilled.

It is possible that David had bound himself to Ittai with a
covenant in the name of Yahweh to protect David and his men
at all costs. Now that he is not in a position to honor his covenant
commitment, David wishes that Yahweh may show "steadfast love
(hesed) and faithfulness *(emet)*" toward Ittai, because Yahweh is
the custodian of the covenant. On *hesed,* see above on 7:14-15.
David, as king, shows his magnanimity here. At a critical time
when he is in distress, the loss of six hundred soldiers (15:18) is
a serious matter. Still he would not compel the Gittites to follow
him, but rather leaves the decision to them. Ittai, too, proves
himself faithful to his covenantal obligation. He is not an opportunist who would desert his protector when the latter is in danger.
As a loyal covenant partner he will go with his master "for death
or for life" (v. 21). Ittai's loyalty is later rewarded when David
makes him commander of one third of his army (18:2). The
presence of "the little ones" in their midst (15:22) might suggest
that David's flight must have been rather slow.

Community weeping ("all the country wept aloud," v. 23) was
an aspect of appropriate religious ritual (cf. Joel 2:17). We have
here perhaps worship elements mixed into a historical account.

"The brook Kidron" (2 Sam. 15:23) is the steep valley to the immediate east of Jerusalem between the city and the Mount of Olives (cf. v. 30). David moves "toward the wilderness." The reference is perhaps meant to suggest that David now becomes a fugitive who is completely at the mercy of God (cf. v. 26; 16:10).

The fact that David was chosen by God as his anointed one and the fact that the LORD bound himself to David with an everlasting covenant did not mean that David was immune to temptations, trials, and hardships. David was now reduced to the level of a fugitive and was driven into the wilderness. His suffering can be compared to the spiritual experience of a believer. In the life of such a one, wilderness experiences are very common, especially when the person finds himself not only forsaken by people but also forsaken by God (cf. Ps. 22:1). At such moments of spiritual desolation or spiritual darkness, total surrender to God is the only right thing to do. This is because God says, "For a brief moment I forsook you, but with great compassion I will gather you" (Isa. 54:7).

The Ark and the Priests Return to Jerusalem (15:24-29). The text appears to be corrupt here. The original account appears to have dealt only with Zadok. Abiathar appears to have been introduced only secondarily. The reference to "the Levites" is an anachronism. A later editor may have introduced it for doctrinal reasons, because later laws required the presence of the Levites at the ark (Num. 3:31; Deut. 10:8; 1 Chr. 15:2). Worship in Jerusalem was closely associated with the kingship in Israel, so the end of kingship meant the end of cultic worship as well (cf. Lam. 2:6). Thus when the king left the country, the priests also decided to follow him with "the ark of the covenant of God" (2 Sam. 15:24), the moving sanctuary of Yahweh. But David urged the priests to go back to Jerusalem, both for theological and for political and practical reasons. Theologically, the return of the ark would reveal that God still had pleasure in David. Politically, it would mean that David's sovereignty over Jerusalem had not been given up, and that his departure was only temporary. Moreover, it would also have a practical advantage. The priests could play the role of spies and let David know what was going on in the city without being under suspicion.

233

In the Hebrew text of v. 24 Zadok is mentioned first, for he is the head of the Levites; elsewhere in the Davidic account Abiathar is mentioned first. In v. 25 it is Zadok who is addressed, indicating that at this stage Zadok had taken over the leadership of the Jerusalemite priesthood. On Zadok, see above on 8:17. On "the ark of the covenant of God," see the introduction to 1 Sam. 4:1b–7:2. Where the RSV reads "they set down" (2 Sam. 15:24), the Hebrew text may have a form of the verb "they poured." This would refer to some ritual of pouring out a libation, as part of the ritual of sanctifying the place where the ark is to be set down. Such ritual pouring is common in most oriental religions.

Behind David's advice to Zadok and Abiathar to return to Jerusalem with the ark of God, and his belief that Yahweh would call him back if he should be pleased in him, is the belief that Jerusalem continued to be the city of Yahweh's "habitation." By submitting himself totally to Yahweh's will, David therefore proves himself to be the ideal king of Israel and the servant of Yahweh. In this he stands in contrast to Saul. At a time of similar crisis Saul resorted to seeking help from sources other than Yahweh (1 Sam. 28:8ff.). David, on the contrary, would rely on Yahweh alone (cf. 2 Sam. 24:14).

The Mourners' Procession to the Mount of Olives (15:30). This verse betrays a cultic background. Weeping, walking barefoot (cf. 19:24), and having the head covered (13:19) are all part of the rituals of national mourning (cf. Jer. 14:2; Ezek. 24:17). They are not fitting for a fleeing band of soldiers and king. The geographical location here also differs from what has been said above. In 2 Sam. 15:23 we are told that all the people passed on toward the wilderness, while in v. 28 David tells Zadok that he would wait at "the fords of the wilderness" until he hears from Zadok. Here David is said to be climbing up "the ascent of the Mount of Olives." His aim seems to be to go to the summit "where God was worshipped" (v. 32). The fact that here the Hebrew word *elohim* is used for God and not Yahweh might suggest that there was a pre-Israelite cultic center at the top of the Mount of Olives, probably a pilgrim center. Thus David and his men went up there for worship. It is possible that the account of such a cultic procession has been combined with the historical account of David's flight. David's going barefoot might indicate that it was actually a penitential ritual.

Hushai and the Counsel of Ahithophel (15:31-37). David learns that his counselor Ahithophel is also among the conspirators with Absalom (v. 31). Disturbed by this news, David prays to God to "turn the counsel of Ahithophel into foolishness." As an answer to David's prayer, God brings Hushai the Archite to accomplish that end (v. 34). Hushai, instead of following David and becoming a burden to him in his flight, is to return to Absalom and pretend to be loyal to him, so defeating Ahithophel's counsel. Just how the counsel of a wise man, when he turns away from God and departs from practicing justice (here Ahithophel's betrayal of his loyalty to David), can become "foolishness" and destructive is well illustrated here. "The fear of the LORD is the beginning of knowledge" (Prov. 1:7); the corollary is therefore that turning away from God is foolishness. The appearance of Hushai turns out to be God's answer to David's prayer, in that David "came to the summit, where God was worshipped."

2 Samuel 15:35-37 picks up what was said in vv. 27-29. Since the priests are the least suspected in the community, secret messages could be passed on through them. "Ahimaaz, Zadok's son," and "Jonathan, Abiathar's son" (v. 36) appear to have served as the messengers of David (cf. 17:17ff.; 18:19ff.). While putting his whole trust on God (15:25-26), David himself does all that he can to thwart Absalom's efforts. Dependence on God's providence does not rule out possible human initiatives.

Ziba Meets David (16:1-4). Ziba, the servant of Saul with whom David entrusted the estate of Jonathan's son Mephibosheth (9:9-12), now comes to meet David with a large supply of food and drink. This is apparently a bid to discredit Mephibosheth in the eyes of David, in that Mephibosheth did not come himself to meet the king, and to win the king's favor for himself. Ziba ascribes a sinister motive to Mephibosheth's absence, alleging the latter to have expressed his intention to get back "the kingdom of [his] father" (16:3). David believes Ziba and promises the transfer of Mephibosheth's estates to the servant, the thing for which Ziba has been conspiring. Ziba's treachery, however, is exposed later when David meets the invalid Mephibosheth in person (cf. 19:24-30). True to the saying "a friend in need is a friend indeed," by helping David at the time of his crucial need, Ziba wins David's goodwill. This may be why David later felt obliged to divide Saul's land between Mephibosheth and Ziba, even after he learned that Ziba had deceived Mephibosheth. Ziba exploits the disability of his master to his own advantage. In this he becomes the typical model of all those who allow vested interests to come in the way of service. Such interests betray love and loyalty, and engender lack of integrity, exploitation, and misappropriation.

The fact that Ziba brought asses "for the king's household to ride on" suggests that the royal household at this time actually possessed neither horses nor chariots (cf. 8:4; 13:29; 15:1).

Shimei Curses David (16:5-14). This account heightens the tragedy that has befallen David, even as the king flees for his life from his son. Shimei adds insult to injury by cursing David. Bahurim (16:5; cf. 3:16; 19:16) is a Benjaminite place in the Jordan Valley on the way from Jerusalem. Shimei the son of Gera is a man of considerable influence; he was probably a leader of a "thousand" (cf. 19:16-17). From Gen. 46:21; Judg. 3:15 we know that Gera too is a Benjaminite name. We may therefore assume that Shimei belonged to the same clan in Benjamin to which Saul belonged (cf. 2 Sam. 16:11). Shimei, being attached to Saul's family, is probably making a protest demonstration against David. Cursing, along with throwing stones and flinging dust on the enemy, are elements in symbolic acts invoking evil upon the enemy. They were not meant to do any physical harm to the enemy. By throwing stones on the king single-handedly and inflicting physical harm on him, Shimei could not have expected to achieve anything except immediate reprisal. Shimei was walking right in the middle of David's men. He was probably in a state of ecstasy so that the people did not dare to stop him or attack him. David's later observation that "the LORD has bidden him" (v. 11) seems to confirm this. David seemed to believe that Shimei could have been speaking under inspiration by the Spirit of God.

Shimei curses David as a "man of blood" (vv. 7-8). In David's overthrow by his son Absalom, Shimei sees the blood of the house of Saul avenged. That David was a man of war and had therefore shed much blood appears to be well established in Israelite tradition (cf. 1 Chr. 22:8; 28:3). "Dead dog" (2 Sam. 16:9) is an abusive term (cf. 3:8; 1 Sam. 24:14). David dissociates himself from the bloodthirsty methods which are characteristic of the sons of Zeruiah (2 Sam. 16:10; cf. 3:26-30). He takes Shimei's curse to have its source in God (16:11). It was believed in Israel that Yahweh was the source of all authentic cursing and blessing. Once the words of cursing or blessing had proceeded from the mouth of the person appointed by God, those words could never be recalled (cf. Gen. 27:30ff.).

In the OT blessings and curses are differentiated from idle chatter. They were words spoken from the heart and with intent. They were like arrows shot from a bow. Once shot, they cannot be recalled, but must reach their target and be effective. But an arrow is a mere artifact. A word spoken with intent is alive because it comes from the heart of a living person. If this is true of mankind, how much more is it true of God. God's word cannot return to him "void," but must inevitably fulfil the purposes for which it is sent (Isa. 55:11). It is this reality which gives us the theology of John 1:1ff.

David believes it would be futile for Abishai to silence Shimei by killing him if Shimei were indeed speaking the authentic word of God. However, if Shimei were not authentic, and his cursing were his own words and thus an expression merely of his own human will, David would still be rewarded "with good" (2 Sam. 16:12) for not repaying evil with evil. That unjust sufferings bring God's blessings is a common biblical motif (cf. the book of Job; Isa. 53; Matt. 5:11-12).

After a while Shimei departs, taking another direction, and goes "along on the hillside" opposite to David (2 Sam. 16:13). More is said about Shimei later in 19:16-23; 1 Kgs. 2:8-9, 36-46. Meanwhile David and his men arrive at the Jordan and refresh themselves (2 Sam. 16:14). The name of the place where they stopped is not mentioned here. According to 1 Kgs. 2:8 it was at Mahanaim, a place E of Jordan and E of Succoth to which David had been heading. However, according to 2 Sam. 17:22 David and the people accompanying him crossed the Jordan only after Hushai had first sent word. The motif of Jordan being a place of refreshment is very real to the Palestinian desert life, and it has become a religious motif also in both Jewish and Christian piety.

Ahithophel and Hushai (16:15–17:23)

This section deals with the counsel of Ahithophel and the counter-counsel of Hushai. The seriousness with which Hushai's counsel is considered shows that Hushai was also a wise man in David's court, though he did not carry any special title as did Ahithophel.

Hushai Joins the Court of Absalom (16:15-19). This text picks up the account from 15:37. Following David's advice, Hushai approaches Absalom with the intention of joining his court. Absalom is aware of the fact that Hushai was a close friend of David. Perhaps David and Hushai had bound themselves with a friendship covenant as in the case of David's covenant with Jonathan (1 Sam. 18:3-4; 23:18). Therefore Absalom questions the validity of Hushai's "covenant loyalty" (*hesed,* 2 Sam. 16:17) to his friend David. Hushai wisely argues that his "loyalty" is to the king and not so much to the person David. His basic loyalty is to Yahweh, and he would serve "whom the LORD and this people and all the men of Israel have chosen" (v. 18), simultaneously boosting Absalom's self-conceit as a king possessing the consent of both God and the people. Absalom was naturally pleased to hear such a theological legitimation of his usurpation, as is the case with all traitors and usurpers, because it vindicated him of the charge of being either an opportunist or a traitor. Moreover, Hushai argues that he has not changed his loyalty to anyone outside the Davidic line. Serving the son with the same loyalty as that shown the father (v. 19) is only proper of a faithful courtier. Hushai's acclamation of Absalom as "the king" (v. 16) with the consensus of God and the people, along with his promise of allegiance to him, perhaps boosted Absalom's self-image, and he readily accepts Hushai into his service.

Ahithophel's First Counsel (16:20-23). Absalom seeks the counsel of his advisors. In his request that Ahithophel "Give your counsel" (v. 20), the Hebrew for "your" is plural, which means that Absalom's order is addressed to a circle of advisors. However, the only word that could count is Ahithophel's. Ahithophel is probably the head of a council of advisors, because his advice is as reliable as that of "the oracle of God" (v. 23). Ahithophel counsels Absalom to have sexual intercourse with David's concubines whom David left behind "to keep the house" (15:16) in Jerusalem. Through this Ahithophel seems to aim at achieving two things. First, it will signal a clear break in Absalom's ties with his father David. Ahithophel is perhaps aware of David's special love for Absalom. This contemptuous act of Absalom against his father will give credibility to his revolt against his father and boost the morale of Absalom's supporters. Second, this action will affirm in the eyes of the public that Absalom has asserted his rights as king. Taking the harem of a king and having intercourse with them seem to have been related to the claims of a king (cf. 3:7; 1 Kgs. 2:22). For the narrator, however, this act of Absalom was in fulfilment of the prophecy given by Nathan in 2 Sam. 12:11-12. Some scholars see in the act of having intercourse under a tent on the roof some sort of ancient religious practice associated with sacral marriages in the cult (Peter R. Ackroyd, *The Second Book of Samuel,* 261; Fritz Stolz, *Das erste und zweite Buch Samuel,* 262).

Ahithophel's Second Counsel (17:1-4). As the next step Ahithophel counsels Absalom to destroy his sole opponent, his father David, without killing the people and thus alienating them from him. Once the leader of the opposition is dead, it is possible to win back the people to one's side. "Strike the shepherd, that the sheep may be scattered" (Zech. 13:7; Matt. 26:31) had been a strategy of war followed in ancient times. Ahithophel's guess based on his sound analysis corresponds to the real situation of David. A surprise attack could have brought victory to Absalom. Ahithophel means to catch David quickly "while he is weary and discouraged"

239

(2 Sam. 17:2). Ahithophel's counsel has the further advantage that Absalom himself need not go to war. Ahithophel himself will lead the foray. This would mean that, even if some disaster were to strike this unit of the army, Absalom is still safely behind to organize an army to fight the enemy. Ahithophel proves himself to be a really wise man, so far as his strategy is concerned. However, there is a possible danger implied in it. Ahithophel is to lead the army, and should he come out the victor that would pose a problem for Absalom (cf. 12:28). This may have been one reason why Absalom seeks a second opinion. That Absalom does not trust Ahithophel fully is confirmed by the fact that Ahithophel later commits suicide when he sees that his counsel has not been followed (17:23). The author sees all this as the work of God (v. 14).

Hushai's Counter Counsel (17:5-14). Hushai could probably read Absalom's fear, and so he takes advantage of it. The main difference in Hushai's counsel is that it is Absalom himself who is to lead the war, and not Ahithophel. Hushai concedes that Ahithophel's counsel in general has been good. But "this time" (v. 7) is an exception: it is "not good." Hushai appeals to Absalom's vanity by suggesting that the success of attack depends much on Absalom's personal leadership. Hushai points out the weakness of Ahithophel's counsel by noting that it was based on miscalculations about David's wisdom and war tactics. He expounds upon David's reputation among his people. David and his soldiers are "mighty men," enraged and vigilant "like a bear robbed of her cubs" (vv. 8, 10; cf. 10:7; 16:6; 20:7). David is "expert in war" (17:8). He is known for his cunning strategies — "even now he has hidden himself in one of the pits, or in some other place" (v. 9a; cf. 1 Sam. 21:12ff.; 23:22; 26:6ff.). David will not be in the midst of the people, to be caught so easily as Ahithophel thinks. Moreover, the whole endeavor can boomerang upon Absalom himself should some warriors in Absalom's army die and the news ("there has been slaughter among the people who follow Absalom," 2 Sam. 17:9b) spread abroad. This can demoralize "even the valiant man, whose heart is like the heart of a lion," because "all Israel knows" that David "is a mighty man, and that those who are with him are valiant men" (v. 10). As a result Absalom's followers might well desert him.

The arguments given by Hushai to discredit Ahithophel's counsel sound sensible and logical, and they appeal to Absalom and his men. Having thus undermined Ahithophel's counsel, Hushai proceeds to offer his own counsel. In reality it is aimed first at giving time for David and his men to move to safety and to organize themselves for war. Second, it will make Absalom's army massive, disorganized, unwieldy, and easily scattered, over against the carefully selected and valiant men of David. Third, Absalom's forces will be cumbersome, and a desert march toward Mahanaim would be difficult (v. 24). Fourth, Hushai's plan will draw Absalom, David's chief opponent, into war (v. 11) and so deliver him into the hands of David's army.

The counsel of Hushai sounds acceptable to Absalom and to his people, and so better than that of Ahithophel. However, as the author says, it was because "the LORD had ordained to defeat the good counsel of Ahithophel, so that the LORD might bring evil upon Absalom" (v. 14). Absalom's story illustrates how people who rely on the counsel of those who do not know the fear of the LORD are doomed to self-defeat and self-destruction (cf. Prov. 16:25; 21:2).

Destroying a city meant in those days pulling down its gates (cf. Judg. 16:3) and its walls (cf. Josh. 6:20). "Ropes" could have been used for such purposes (2 Sam. 17:13). Mahanaim was apparently just such a walled city with gates (cf. 18:4, 24; 19:8).

Hushai's Message to David (17:15-20). As advised by David earlier (cf. 15:34-37), Hushai passes on to "Zadok and Abiathar the priests" (17:15) the message that is to be given to David. The priests in turn convey the message through "a maidservant" to Jonathan and Ahimaaz (v. 17), who are waiting at En-rogel, at the border of the city. Hushai apparently is not aware of Absalom's final decision as to whether he took Ahithophel's counsel or his. He fears that if Ahithophel's counsel were followed, the king and his people would be taken unawares and be destroyed. So, as a matter of precaution, Hushai urges them to move to safety quickly. En-rogel means "Fuller's Spring"; it lay on the southern side of

Jerusalem at the junction of the Kidron and Hinnom valleys. It
was probably a well from which the people drew their water. "A
maidservant" coming to the well to draw water would not be
suspected, so that is why she is employed to carry the message.
On God's using "servants," the "little people" of society, in his
economy of salvation, see above on 1 Sam. 9:6ff. The "man at
Bahurim" may be a friend of David (2 Sam. 17:18); "the woman"
here is probably the housewife (v. 19). The daring way in which
this woman saved David's spies (vv. 18-20) resembles the way in
which Rahab saved the spies of Joshua (cf. Josh. 2:1ff.). Jonathan
and Ahimaaz enter an open well with steps leading downward;
the woman then spreads a covering over the well's mouth, scatters
grain upon it (2 Sam. 17:19), and thus camouflages it. The
servants of Absalom, informed by a boy who saw the spies, come
searching for them, but when they cannot find them they return
to Jerusalem (v. 20). The Bible records many such heroic deeds
done by women who thus shared in God's work of salvation (cf.
Josh. 2:1ff.; Judg. 4:4ff., 17ff.).

David and His People Cross the Jordan (17:21-22). The spies report
to David apparently only the message regarding Ahithophel's
counsel and its consequence, since it is a matter of great importance. David and his men must immediately get out of the reach
of Absalom's army. If they are able to cross the Jordan and reach
a place of safety in the desert, it will make things difficult for
Absalom's large army. David therefore now takes Hushai's advice
and acts quickly: "and they crossed the Jordan; by daybreak not
one was left who had not crossed the Jordan" (2 Sam. 17:22).
In biblical thinking the river Jordan plays an important role, as
noted above. For many Jews and Christians it becomes a symbol
of solace and comfort. Whether here the author sees any spiritual
significance in David's crossing the Jordan is not clear. However,
it becomes a line of protection for David and his forces.

Ahithophel Commits Suicide (17:23). This verse interrupts the narrative of David's escape to Mahanaim. Perhaps since this is the
point where it becomes evident that Absalom has rejected
Ahithophel's counsel, the author found it fitting to mention

Ahithophel's suicide here. As a wise man, Ahithophel knew that Absalom would be courting disaster if he followed Hushai's plan. Moreover, Ahithophel was acutely aware what would happen to himself if David succeeded in quelling the rebellion. He would be accused of being a traitor by openly supporting Absalom. Accordingly, Ahithophel "sets his house in order." That is, he fulfils his responsibilities before his death, and then commits suicide.

In David's flight before Absalom and all his sufferings, certain NT writers may have seen an analogy with the persecution and sufferings of Jesus, "the son of David." As Peter R. Ackroyd notes, the narrative of Jesus' passion is deeply enriched with allusion and analogy from the Davidic account. Crossing the Kidron (15:23; cf. John 18:1), the route toward the Mount of Olives, and the weeping and the praying (2 Sam. 15:30) are all suggestive of Gethsemane. The suicide of Judas also (Matt. 27:5) is described in words which are exactly those of the LXX (Greek) text of 2 Sam. 17:23 (Ackroyd, *The Second Book of Samuel*, 162).

Absalom's Defeat and Death (17:24–18:32)

"David came to Mahanaim" (2 Sam. 17:24), his ultimate goal (cf. 1 Kgs. 2:8). This city was Ish-bosheth's capital (cf. 2 Sam. 2:8). Formerly the capital of Gilead (see above on 2:8), it possessed suitable fortifications (cf. 18:24). At this point, however, the narrator switches over to tell us what was happening on Absalom's side. Having gathered "all the men of Israel" (17:24), Absalom too crossed the Jordan, presumably having heard that David had gone over to Mahanaim. Does the statement that "Absalom had set Amasa over the army instead of Joab" (v. 25) indicate that Joab was on the side of Absalom for some time? The fact that Joab later on had a demoted status in David's army (cf. 18:1-5), and that David thought of making Amasa the commander in place of Joab (cf. 19:13) and had actually appointed him to that position (cf. 20:4), tends to support this view. This would also explain Joab's absence from David's camp until now. Joab's earlier sympathy for Absalom is known (cf. 14:1ff.). He had probably supported Absalom's claim for the throne initially, but later broke away when he realized that Absalom intended to usurp his father. Thus when Absalom appointed Amasa as his commander, Joab finally deserted him and joined David. This would also explain why Joab was merciless toward Absalom — even when the king wanted his life to be spared — and why he was ruthless in killing Amasa (20:9-10).

In view of the account in 20:4-13, one wonders whether the subject "Absalom" in 17:25a is an error for "David." Verse 25b explains Amasa's identity: he is Joab's cousin, with Ishmaelite connections. The Hebrew text reads "Israelite" in place of "Ishmaelite." Since in the OT no Israelite is specifically described as such, it is suggested that we read in its place "Ishmaelite" with the Latin Vulgate and 1 Chr. 2:17.

In place of the RSV reading "married" in v. 25b the Hebrew text reads literally "went in," the common Hebrew expression for having sexual intercourse. Scholars think that this is a reference to the *binah*-marriage or *tsaddiqah*-marriage (cf. Charles F. Burney, *The Book of Judges*, 263, 354-55; Hans Wilhelm Hertzberg, *I and II Samuel*, 357). These marriages are a type of union in which the wife does not leave her father's house. Instead, the husband takes up residence in her home and severs his connections with his own clan. Ethnographers have identified this type of marriage in Sri Lanka, where it is called *beena* marriage. Among Palestinian Arabs it is known as *tsadiqa* marriage, from *tsadiqa*, meaning "lover" or "mistress." It is a true marriage but without permanent cohabitation. The woman is mistress of her own house and the husband comes as a guest, bringing presents (R. de Vaux, *Ancient Israel*, 29, 283). Zeruiah herself could have been married under such a custom. This would explain why her three sons are always called by the name of their mother.

In 19:13 David asks the elders of Judah, whom he describes as "my bone and my flesh" (v. 12), to tell Amasa that he also is David's bone and flesh. This may indicate that Amasa was a person from Judah.

The name Nahash (17:25) appears again in v. 27 referring to the Ammonite king. Some scholars wonder whether the name in v. 25 is a scribal error for some other name (Hertzberg, 357; William McKane, *I and II Samuel*, 262).

Verses 27-29 explain how God feeds David and his men "in the wilderness." Shobi the son of Nahash from Rabbah, Machir the son of Ammiel from Lo-debar, and Barzillai the Gileadite from Rogelim (v. 27) bring all kinds of food "for David and the people with him to eat" (v. 29). Shobi appears to be a man from the Ammonite royal family who was apparently the local deputy through whom David exercised his rule. Perhaps he was the brother of Hanun (cf. 10:1). On Machir, see above on 9:4. Perhaps we are to relate Machir's loyalty to David's kind treatment of Mephibosheth. Barzillai the Gileadite was "a very wealthy man" (19:31-32). 2 Sam. 21:8 speaks of another Barzillai "the Meholathite." The location of Rogelim is not known with certainty. Later when David mentions his gratitude, he refers only to Barzillai (1 Kgs. 2:7). The other two persons are perhaps included here to make the number of persons meeting David three. On the use of the mystic numbers in Israel, see the Introduction. Here the author perhaps sees a spiritual meaning — the LORD feeds his people in the wilderness. The reason why they brought food is that "the people are hungry and weary and thirsty in the wilderness" (2 Sam. 17:29). Perhaps this is a reference to a sort of law of natural justice demanded of them. Anyone "hungry and weary and thirsty in the wilderness" has to be fed. If this law of natural justice could only be followed by the generation today, the poverty in the world could be eradicated in no time.

Preparations for Battle (18:1-5). Having withdrawn to safety, David plans measures to crush Absalom's rebellion. David takes up the overall command of the army. He divides it into different units of thousands and hundreds and sets them under three commanders — Joab, Abishai, and Ittai the Gittite. This may be for strategic reasons; even if one of the commanders turns out to be a traitor and joins the enemy, the other two can still fight against the enemy. This further makes us wonder if David doubted the loyalty of Joab. In the account of David's flight, Joab is mentioned now for the first time, and in a demoted position. He is no more the general commander of David's army. See above on 17:25.

Appointing "commanders of thousands and commanders of hundreds" (18:1) corresponds to the judicial order evolved during

245

the time of Moses (cf. Exod. 18:21). On Abishai, see above on
1 Sam. 26:6; on Ittai the Gittite, see above on 2 Sam. 15:19-23.
David offers to take up the overall command of the army himself
(18:2), either because of his distrust of Joab or because of the
fact that on the enemy side Absalom bears the general command.
However, David's men will not allow him to go into the battle
in person because David's life is of more value than that of
common people: "you are worth ten thousand of us" (v. 3).
Perhaps here is an allusion to Ahithophel's strategy of singling
out David and then killing him (cf. 17:2). Here is the beginning
of a tendency toward making the person of a king sacrosanct (cf.
1 Sam. 24:4ff.; 25:29; 26:9). The king becomes "the lamp of
Israel" that should not be quenched (2 Sam. 21:17): the end of
the kingship means the end of the nation (Lam. 2:6). Therefore
it appears that, already even during the early days of the reign of
David, a rule is evolving that the king should not go to war
personally. This special image of kingship in Israel obviously contributed to the development of the spiritual image of the Messiah.

"The gate" in 2 Sam. 18:4 is probably the gate of the city.
Mahanaim appears to have been a fortified city (see above on
17:13). David's special concern for sparing the life of Absalom
(18:5) shows that he is not only a warrior and a king, but also
an affectionate father. Fatherly love reaches out to the son in spite
of the son's hostility. We are here reminded of the parable of the
Prodigal Son (Luke 15:11-32) and its teaching on God's love
toward sinful humanity. The note "and all the people heard"
(2 Sam. 18:5) prepares the ground for v. 12.

Absalom's Demise (18:6-18). Verses 6-8 explain the general course
of the battle. Verses 9-15 deal with the tragedy of Absalom's
death.

18:6-8 A crack in the facade of the United Monarchy under
David can already be seen here. The fighting is between "Israel,"
meaning the northern tribes (vv. 6-7; cf. 15:6; 17:4, 24, 26), and
David and his men. David's forces presumably came from Judah
along with the foreign personnel in David's bodyguard. The battle
is fought "in the forest of Ephraim" (18:6), and "the men of Israel

were defeated there by the servants of David" (v. 7). "The forest devoured more people that day than the sword" (v. 8); in the dismay of defeat the soldiers seem to have run helter-skelter in the forest, and got lost or were caught in the bushes or branches (as in the case of Absalom) and so died. Behind the expression "the forest devoured" seems to be some popular notion such as that found in the fable of Jotham (Judg. 9:15). The author is perhaps trying once again to show that the victory was actually wrought by the hand of God.

18:9-18   Absalom retreats from "the servants of David . . . riding upon his mule." That Absalom rides a mule may have been a deliberate choice to symbolize his royal claims (cf. 2 Sam. 13:29). The description is vivid: "his head caught fast in the oak, and he was left hanging between heaven and earth." His long and thick hair (cf. 14:26), once the object of his pride and joy, now becomes the snare of his death. Joab hears about it and mercilessly kills him. "A certain man" (18:10) who sees Absalom hanging would not dare to kill him because of the king's warning (v. 5) and of the danger involved in ignoring that warning (vv. 12-13). From what happened when the Amalekite who killed Saul on humanitarian grounds brought the news to David (cf. 2 Sam. 1:6-16), such a fear of David was justified. "And there is nothing hidden from the king" (18:13) is a motif commonly associated with David's greatness: David "has wisdom like the wisdom of the angel of God to know all things that are on the earth" (14:20; cf. 19:27; see above on 18:3).

"Ten pieces of silver and a girdle" (v. 11) probably represent both a monetary gift and a mark of military honor. Joab's ruthlessness and rashness in getting rid of his opponents is once again illustrated here (he kills Abner, 3:26-27; and Amasa, 20:10). For a possible reason, see above on 17:25. As a seasoned politician and warrior, Joab probably did not believe in sentimentality and forgiveness. Having understood Absalom (cf. 14:28ff.), Joab probably knew that sparing him would be just inviting further troubles. Like a wounded cobra Absalom might wait for the next opportunity to attack David. Joab thrust three darts "into the heart of Absalom" and thus killed him (18:14). Joab's act of killing

Absalom as he hangs defenseless does not display any heroism. Rather, his action appears as a third-rate act of vengeance. Verse 15, which speaks of "ten young men" surrounding Absalom and killing him, is superfluous and is probably secondary in the present context.

Once the leader is killed, his people are scattered (vv. 16-17). David's army would not want to pursue those who followed Absalom and destroy them, because they are to be wooed back to David's side later. Although he is the king's son, Absalom is not even given an honorable burial, an act which reveals Joab's bitterness against Absalom and his utter disregard of the feelings of David the king. The "heap of stones" (v. 17) over Absalom's grave is not made in his honor; such cairns appear to have been raised over bodies of people who had greatly offended against their people and country (cf. Achan, Josh. 7:26; the king of Ai, 8:29). Such cairns may have been erected for the purpose of restraining the spirits of the dead from troubling the community further. They could also have been intended to serve as a warning to others.

In 2 Sam. 18:18 the editor refers to "Absalom's monument." Absalom is said to have set up a pillar in "the King's Valley" to preserve his own remembrance because he had no children. The veracity of this tradition is questioned by the fact that according to 14:27 Absalom had three sons and a daughter. The editor is perhaps unable to imagine why a person should seek to perpetuate his memory on lifeless stones if he had a living family to keep that memory alive. Thus he assumes that Absalom had no children. The erection of a funeral stela was not normal in Israel. Absalom did this perhaps because of the Aramean connections on his mother's side (William F. Albright, *Archaeology and the Religion of Israel,* 106).

David Receives News of Absalom's Death (18:19-32). The account of how the ambiguous message of Absalom's defeat and death was brought to David is given in detail. While the message of victory over the rebel is a matter of joy for David, the message of Absalom's death is a matter of deep distress to him. Ahimaaz the son of Zadok (18:19) was one of David's messengers, presumably a fast runner (cf. 15:36; 17:17ff.) and a staunch admirer of David. He is keen on carrying the happy part of the message. The Hebrew word used here for "carrying tidings" *(bashar)* is used often for carrying "good tidings" (18:19, 25, 27; cf. Isa. 40:9; 41:27; 52:7; 61:1). Good tidings are meant to be carried only by a good man (2 Sam. 18:27). Since the message being brought is not clearly a message of happiness, Joab does not want a "good man" like Ahimaaz to carry it. A foreigner would be a more probable carrier for sad news. Accordingly, Joab sends a Cushite, an Ethiopian who is black and probably a slave. However, Ahimaaz, a restless youth, persists that he should carry the news, with utter disregard for what it would bring for him, whether reward or punishment. So Joab finally allows him to run. Because he was a fast runner, and since he knew the quicker routes through "the plain," Ahimaaz "outran the Cushite" (v. 23).

David was "sitting between the two gates" (v. 24), waiting for news of the outcome of the war. The gates here refer to the two gates of the room at the city gate. Square or rectangular in shape at the ground level, it had a towerlike stone structure above it that was integral to the city wall, with projections beyond the line of the wall. The room in the ground floor offered space for city councils to meet. In the tower above stood the watchman. David sits at the center of the room on the ground floor, with the watchman apparently shouting from the watchtower from time to time what he was able to observe from above. It is up to the king to interpret the messages thus communicated.

In accordance with his reputation, Ahimaaz announces only the good part of the news: "All is well" (v. 28). *Shalom* is the Hebrew word used here; it can mean health, welfare, prosperity, and peace. It was used among the Israelites as a conventional form of greeting. However, to David's inquiry regarding the welfare of his son Absalom, Ahimaaz, as a wise and cautious messenger, gives an evasive answer (v. 29). In this way he conveys some forebodings of a possible tragedy, and thus prepares David for the shocking news brought by the Cushite. The Cushite also first utters the good side of the message (v. 31), whereupon David repeats his inquiry regarding Absalom. The Cushite, as a foreigner and thus probably unaware of David's feelings, invokes the fate of Absalom on all adversaries of David. He thereby indirectly conveys to David the still worse tragedy that had happened to Absalom.

David's Grief and Joab's Counsel (18:33–19:8a)

On hearing the news about Absalom's death, David "went up to the chamber over the gate" and began to mourn Absalom's death (18:33; numbered 19:1 in the Hebrew text). It is possible that over the gate was a room which the king could use for his privacy. David apparently utters a mourning song over Absalom (18:33b; 19:4b). "Would I had died instead of you . . ." is a common theme still used in mourning in traditional societies. Joab is annoyed over David's personal, emotional reaction, which prevents him from seeing the realities as head of a nation. The victory over Absalom is a national victory, and it is an occasion for national rejoicing. But the king's grief for his son, who was actually the national enemy, turns it into a day of mourning (19:1-2). People who participated in the fighting and who had saved David's life, instead of being welcomed by the citizens as heroes with jubilation, have to steal into the city as people "who are ashamed when they flee in battle" (v. 3). Joab sees that David's sorrow is not justified. In fact Absalom had been after David's life (17:2), and had it not been for the valiant courage of David's men, he himself would have been killed by this time. Sparing the life of Absalom would have meant giving themselves into his hands and being killed. Joab accuses David, saying he would have been happier to see such a thing occur (19:6). If this situation were to continue, Joab fears, not many warriors would stick by David. He therefore urges David to give up his mourning and present himself to the people as a sign of welcoming them back, and of appreciating and thanking them for what they had done (v. 7). David sees Joab's point, gives up his mourning, and takes up his position at the gate to meet the people. What Joab stresses here is that people in public office should not allow themselves to be carried away by personal sentiments and emotions. The author again presents David as a person who combines in himself a real father and a leader. True leaders must really lead a life of sacrifice. For the sake of the welfare of the public, they are expected to suppress many of their emotions and feelings, and to sacrifice many of their personal likes and dislikes for the common good.

David's Return to Jerusalem (19:8b-43)

This section completes the story of Absalom's rebellion. David is restored to the throne as the anointed king of Israel. That loyalty and submission to him are required of all is stressed by citing the reconciliatory efforts of Shimei (vv. 16-23), Ziba (v. 17), Mephibosheth (vv. 24-30), Barzillai the Gileadite (vv. 31-40), and also of Judah and Israel (vv. 41-43). David's kingdom is presented here as a kingdom for all the people. Being reconciled to him, all now find their place in it — an enemy (Shimei), a servant (Ziba), a disabled person (Mephibosheth), and one who is aged (Barzillai).

Israel Thinks of Recalling the King (19:8b-10). Verse 8b picks up the account of the flight of Israel's warriors from 18:17. Though Joab restrained his army from pursuing the fleeing troops of Israel, they all "fled every man to his own home." Now that Absalom is dead, the hopes of a better regime he had kindled (15:3-6) fade away and the sense of gratitude to the old king is revived. The people ask their leaders why they were not taking any steps for "bringing the king back" (19:9-10). Such an initiative could give Israel considerable influence over David.

Judah Brings David Back (19:11-15). The elders of Israel, in accordance with the popular wish, seem to have sent word to David, inviting him to return to Jerusalem and to assume his kingship anew (vv. 11b, 43). However, David feels that it is the people of Judah who should bring him back. So he sends word to the priests Zadok and Abiathar, who are still at Jerusalem (cf. 15:29). David appeals to his kinship with the Judahites, to his tribal solidarity with them: "You are my kinsmen [Hebrew, "brothers"], you are my bone and my flesh" (v. 12; cf. 5:1). He seems to be claiming from the Judahites, who were his kinsmen, their right to act as his "redeemer" (*go'el*) and so to restore him to his old position. They were to do so quickly, lest the Israelites in the north act first and so claim that it was they who had brought David back to the throne. Such an action would be an insult both to David and to Judah.

In order to woo the Judahites to his side, David offers to make Amasa the commander in the place of Joab (19:13). This again raises the question regarding the roles of both Amasa and Joab. After the reference to Absalom's appointment of Amasa as commander instead of Joab in 17:25, we hear of Amasa only here. No mention is made of his taking part in the battle. Moreover, why does David come to this radical decision? Is it because Joab originally cast his loyalty on the side of Absalom (see above on 17:25)? Or is it because Joab killed Absalom in spite of the king's caution against doing so? It is possible that this verse is an interpolation, entered here partly because of the verbal link ("my own flesh and blood") with 19:12 and also to provide grounds for the murder of Amasa by Joab in 20:4-13. The editor is evidently endeavoring here to reconcile elements of the tradition which were in fact contradictory.

In David's overdependence on his tribal solidarity may lie the seed of the hostility between the southern and northern tribes (19:41-43) which later resulted in the division of the kingdom (1 Kgs. 12:16ff.). David, as king of all Israel, could not outgrow his tribal solidarity. Such feelings of caste/tribal/racial kinships are becoming stronger even in these modern days, at a time when we look for a global human community. This kind of kinship alliance which blinds one's sense of justice is detrimental to human solidarity. It is for this reason that Jesus refused to be swayed from his commitment to the human community by any appeal to his kinship loyalty, when he asked, "Who is my mother, and who are my brothers? . . . Here are my mother and my brothers! For whoever does the will of my Father in heaven is my brother, and sister, and mother" (Matt. 12:48-49). The community in Christ knows no barriers whatsoever (cf. Col. 3:11). All those who are divided by kinship alliances are reconciled to God "in one body through the cross, thereby bringing the hostility to an end" (Eph. 2:16).

The Reconciliation Efforts of Shimei and Ziba (19:16-23). "Shimei the son of Gera, the Benjaminite," who had cursed David at

Bahurim (2 Sam. 16:5-8), sees that the course of events has changed from what he expected. Shimei realizes that he had been put in a dangerous position because of what he had done earlier to David. Accordingly, he rushes to be the first to welcome David back and thus to win his favor and forgiveness. David spares Shimei's life, but only temporarily, for later he dies at the hands of Solomon (1 Kgs. 2:36-44).

The account of Shimei is interrupted in 2 Sam. 19:17 by the reference to Ziba, who also rushed to meet David, probably for fear that David had found out about his treachery against his master and would now decide to retaliate. Ziba tries to placate David by doing "his pleasure" (v. 18). This anticipates the appearance of Mephibosheth in vv. 24ff. Before the handicapped Mephibosheth could meet David and disclose to him the truth, Ziba tries to meet the king and "please" him.

Shimei, with a "thousand men from Benjamin" (v. 17), joins "the men of Judah" to meet King David (v. 16). He thereby shows David that he has changed his loyalty to the house of Judah, as an act of repentance for what he had done to David in the name of the house of Saul. Perhaps this is the beginning of the alliance between Judah and Benjamin over against the ten tribes of the north. The prophecy of Ahijah in 1 Kgs. 11:29-39 allots ten tribes to Jeroboam (Israel) and one tribe to Solomon (Judah), apparently the tribe of Benjamin (12:21; 2 Chr. 11:12).

"All the house of Joseph" (2 Sam. 19:20) is here a reference to the northern tribes, although the Joseph tribes actually are only Ephraim and Manasseh (cf. Gen. 48:7ff.). On Abishai's attitude and David's response (2 Sam. 19:21-22), see above on 16:10. David sees Abishai "as an adversary" (19:22). *Satan* is the Hebrew word used here for "adversary." Satan was first used of human adversaries (cf. 1 Kgs. 11:14); later it came to be used of a member of the heavenly council whose duty it was to test the people on earth (cf. Job 1–2). Only later did Satan become an evil figure who incited people to disobey God (cf. 1 Chr. 21:1).

David declares an amnesty on the occasion of regaining his kingship in Israel: "I am this day king over Israel" (2 Sam. 19:22). This recalls the *misarum* institution known in the ancient Near East (Sumerian *niq.si/sa*), by the proclamation of which kings

ascending their thrones often proclaimed an amnesty and declared
release for all slaves, debtors, and prisoners (Gnana Robinson, "A
New Economic Order," 375). David's amnesty on Shimei ("You
shall not die," v. 23) seems to imply "you shall not die from my
hand." Thus it absolves Shimei from the punishment of death at
David's hand. According to 1 Kgs. 2:8 David swore to Shimei,
"I will not put you to death with the sword." Solomon later curbs
Shimei's freedom of movement within Jerusalem, and executes
him for breaking the royal order by going outside the walls of
the city (1 Kgs. 2:36-46).

Mephibosheth Comes To Meet David (19:24-30). Mephibosheth goes
down to the Jordan to meet David. However, he seems to have
missed David, and so turns back and overtakes him on the point of
David's entering Jerusalem. 2 Samuel 19:25 should read "and when
he came to Jerusalem" (RSV mg). By his very appearance Mephibosheth shows to David that he had been very much affected by
David's leaving, and that he was anxiously waiting for the king's
return. In this way he tries to disprove the allegation made by Ziba
(cf. 16:3). Mephibosheth presents himself in the state of mourning
— without dressing his feet (cf. 15:30), without trimming his
beard, and without washing his clothes "from the day the king
departed until the day he came back in safety" (19:24; cf. 12:20;
14:2). Similar neglect of care for one's body as a sign of grief is much
practiced in the East even today (cf. Lev. 19:27; Job 1:20).

David is obviously not persuaded by this outward appearance.
He asks why Mephibosheth did not go with him (2 Sam. 19:25).
David could have expected Mephibosheth, as one sitting at table
with him, to go with him. Mephibosheth puts the blame on his
servant Ziba. Because he is so handicapped, Mephibosheth cannot
saddle his ass and ride it without the assistance of someone else,
and Ziba was expected to do that. However, instead of helping
his master to go with the king, Ziba himself went down to meet
David. Mephibosheth was perhaps compelled to watch all these
movements helplessly, because he was "lame" (v. 26). Thereupon
Ziba not only deceived Mephibosheth but also "slandered" him
to the king (the reference here is to 16:3b). How Mephibosheth
came to know all about it is not indicated.

On the phrase "my lord the king is like the angel of God," see 14:17, 20; 18:13. Mephibosheth realizes that David is angry. Although he was aware that Ziba had played a double game, David might still have felt that Mephibosheth could have followed him, if he had really sought the assistance of some others. Therefore Mephibosheth submits himself to David's decision: "Do therefore what seems good to you" (19:27). Mephibosheth further acknowledges his gratefulness to David, recognizing that he lives more by David's mercy than by any merit or right of his own. He has no "further right" to "cry" to the king (v. 28).

David seems to find both Ziba and Mephibosheth equally guilty, and so divides Mephibosheth's land equally between them (v. 29). This is, of course, a departure from what David had promised to Ziba earlier (16:4). David will not be held bound by his promises to a fraud. Nevertheless, he is grateful for what Ziba had done for him at a time of great crisis. Mephibosheth further tries to prove his innocence by refuting Ziba's accusation that Mephibosheth was after his father Saul's kingdom: he is not even interested in his own land. Ziba can have it all, for Mephibosheth has cast his lot with the king, and he is happy that David is safely back. Without Ziba and his children to work on the land, perhaps Mephibosheth finds no use for it. That too could have been why he shows no interest in his own land.

Barzillai Escorts David to the Jordan (19:31-40). Barzillai was one of the three who brought food and materials to David during his stay in Mahanaim (17:27-29). More particulars about Barzillai are given here. He is eighty years old and "a very wealthy man" (19:32). As a sign of his gratitude, David invites Barzillai to go with him and spend the rest of his life with David as his guest (v. 33). But Barzillai turns down the offer on the ground that he is too old to be a royal guest, to enjoy the choicest food and the music of the king's court (vv. 34-35). These verses echo Eccl. 12, where the signs of aging are described. In remarking "I am this day eighty years old" (2 Sam. 19:35), Barzillai probably alludes to the view that commonly reckoned seventy years as the span of human life. Eighty years then is only "by reason of strength" (Ps. 90:10). Barzillai holds that he has already enjoyed the fullness of his life. The fact that his faculties are weakening reveals that his strength is declining, so that Barzillai cannot expect many more years of life. Consequently he does not want to become an "added burden" to the king (2 Sam. 19:35). However, he offers to accompany David "a little way over the Jordan." He sees David's generosity in inviting him to live at the court as a "reward" quite out of proportion to what Barzillai had done for David (v. 36). Behind this decline of David's offer is the basic desire of Barzillai to die in his "own city" and to be buried by the grave of his father and mother (v. 37; cf. 21:14), a desire which many people cherish even today.

Barzillai offers the young man Chimham to go with David (19:37-38). In the light of 1 Kgs. 2:7 we may assume that Chimham was one of Barzillai's sons. David and his people cross the Jordan, and David bids farewell to Barzillai by kissing and blessing him (2 Sam. 19:39). David, as priest-king, could thus bless Barzillai, even though Barzillai is much older than David.

David and his people are then said to have gone to Gilgal (v. 40). It was at Gilgal that the first encampment of the Israelites had taken place after crossing the Jordan (Josh. 3–4). Also, Saul was made king there (1 Sam. 11:14-15). According to the eighth-century prophets, Gilgal and Bethel were popular centers of worship which the Israelites were accustomed to visit frequently (cf. Hos. 4:15; Amos 4:4; 5:5). It is possible that the sanctuary at Gilgal had some special connection with kingship, for David went there to offer his thanks to God for bringing him back as king. The later prophetic traditions, however, condemned the worship that was carried on in Gilgal and Bethel. According to Hosea, Yahweh "began to hate" Israel in Gilgal. This then is part of the anti-kingship tradition, and the reference is obviously to Saul's appointment as king at Gilgal (cf. Hos. 9:15; 12:10-11). Pagan ceremonies seem to have been carried on in these places in the days of Amos and Hosea. If so, these ceremonies were blasphemous misappropriations of the twelve stelae which Joshua had erected to the glory of Yahweh, in thanksgiving for bringing the twelve tribes into the Promised Land (Josh. 4).

Rivalry over Claims on the King (19:41-43). According to 2 Sam. 19:40, only "half the people of Israel" brought up the king. Now at v. 41 it is "all the men of Israel" who came to him. "All" Israel now seeks to enforce its case for ownership of the king. This is a prelude to the developing tension between the Israelites and the Judahites and the final division of the kingdom. It serves as a link between David's return (v. 40) and the narrative of rebellion which follows in ch. 20. Because of their ethnic kinship to David, the Judahites feel that they have a special claim on him as their king, and David himself fanned such feelings. But the Israelites, because of their numerical superiority, claim the greater right to him — "we have ten shares in the king" (19:43). Though David is a Judahite, the Israelites make more claim on him because they were "the first to speak" of bringing him back. But the Judahites react fiercely (v. 43), because "the king is near of kin" to them (v. 42). Clearly a true leader should be neutral to all people under his jurisdiction. In this respect David apparently failed by asserting his kinship with the Judahites and thereby alienating the tribes of the north. The result was inevitably the division of the kingdom.

David, although the chosen of the LORD, is revealed in the books of Samuel as a very human person, with human hopes and fears. What is revealed here is that God overrules David's lack of understanding of all that Nathan the prophet had interpreted to him about his election and that of his house "for ever!" (ch. 7). David had at first been faithful to God's revealed word and had "reigned over all Israel" (8:15). Here the name Israel is the theological term for the whole people of God, rather than the political title of the northern tribes. David had "administered justice and equity to all his people." But David's loyalty to God's covenant with him was not to last. The prevenient love of God for Israel and God's concerned plan for the use he was determined to make of "all Israel" in days to come are revealed as the real factor in the story. Moreover, they are evidence of God's elective love, which he can actually take up and employ in his plan for the redemption of the world — even the sinful disloyalty of his chosen king.

Sheba's Rebellion Crushed (20:1-26)

This is an independent account, which the compiler chose to insert at this point probably because of the preceding narrative about the rivalry between Judah and Israel. Within the account of Sheba's rebellion is also that of Amasa's death at the hands of Joab (20:8-13), a memory of an event that probably belonged in some other context. The account of the wise woman of Abel of Beth-maacah in vv. 14-22 exposes once again the influence of the Wisdom school on the Succession narratives.

20:1-2 The phrase "Now there happened" in v. 1 indicates that what follows is an independent account. Verse 1 follows 19:43, according to which the Judahites were gaining the upper hand and the men of Israel were feeling neglected and insulted. This leads to the rebellion led by a certain "Sheba, the son of Bichri, a Benjaminite." Thus Sheba belongs to the tribe of Saul and Shimei. According to 19:16 Shimei and a group of Benjaminites had promised their allegiance to David. Sheba apparently belonged to another group which was hostile to David. Hebrew *ben* can mean that he is "the son" of Bichri or possibly "a descendant" of Bichri. According to Gen. 46:21; 1 Chr. 7:6, 8 "Becher" is the name of a Benjaminite; according to 1 Sam. 9:1 "Becorath" (KJV "Bechorath") was an ancestor of Saul. Sheba is perhaps presented this way as a member of the family of Saul to indicate that the enmity of the family of Saul continued.

"The trumpet" was blown normally both to assemble the people — warriors in particular, as is the case here — and to disperse them (cf. 2 Sam. 20:22). When a person not authorized by the king blew the trumpet, it obviously indicated rebellion and announced the establishment of a rebel kingdom (cf. 15:10). "Portion" and "inheritance" (20:1) normally refer to the property (land) inherited by every Israelite, and this was inalienable (cf. 1 Kgs. 21:3). Sheba holds that the Judahites by their exclusive claim on David had made David a king of their own (i.e., only of Judah), and thus Israel has no "portion" or "inheritance" in David's kingdom. "Every man to his tents" is the ancient cry remembered from the days of the Conquest, used to disperse the troops (cf. Judg. 7:8). David's kingdom, without the northern tribes, was reduced to Judah only. "From the Jordan to Jerusalem" (2 Sam. 20:2) indicates the boundary of the territory of Judah at that time.

20:3 The reference to David's return to Jerusalem and to his dealings with ten of his concubines interrupts the narrative of Sheba's rebellion, once again indicating the secondary nature of Sheba's account here.

David returns "to his house at Jerusalem." As a first act after his return, he attends to those of his concubines who had been humiliated by his son Absalom (15:16; 16:21-22). He puts them in a separate house and provides for them. They are made to live "as if in widowhood," cut off from himself as well as from other men. This, however, does not mean that remarriage for widows was not practiced in Israel. Indeed, David married the widows Abigail and Bathsheba. Since Absalom had humiliated these women and had thereby humiliated David, David keeps himself away from them. Moreover, because sexual relations with the concubines of a king stake a claim on the kingdom, these concubines cannot have sexual relations with any common man either.

20:4-5 David calls Amasa, whom he had newly appointed as commander of the army in place of Joab (cf. 19:13), and orders him to bring together the men of Judah. Along with the troops, Amasa is also to present himself to the king in three days' time. But Amasa cannot keep to the appointed time. Why is this unusual stipulation of time made here? Is it to justify Amasa's murder by Joab (cf. 20:8-10)? Peter R. Ackroyd considers it possible, though it is not in any way clear in the text "that Amasa was taking advantage of his position and of the duty entrusted to him to engage in rebellious activity on his own, to continue Absalom's revolt" (*The Second Book of Samuel*, 189).

It is not clear why David wanted the men of Judah, when his mercenaries alone were quite capable of crushing the rebellion (vv. 6-7). Perhaps he wanted to give the Judahites an opportunity to defend the kingdom and to establish their claim over it. (On David's reliance on his tribal solidarity, see above on 19:11-15.)

20:6 David is personally anxious to stop the move made by Sheba. He fears that if Sheba gets into one of the fortified cities, as David himself did in Mahanaim, it would be difficult to crush his rebellion. Since Amasa fails to return within the appointed time, David commands Abishai instead to take "your lord's servants," David's personal mercenaries, and to pursue Sheba. It is worth noting that here again Joab is ignored, further indication of a possible rupture in the relationship between David and Joab (see above on 17:25).

20:7 Joab, however, does not seem to be offended by David's preference for Abishai over himself. Joab's loyalty and commitment to the kingdom seem to be stronger than his reliance upon personal relationships. It is a pity that today we come across many people, both in the Church and in society, who put their personal interests before the interest of the institution which they are called to serve.

Joab follows Abishai, along with the mercenaries — "the Cherethites and the Pelethites" (see above on 8:18) and "all the mighty men" (cf. 23:8ff.). However, for all practical purposes, Joab assumes the command (cf. 20:11, 13). Between the brothers there seems to be no grudge over the leadership. Abishai seems to acknowledge and respect the superiority of his elder brother, an attitude characteristic of people in the East.

20:8-10 Joab kills Amasa by treachery. The Hebrew text is corrupt here. We can only guess the nature of Joab's treachery. While Joab and his men were on the way, Amasa returns, presumably with the men of Judah (cf. vv. 11, 13). Joab deliberately lets his sword fall out of its sheath so as to be visible to all, probably in order to remove from Amasa's mind any suspicion of foul play. Apparently Joab has a second sword concealed under his military cloak (cf. Ehud, Judg. 3:16-23). Under the pretext of kissing Amasa, Joab stabs him with his hidden sword and kills him. This cold-blooded act appears to be more an act of personal vengeance on Joab's part than an act of punishing Amasa for not keeping the appointed time, which should have been the king's responsibility. Joab's ruthlessness in dealing with his rivals is already known (cf. 2 Sam. 3:27). His treachery toward Amasa is often compared to the treachery of Judas toward Jesus. His greeting to Amasa is described as "the OT kiss of Judas" (Karl Budde),

Gibeon was a noted holy place, and "the great stone" there

was probably the altar on which Solomon later offered his burnt offerings (cf. 1 Kgs. 3:4-5).

20:11-13   Those who came with Amasa also join and pursue Sheba. One of Joab's men takes his stand by the dead body of Amasa, and commands all those who favor Joab and are loyal to David to follow Joab. However, the people who followed Amasa stop as they come to the body of Amasa. Whether they did so because of respect for their dead leader or whether behind their behavior lay some ancient religious belief connected with the dead, we do not know for certain. This delays the movement of the army, and so "the man" mentioned in 2 Sam. 20:11 covers Amasa's body with a garment. Then all the people go after Joab to pursue Sheba.

The breadth and depth of God's covenant love for David is shown here. God accepts and employs even the treachery of Joab in murdering Amasa for God's purposes of the salvation of the world. How extraordinary God is.

20:14-15   As feared by David (cf. v. 6), Sheba manages to reach security in a fortified city, Abel of Beth-maacah, with "all the Bichrites" who followed him. Sheba "passed through all the tribes of Israel," probably in an attempt to gain their support for his rebellion, but he could only succeed in getting the support of his own clan. Abel of Beth-maacah has been identified as modern Tell Abil near Dan, N of Lake Huleh. Joab and his men set up "a mound against the city," apparently to stand on it and attack the wall of the city and "throw it down." A "mound" is a raised earthwork to facilitate a siege and the capture of a city.

20:16-22   A "wise woman" from Abel intervenes and prevents the shedding of innocent blood. "Let them but ask counsel at Abel" (v. 18) appears to be a proverbial saying which indicates the reputation of Abel as a center of wisdom. The woman presents herself as one of those "who are peaceable and faithful in Israel." Her city she calls "a mother in Israel" and "the heritage of the LORD" (v. 19). The destruction of such a city is therefore against the will of God. Joab makes it clear to her that it is not his intention to destroy the city. If the city would but deliver to him Sheba, the man who had revolted "against King David," Joab would withdraw (v. 21).

The certainty of the woman that she could persuade her people to execute Sheba, who had sought asylum in the city, raises the question of the city's obligation to such people. Perhaps the supremacy of wisdom over legal rights is implied here. Is it right to allow a city with innocent people — women, children, and the aged — to be destroyed for just one disloyal person, or ought one hand over that person and so save the others from destruction? "It is better for one person to die to save many" (cf. John 11:50) seems to be the principle that prevailed here. That Sheba was a criminal acting against the king could certainly have made it easy for the wise woman to persuade her people. Once again we meet with a woman who participates in God's work of salvation (see above on 2 Sam. 17:18-20).

On seeing what happened to their leaders the Bichrites surrendered. Joab "blew the trumpet" (see above on 20:1) as a sign that the war was over, the people dispersed to their homes, and Joab "returned to Jerusalem to the king." Joab's role in crushing the rebellion of Sheba could well have vindicated his loyalty to David.

20:23-26 This section speaks about the royal household and probably comes from the editor. It is placed at this point because of Joab's restored position. Similar information is given in 8:15-18. "Israel" here is the theological name for all twelve tribes. The additional information offered here is that "Adoram was in charge of the forced labor" (20:24), "Sheva was secretary" (v. 25), and "Ira the Jethrite was also David's priest" (v. 26). The ministry of "forced labor" was probably a new appointment. The former secretary Seraiah (8:17) is either dead or has been replaced by Sheva. It is also possible that both these names refer to the same person, and that the name "Sheva" is a corruption of "Seraiah." In 8:18 it was said that "David's sons were priests"; but here it is said that "Ira the Jethrite" is David's priest. This indicates that in David's court there were extra priests, apart from the official priests Zadok and Abiathar. Ira is presumably to be identified with Ira "the Ithrite" or "Jethrite" of 23:38, one of the mighty men of David. He may well later on have taken over the functions of David's sons.

"Forced labor" is one of the evils already foreseen in the introduction of the institution of kingship (1 Sam. 8:17). As the kingship becomes established in Israel and as urbanization gradually takes place, forced labor becomes an essential part of the life of Israel. This situation becomes even worse during the reign of Solomon. Great monuments of ancient kingdoms, such as the pyramids of Egypt and the Great Wall of China, remind us of the vast amount of forced labor that was put into their construction. They stand as symbols of the sweat and blood of thousands of human lives. The gospel of Jesus Christ not only proclaims release to those captives who may be reduced to such forced labor (Luke 4:18), but it also offers rest to such unhappy people (Matt. 11:28).

VI. APPENDIX
2 Samuel 21:1–24:25

The proper continuation of 2 Sam. 20 is to be found in 1 Kgs. 1. 2 Samuel 21:1–24:25 is a collection of different materials coming from different hands — anecdotes (21:15-22; 23:8-23), a list of names (23:24-39), two sagas (21:1-14; ch. 24), and two poetical compositions (ch. 22, a royal thanksgiving identical with Ps. 18; 2 Sam. 23:1-7, a royal statute spelling out the principles to which a king faithful to Yahweh should hold fast). One or more editors could have been responsible for placing these separate items here at the end of the book. They have placed them between the books of Samuel and Kings, because they could not fit them in easily within the main section of the books of Samuel.

FAMINE AND BLOODGUILT OF THE HOUSE OF SAUL (21:1-14)

The contents of this account concern David's dealings with the house of Saul. The context here is a famine which continues for three years. Its root cause is identified as the unavenged bloodguilt of the house of Saul. Behind this saga lies an element of a primitive theology which sees every misfortune as the work of God and as the result of sin (see above on 1 Sam. 26:19). According to Israelite belief, unavenged blood cries to God (see above on 1 Sam. 15:32-33; cf. Gen. 4:10; 2 Sam. 1:16). God brings adversities on the people because of unavenged blood. Therefore it is the people's responsibility to see that the bloodguilt is removed. Famine, pestilence, and sword (war) are the three divinely ordained adversities (cf. 24:12-13). Here the adversity comes in the form of famine caused by drought. As king David must bear the responsibility for averting the famine by avenging the bloodguilt of the house of Saul.

21:1-2 The expression "David sought the face of the LORD" probably refers to David's visit to a sanctuary. At the shrine in Jerusalem, in the days before Solomon built the temple, the priest could have used the oracle device known as Urim and Thummim and interpreted its meaning for David. How this device could have given a descriptive answer is not clear. "The face of the LORD" always refers to the benign disposition of God. Saul is said to have put the Gibeonites to death (21:1), "in his zeal for the people of Israel and Judah" (v. 2). However, we have no record of such a massacre of the Gibeonites by Saul. Saul may well have massacred them out of his zeal for the fulfilment of the *herem* institution, which the Gibeonites escaped earlier by playing a trick on the Israelites (cf. Josh. 9). Saul is presented here as one to whom preservation of the purity of the people and their religion was of primary importance.

21:3 David consults the Gibeonites as to what he should do for them in order to "make expiation" for the sin committed by Saul, so they may "bless the heritage of the LORD." "The heritage" here is a reference to Judah and Israel together. David wishes that the Gibeonites might bless Israel. What Saul in his zeal had done for Israel and Judah turned out to be a curse on Israel. Now David, the true king, must avert the cause of this curse and turn it into blessing. Perhaps the Gibeonites, as per the original treaty, were obliged to exercise some kind of ministerial function of blessing Israel. This they no longer did after Saul's massacre of the Gibeonites. Behind David's desire for the blessings of the Gibeonites lies the Israelite belief in the efficacy of words of blessing or curse once uttered (cf. Gen. 27:1ff.).

21:4-6 The Gibeonites seem to hold that what Saul had done to them was of a spiritual nature and could not be rectified by any form of compensation, neither with "silver or gold" nor by executing any human person in Israel (2 Sam. 21:4). More than the act, it was the intention behind the act that was serious: Saul had intended to destroy them completely that they might have no place in the territory of Israel (v. 5). Here we are reminded of how Hitler sought to extirpate all Jews from the soil of Germany, and the millions of other people such as the Palestinians who in today's world are being removed from their rightful territories and therefore cry for justice!

The Gibeonites demand seven sons of Saul to be hanged "before the LORD at Gibeon on the mountain of the LORD" as rectification for the bloodguilt (v. 6). David grants their request. The mystical number "seven" (on mystical numbers in Israel, see the Introduction) indicates wholeness. "Seven sons" probably here refers to all the males born in the house of Saul. The evil that Saul intended on the Gibeonites is thus turned onto him — his house (or family) will have no portion in the territory of Israel.

In Gibeon was a famous shrine of Yahweh which played an important role even during the time of Solomon (1 Kgs. 3:3ff.). This "temple" was probably located on a hill and so became known as "the mountain of the LORD."

21:7 David spares Jonathan's son Mephibosheth, "because of the oath of the LORD which was between them." Though it was a friendship covenant, because it was made in the name of Yahweh it became "the oath of the LORD." The reference is to the covenant between David and Jonathan in 1 Sam. 20:14-17.

21:8-9 David hands over to the Gibeonites seven men from the house of Saul — two sons born to Saul's concubine Rizpah and "the five sons of Merab the daughter of Saul." Strictly speaking, Merab's offspring should not have been considered as the "sons of Saul." According to Israelite custom, children reckoned through the male line alone could be considered as heirs. Perhaps because the other male heirs of Saul except Mephibosheth had been killed in battle (cf. 2 Sam. 4:4; 9:1ff.) an exception is made here. Mephibosheth could be exempted because of "the oath of the LORD" with which David and Jonathan had bound themselves.

"They were put to death in the first days of harvest, at the beginning of barley harvest" (21:9). This is the beginning of the *massoth* festival, the Feast of Unleavened Bread. That the men were executed at the time of the *massoth* festival and that they were hanged "before the LORD" indicate that this was obviously a religious sacrifice. We see here how a primitive religious belief can cause great damage to the lives of innocent people. Similar things happen even today in many primitive religions. Bringing people to the right knowledge of God is therefore an important task of the Church's mission today. The revelation in Jesus Christ focuses attention on the salvation of humanity as a whole. The Son of Man came to save sinners, not to destroy them, "that they may have life, and have it abundantly" (John 10:10).

21:10-14 Different traditions appear to have been brought together here. The immediate context is Rizpah's mourning over the killing of her two sons. Rizpah spread the sackcloth on the rock and probably sat on it, and did not allow birds by day or beasts by night to come upon the dead bodies of her sons. It is said that she did it "from the beginning of harvest until rain fell upon them" (2 Sam. 21:10), which in fact is a long period. What the original intention of Rizpah's act was is not clearly told. In its present context it is made to appear that Rizpah wanted a decent burial for the dead bodies. Verses 12-14 deal mainly with the secondary burial of "the bones of Saul and the bones of his son Jonathan" (repeated three times), "in the land of Benjamin in Zela, in the tomb of Kish his father."

The only thing which links vv. 12-14 with vv. 10-11 is the sentence "and they gathered the bones of those who were hanged" (v. 13), which is secondary in its present context. The original tradition in vv. 12-14 spoke only of the secondary burial of the bones "of Saul and his son Jonathan." By adding the above sentence, a redactor made the account include the burial of the seven sons hanged now and also the other sons of Saul hanged earlier with Saul and Jonathan. Once this was done, the famine was lifted and there was rain.

Behind this account are traces of primitive beliefs coming from the fertility cult, which saw a close connection between the harmonious human life and the harmonious order of nature. That human sin affects the harmony of nature is a fact underlined by biblical teaching on sin (Gen. 3:17). Religious traditions sought to restore the harmony of nature by rectifying the disorder in human relations. This teaching, that human sin affects the order of nature, gains relevance today as well. Ecological scientists confirm the fact that human greed and avarice and the consequent plunder and destruction of nature are the root causes for drought and famine in many parts of the world.

DAVID'S MIGHTY MEN AND THE PHILISTINE GIANTS (21:15-22)

Here are four anecdotal episodes, each telling about the killing of a Philistine giants of unusual size by one of the mighty men of David. The accounts are preserved in stereotyped form. These episodes probably existed in fixed form and were preserved in the royal archives. It is possible that "the Book of the Wars of Yahweh" mentioned in Num. 21:14 contained such accounts. David's mighty men had to "go down" in each case from the hill country in which they lived to the coastal plain that was occupied by the Philistines. It should always be kept in mind that Jerusalem lies some 760 m. (2,500 ft.) above sea level.

The description of the giants given here appears to have influenced the description of Goliath in 1 Sam. 17. All four men who killed the giants — Abishai, Sibbecai the Hushathite, Elhanan, and Jonathan — appear to have been among the "mighty men" of David mentioned in 23:8-39. These accounts indicate that the Philistine menace continued throughout the reign of David.

21:15-17   The account of Abishai's killing the giant Ishbi-benob is given as the occasion for the origin of the famous royal dictum, "You shall no more go out with us to battle, lest you quench the lamp of Israel." Ishbi-benob, a descendant of the giants of Gath (21:16, 22), had attempted to kill David, but Abishai the son of Zeruiah (cf. 2:18) came to David's aid and killed the giant. "The descendants of the giants" (literally, "the sons of Raphah") were usually known as "Rephaim" (1 Chr. 20:4; cf. Gen. 14:5; 15:20; Josh. 12:4; 13:12).

That the king should not venture into the hazards of battle and risk his life (2 Sam. 21:17) is something which the people learned out of their experience, and which came to be well established in Davidic kingship (see above on 18:3). In Israelite thinking "the lamp" is the symbol of life. A burning lamp in the sanctuary symbolized the abiding presence of Yahweh, the source of life, in the midst of his people (cf. 22:29; Exod. 27:20-21; Lev. 24:2; 1 Sam. 3:3). A king in the Davidic line, because of God's covenant with David, is the guarantor of the welfare and security of the community, and thus became "the lamp" of Israel (cf. 1 Kgs. 11:36; 15:4; 2 Kgs. 8:19; Ps. 132:17). His light, however, is a derived light — light derived from the true lamp, Yahweh (2 Sam. 22:29). The death of a righteous king in Israel amounted to the quenching of the lamp of life in Israel. Therefore the king was prevented from entering into the hazards of the battle (cf. 11:1). However, it was the king's prerogative to claim the victory of the battle fought by his servants (cf. 12:28).

Ishbi-benob's spear weighed "three hundred shekels of bronze" (21:16) — about 3,450 g. (122 oz.). This is reminiscent of the story of Goliath, whose spear was twice as heavy as this (1 Sam. 17:7).

21:18   Sibbecai the Hushathite slew the giant Saph. 1 Chronicles 20:4 gives the name of the giant as Sippai. 2 Samuel 23:27 mentions Mebunnai the Hushathite as one of David's mighty men; perhaps Mebunnai is another name for Sibbecai.

21:19   "Elhanan the son of Jaareoregim, the Bethlehemite, slew Goliath the Gittite." Scholars have had difficulty in reconciling this account with that in 1 Sam. 17, according to which it was David who killed Goliath. The Chronicler tries to reconcile the problem by making the giant here to be the brother of Goliath, by reading the Hebrew word for "Bethlehemite" as *et-lahmi,* "Lahmi the brother of Goliath" (1 Chr. 20:5). The prevailing view, however, is that the fame of victory over this apparently deadly warrior was in the course of time transferred from the unknown Elhanan to the much more popular David. Some scholars try to show that Elhanan was the original name of David, which at an early stage was forgotten in view of his title as leader (Martin Noth, John Bright,

George Ernest Wright). In the list of David's mighty men, Elhanan is said to be "the son of Dodo of Bethlehem" (2 Sam. 23:24); Dodo is probably another name for Jaare-oregim (Fritz Stolz).

21:20-21 "Jonathan the son of Shimei, David's brother," kills another giant "of great stature" with twelve fingers and twelve toes. This nephew of David is not known otherwise. Perhaps this is a corruption for "Jonadab the son of Shimeah, David's brother" (13:32). Shimeah is probably another form of Shammah (1 Sam. 16:9).

21:22 A summary statement concludes the account of the exploits of David's mighty men. The victory of the servants is ascribed to the king (see above on 2 Sam. 21:15-17). It is possible that the account originally began with the valiant exploits of David, perhaps with his encounter with Goliath and Ishbi-benob.

"Giants" in the Bible are held to be the embodiment of godlessness, arrogance, and violence. Destruction of the giants is therefore part of the mission of God in establishing righteousness and peace in this world. David fulfils this task as the faithful servant of the LORD. Today we are no longer threatened by individual giants who are physically of unusual size and strength. Rather, we are threatened by giant structures of godlessness, arrogance, and violence, and to fight against them is now the mission of the children of God.

DAVID'S PSALM OF THANKSGIVING (22:1-51)

Verse 1, and also probably v. 51, come from the editor. Both verses are in the third person, whereas the rest of the psalm is in the first person. Verses 2-51 are found in Ps. 18:2-50 with only slight variations. The poem is an individual royal thanksgiving psalm. Except for 2 Sam. 22:51, which speaks specifically of David, the rest of the psalm deals with general themes in pictorial language that could be applied to a variety of situations in which God is recognized and acknowledged. In its present context the psalm is made to apply to David. David acknowledges God as his deliverer from all his enemies, both internal and external, and

270

gives thanks to God for preserving his life. It is possible, though we cannot say with certainty, that the psalm originated with David, but in the course of time it developed independently in the liturgical circles of the Israelite congregation. Several Psalms are associated with the name of David (e.g., Pss. 3, 7, 34, 51), but Ps. 18 is included here in the books of Samuel because through it the compiler intends to give a theological commentary to the history of David as a whole. The history of David is to be read and heard in the light of this psalm.

The psalm can be divided into five parts:

2 Sam. 22:1-7	Introduction: Confession of Faith and a Cry in Distress
Vv. 8-20	An Experience of Deliverance
Vv. 21-25	A Reflection on Deliverance
Vv. 26-31	A Reaffirmation of Faith
Vv. 32-51	An Acclamation of Faith

Thus, in the development of the psalm we see the spiritual development of the psalmist. On the basis of his faith, the psalmist cries to God in distress, experiences God's dealings both in his own life and in the world, experiences God's deliverance both in his life and in the lives of others, examines himself in the light of God's revelation through his experiences, affirms his faith, and finally acclaims it.

Introduction: Confession of Faith and a Cry in Distress (22:1-7)

Verse 1 is the editor's introduction to the chapter. He explains why he found it appropriate to place this psalm at this place. David has finished all his wars, and his kingdom is now established — enemies conquered, curses removed, and blessings ensured (cf. 21:3). David is now ready to thank God for all his deliverances and blessings. The phrase "from the hand of Saul" (22:1) is parenthetical to "from the hand of all his enemies," because most of David's opposition had originated from Saul and his family.

Verses 2-3 represent a strong affirmation of faith on the relia-

271

bility of Yahweh as deliverer. In Ps. 18:1 this affirmation is preceded by the confession "I love thee, O LORD, my strength." The relationship between the psalmist and God is one that is based on love. It is not a mystical union with God, but an active relation in life based on full trust and total surrender to God (cf. Deut. 6:5; 10:12; Josh. 22:5). In this relationship of love the psalmist experiences the reliability of God which he expresses by the use of the images of "rock" (2 Sam. 22:3, 32, 47), "fortress" (v. 2), and "stronghold" (v. 3). "Shield" (vv. 3, 31) is the symbol of defense and protection; the psalmist finds his protection in the LORD. "Horn" (v. 3) is the symbol of royal power; it is the LORD who gives strength and power to the king (cf. 1 Sam. 2:10). David thus owes all his success to the LORD. Out of his deep trust in the deliverance of the LORD, the psalmist called "upon the LORD" and was saved from his enemies (22:4). However, a loving relationship to God does not make one immune to troubles in this world. Troubles are part of this sinful world, but in the face of troubles the faithful ones find immediate access to the God of love from whom deliverance comes.

In vv. 5-6 the psalmist describes the sufferings he had undergone in terms of the primordial chaotic waters, which in the ancient Babylonian myths are personified as Tiamat. It is Yahweh who in the beginning overcame the power of chaos, and created life and order in the earth. Now once again when the powers of chaos threaten life, it is Yahweh who is capable of overpowering them and delivering his people (cf. Ps. 89:10ff.; Job 38:4ff.). The psalmist sees his sufferings as the effect of the powers of the chaotic forces of death on him. Thus he cries to Yahweh, his deliverer, the God of life and order, and Yahweh responds to him "from his temple" (2 Sam. 22:7) and saves him from his enemies (v. 4).

The reference to the temple here might suggest that the psalmist is in the temple and the answer to his prayer is communicated to him through some priestly oracle (cf. 1 Sam. 1:17). The temple here can refer both to the temple in Jerusalem and to the heavenly temple, the heavenly abode of God, which indicates the universal sovereignty of the God of the biblical revelation. God's salvation is for all people in this world (cf. John 4:21-24).

An Experience of Deliverance (22:8-20)

Yahweh's theophany is often described in the OT as taking place in and through nature. The psalmist experiences the majesty of God, the grimness of God's anger, and the glory of his mercy, all in the context of the cult. The theophany here recalls the theophany on Mt. Sinai (cf. Exod. 19; Deut. 33:2; Judg. 5:4ff.; 1 Kgs. 19:11-12). What happens here is therefore the concretization of what had already happened in the history of God's salvation *(Heilsgeschichte)*.

In response to the psalmist's supplication, Yahweh here rises up from his temple and appears in what can only be a volcanic eruption, accompanied by earthquake and storm. Disturbance in the order of nature was seen in those days as a sign of God's anger (2 Sam. 22:8). In the midst of the "smoke," "fire," and "coals" of an volcanic eruption, Yahweh is believed to come down from heaven (v. 10). "The heavens" are here conceived like an umbrella set up above the earth, with their "foundations" (v. 8) fixed deep into the earth. Yahweh "bows" the heavens and comes down (v. 10), rides on "a cherub," and flies "upon the wings of wind" (v. 11). The "cherub" is the seat and the vehicle of Yahweh; it is often mentioned in the plural as "cherubim" (see above on 1 Sam. 4:4). Here the cherub is identified with the wind. Yahweh is often described as riding upon the clouds or winds (2 Sam. 22:11; Exod. 19:9; Ps. 104:3; Isa. 19:1). Thunder is seen as the voice of his wrath (2 Sam. 22:14; cf. 1 Sam. 7:10; Joel 3:16; Amos 1:2) and "lightning" as his arrows (2 Sam. 22:15; cf. Zech. 9:14). Fully equipped thus, Yahweh fights against his enemies symbolized by such chaotic forces and so routs them (2 Sam. 22:15). "Darkness" is associated with Yahweh (vv. 10, 12), and it is expressive of the mystery which surrounds Israel's God (cf. 1 Kgs. 8:12).

This account reveals a primitive view of the universe — heavens above, earth in the middle, and the waters in the deep underneath. The earth is supported by pillars and primordial mountains having their foundations in the underworld (cf. Isa. 24:18; Jer. 31:37; Job 38:4ff.).

In 2 Sam. 22:17-20 the psalmist expresses his experience of

deliverance: from on high Yahweh reaches down his hands and draws him out of "many waters" (v. 17). "Many waters" here are obviously the chaotic waters (vv. 5-6) which are symbolic of the psalmist's "strong enemy" and "those who hated" him, who were too strong for him (v. 18) and who came upon him in the day of his calamity (v. 19).

"But the LORD was my stay" (v. 19) expresses the psalmist's deep experience of faith, which in fact is the experience of every true believer. The experience of salvation is described here in terms of being lifted up from the deep (v. 17; cf. Ps. 9:13; 30:3; Jonah 2:3-6) and being brought forth "into a broad place" (2 Sam. 22:20), in contrast to the restriction of "distress" (v. 7) hitherto experienced. Those Israelites who lived in the narrow east-west valleys of the desiccated plateau that was "the hill country" of Judah longed to inherit the flat plains presently inhabited by the Philistines. There they could see for miles and know if an enemy was anywhere near, not just over their shoulder on the ridge above their little valley. Therefore the relief they would feel if they were to dwell in a "broad place" became their theological picture of salvation.

The psalmist sees the ground for his deliverance in the delight of Yahweh: "because he delighted in me" (v. 20). Yahweh rejected Saul from being the king over Israel, because he had no "delight" in what Saul did in rejecting Yahweh's word (cf. 1 Sam. 15:22-23, 26). But Yahweh is delighted in David, because David has been faithful to his covenant with Yahweh. David's hope lies in the "everlasting covenant" which Yahweh has made with him (2 Sam. 23:5; cf. 7:12ff.).

The biblical view of the nature of the heavens and the earth, as revealed in 2 Sam. 22:17-20, need not cause modern mankind to suppose that the biblical view of God is "outdated." For one thing, this view of God was accepted right up till the Middle Ages in Europe, when great theologians such as Martin Luther and John Calvin had to work from it. A parallel today would be an observance of some of God's mighty works taking place now on the surface of Mars or Venus. More to the point, these divine activities in vv. 17-20 are shown to be mere symbols of the majestic power of God's love and creativity.

A Reflection on Deliverance (22:21-25)

In this and in the next section, it sounds as though the psalmist is taking a Pharisaic attitude in boasting over his self-righteousness. He appears to be relying on the popular Deuteronomic view of reward and retribution (cf. Deut. 28), according to which every just act is rewarded by God and every unjust act is punished by God. This, however, seems not to be the case here. Here the psalmist is relying on the covenant loyalty of God (cf. 2 Sam. 22:26). Yahweh is faithful to his covenant promises. He is faithful to those who are faithful to his covenant. The "righteousness" of the believer is his faithfulness to his covenant with God. Verses 21-24 explain the psalmist's "righteousness" by using different terms — his hands were clean (v. 21); he kept "the ways of the LORD" (v. 22); he did not "turn aside" from the "ordinances" and the "statutes" of God (v. 23); he kept himself "blameless" before the LORD (v. 24). Cleanness of hands is the same as being righteous (vv. 21, 25), a necessary qualification for entry into the temple (cf. Ps. 24:4).

A Reaffirmation of Faith (22:26-31)

An experience of deliverance by God leads a believer to gain new insights into the nature of God, to reaffirm his faith, and to bear testimony to the same. The psalmist here is doing exactly the same. "With the loyal thou dost show thyself *loyal* [a word derived from *hesed*]" (2 Sam. 22:26a). This is in brief the new insight of faith the psalmist has gained out of his salvation experience. God is always faithful to his covenant love (*hesed*; see above on 7:15). It is true that God is not indifferent to human actions, but God is not bound by human actions. God's actions are dictated by his covenant love in the light of human actions or responses. Thus another psalmist could assert, "The LORD is merciful and gracious, slow to anger and abounding in steadfast love. He will not always chide, nor will he keep his anger for ever. He does not deal with us according to our sins, nor requite us according to our iniquities" (Ps. 103:8-10; cf. Jas. 5:11). It is this message of the abounding love of God which becomes flesh in the NT. "While we were yet sinners Christ died for us" (Rom. 5:8) is the central message of the NT.

275

The nature of a God-fearing person is described with different adjectives: they are "the loyal," that is, those who keep *hesed,* "covenant love"; "the blameless" (2 Sam. 22:26); "the pure" (v. 27); and the "humble" (v. 28). The wicked, the godless ones, are "the crooked" and "the haughty" (vv. 27-28). Verse 28 recalls the Song of Hannah (cf. 1 Sam. 2:4) and the Magnificat (cf. Luke 1:52-53). The God of the Bible is the God of the humble and the lowly.

Yahweh is the "lamp" of Israel (2 Sam. 22:29). The king who lives in fellowship with him draws the light from Yahweh and thus becomes the "lamp of Israel" (cf. 21:17; Ps. 132:17). Not only the light, but the strength of a king is also derived from Yahweh (v. 30). The dependability of God is repeated time and again in the psalm: "his way is perfect"; his promise "proves true"; "he is a shield for all those who take refuge in him" (2 Sam. 22:31). This might imply that even the wicked (mentioned in vv. 27-28), if they return to Yahweh, will find their refuge in him: "The sacrifice acceptable to God is a broken spirit; a broken and contrite heart, O God, thou wilt not despise" (Ps. 51:17).

An Acclamation of Faith (22:32-51)

The acclamation of faith takes the form of a hymn of praise. The experience of the psalmist becomes a demonstration of the glory of God. The psalmist experiences the dependability and the covenant loyalty of God in equipping him for his "war" against his enemies (2 Sam. 22:34-37, 40a) and in leading him to victory over them (vv. 38-39, 40b, 41, 43). Out of these experiences the psalmist realizes that there is no other God "but the LORD" (v. 32). The enemies "looked" for help, "but there was none to save" them (v. 42). Yahweh "did not answer them" because they were "men of violence" (v. 49; cf. vv. 27b, 28b).

Not only did Yahweh deliver the psalmist from his enemies, but Yahweh also exalted him above people, including foreigners, "as the head of the nations" (vv. 44-46, 48-49). These verses refer probably to David's victories over his enemies and to his rule over the United Monarchy.

Yahweh, being a warrior God, is capable of training (v. 35)

and equipping (v. 40a) his people for war. Bending a bow is an act of heroism (cf. v. 10); bending "a bow of bronze" is still a great achievement (v. 35). "The shield of salvation" is another image for Yahweh (v. 36). Paul speaks of the "shield of faith" and the "helmet of salvation" (Eph. 6:16-17). Deliverance from enemies is seen here primarily as salvation by God (2 Sam. 22:49). "A wide place for my steps" (v. 37) is once again the condition of freedom in which the psalmist is able to move after his deliverance (cf. v. 20). People who are under oppression are compelled to walk through narrow, slippery paths.

The psalmist proclaims the salvation experienced in the LORD (vv. 47-49) "among the nations" (v. 50). Thus the salvation wrought through the Davidic king is not confined to the people of Israel. It is ultimately for all the people of the world. The NT sees this vision of salvation as being fulfilled in Jesus Christ, the Anointed One from the house of David. Verse 51 is obviously a reference to God's covenant with David, which has come to be known as "an everlasting covenant" (23:5; cf. Ps. 89:3; 132:11-12; Isa. 55:3; see above on 2 Sam. 7:14-15).

DAVID'S LAST WORDS (23:1-7)

This poem is generally held to be of late origin and not composed by David. It portrays David as an ideal king. Future kings in the Davidic line were probably expected to live up to this image. 2 Samuel 23:1 probably comes from the editor and introduces the song. Here David is spoken of in the third person, whereas vv. 2-7 are given in direct speech and the name David does not occur in them.

23:1 The poem is introduced as "the last words of David," and it is presented as "the oracle of David." The Hebrew word used here for "oracle" is the one normally used as the concluding formula in prophetic oracles, except in certain sayings of early prophetic seers (Num. 24:3; cf. Prov. 30:1). This verse emphasizes the king's close relation to God: he "was raised on high" and was "the anointed of the God of Jacob." "Raised on high" is a shortened form of "raised by the one who is on high," which would

277

still parallel "the anointed of the God of Jacob." Thus the king draws his authority directly from God, and he stands ultimately responsible only to God. "The sweet psalmist of Israel" means literally "Darling of the songs of Israel" (L. Koehler-W. Baumgartner, *Lexicon in Veteris Testamenti Libros*). It may imply that David was the subject of many songs in Israel (e.g., 1 Sam. 18:7) or that David himself composed many songs (cf. 2 Sam. 1:17ff.). It is David's popularity as a great composer and singer which caused many psalms to be associated with his name in the course of time.

23:2-3a The king, the anointed of the LORD, is endowed with "the Spirit of the LORD" (cf. 1 Sam. 16:13). Therefore, when the king speaks, he speaks by the Spirit of the LORD and his words come with the authority of God. Therefore, the king's words cannot go wrong. "Rock of Israel" is used parallel to "God of Israel" (2 Sam. 23:3a), indicating the reliability of God (see above on 22:32) and therefore the dependability of his word.

23:3b-4 The special quality of the rule of such a king whose spirit is in harmony with the Spirit of the LORD is described here. It will be a just rule. The king will be "ruling in the fear of God" (23:3b). Such a rule dawns upon the people soothingly "like the morning light" and "like rain that makes grass to sprout from the earth" (v. 4). It is worth noting that Israel sees its distinction from other nations and peoples, not so much in its worldly power and strength as the elected people of God, but in terms of the just rule of its leaders (cf. Deut. 4:7-8).

23:5 The great confidence in God's goodness to the Davidic house rests on God's "everlasting covenant" with David. The reference here is obviously to 2 Sam. 7:14 (see above). It is faith in the "covenant love" *(hesed)* of Yahweh which had sustained the people of Israel throughout their hardships and frustrations in history (Ps. 89:1-4; 132:11-12).

23:6-7 "The righteous" in the Psalms are always compared to "the godless," who are the wicked. The Hebrew word used here for "the godless" is *beli'al,* which means "the worthless." The enemies of righteousness are here compared to "thorns" which are to be "thrown away" and "utterly consumed with fire." Thorns in the Bible symbolize divine curse (Gen. 3:18), and the term is used symbolically of unjust rule (cf. Judg. 9:14-15). Because physical contact with thorns can hurt people, they are removed "with iron and the shaft of a spear." If thrown out, they can still hurt those who tread on them; therefore thorns are to be "utterly consumed with fire." The implication here is that in a just rule elements of injustice which prick and hurt people like thorns must be removed, where necessary, with force. Jesus, by accepting a crown of thorns, took upon himself the curse of the world caused by sin (cf. Gen. 3:18) and thus redeemed humanity.

DAVID'S MIGHTY MEN (23:8-39)

Sagas and anecdotes about some "mighty men" of David are given here. This account is similar to 2 Sam. 21:15-22, which preserves the exploits of David's mighty men who killed the giants. 2 Samuel 23:8-12 speaks of his top three mighty men; vv. 13-17 report an adventure of the three mighty men in Bethlehem, and vv. 18-39 list the thirty mighty men. These mighty men belong to the close circle of David. Historically these accounts belong to the early period of David, when David moved around as a guerilla fighter and when duels were an important part of military encounters.

The Three Mighty Men (23:8-12)

Among David's mighty men were three who had top rank. Each distinguished himself with heroic achievements in fighting against the enemies of Israel. The first among them, Josheb-basshebeth slew eight hundred at one time with his spear (v. 8). Eleazar the son of Dodo is second in rank. He stood with David at a crucial time during a battle with the Philistines. When all the Israelites withdrew, Eleazar stood with David and struck the Philistines until they were defeated (vv. 9-10). Shammah, the son of Agee the Hararite, is the third in rank. He defended "a plot of ground full of lentils" against the Philistines at a time when all the other men had fled (vv. 11-12).

It is not clear whether these three men are included below in the list of the thirty. Eleazar is said to be "the son of Dodo"; v. 24 speaks of a "son of Dodo" whose name is Elhanan. Whether Elhanan and Eleazar are the same is not certain. Perhaps Shammah, the son of Agee the Hararite, the third among the three, is the same as Shammah the Hararite mentioned among the thirty (v. 33). Verse 13 seems to imply that they were included in the list of the thirty.

These mighty men were just instruments in the hand of God. It was in fact the LORD who wrought the victory through them (vv. 10, 12; cf. 1 Sam. 11:13; 14:45; 19:5).

Three Mighty Men in Bethlehem (23:13-17)

David longs to drink the water from "the well of Bethlehem which is by the gate" (2 Sam. 23:15). Bethlehem is presented here as a walled city. Since the gate is likely to be guarded by the Philistines, drawing water from the well there should have been a very dangerous task. Risking their lives, the three mighty men break through the camp of the Philistines and bring water from the well as desired by David. But David will not drink it, because he sees it as "the blood of the men" who risked their lives to get it. Blood, according to Israelite belief, is life itself and therefore belongs to God. Accordingly, David "poured it out to the LORD," obviously as a sacrifice.

Why did David long to drink from the well of Bethlehem? Was it because he could not get water in the place where he was? That is very unlikely. Surely when camping to fight against the Philistines David and his men would have taken care to have enough water to drink. The fact that later David poured out the water as an offering to God also might indicate that it was not because of thirst that he longed for the water of Bethlehem. Bethlehem was the native place of David, but now David is standing outside the city as a fugitive. The water from the well there is his birthright, and his longing to drink from this well is an expression of his longing to assert his right over Bethlehem. David's act of pouring out the water for the LORD could have involved a vow or prayer for the restoration of Bethlehem. We are here reminded of the millions of refugees who are today driven out of their homelands. Like David they long to drink from their own wells. Such is God's will: "They shall sit every man under his vine and under his fig tree, and none shall make them afraid" (Mic. 4:4).

The Thirty Mighty Men (23:18-39)

Here again two men are highlighted with special descriptions. "Abishai, the brother of Joab, the son of Zeruiah" (cf. 1 Sam. 26:6ff.), was the "chief of the thirty" (2 Sam. 23:18). He was "the most renowned of the thirty," but he did not "attain" to the level of the three mentioned above (v. 19). Joab is not among the mighty men. Perhaps as commander of the army he belonged to a different cadre altogether and hence is not included in the list.

Next in rank is Benaiah the son of Jehoiada (vv. 20-23). Earlier he was introduced as the commander of the Cherethites and the Pelethites (8:18; 20:23). His heroic exploits are given in some detail: "he smote two ariels [meaning unknown] of Moab," "slew a lion in a pit," and fought with a staff against an Egyptian and killed him with his own spear, which is reminiscent of David killing Goliath (1 Sam. 17:40-51). Later in the Succession account Benaiah plays an important role (1 Kgs. 1:26ff.).

2 Samuel 23:24-39 list the names of the thirty mighty men. Verse 39 says "thirty-seven in all." Perhaps the original list included more who were killed in the meantime. Except for Asahel (v. 24) and Jonathan (v. 32), all the other names are given in some fixed format. Each one is specified by the place of his origin, and some also by their clan. The name Jonathan appears without any other qualification. Some take it together with the following name and read "Jonathan, the son of Shammah the Hararite" (Fritz Stolz). Asahel is qualified as "the brother of Joab," and is specified as "one of the thirty." Without Asahel the list contains thirty names. Perhaps Asahel did not belong to the original list. Without Asahel, Elhanan stands first in the list of the thirty. According to 21:19 a man by the same name killed Goliath, but his father's name there is different. Two men are said to be from Harod (23:25),

a place about 5 km. (3 mi.) SE of Jerusalem. Tekoa (v. 26), about
8 km. (5 mi.) S of Bethlehem, was the birthplace of the prophet
Amos. Anathoth (v. 27) is about 5 km. (3 mi.) N of Jerusalem
and was the birthplace of the prophet Jeremiah. On Mebunnai
the Hushathite (v. 27), see above on 21:18. Eliam (23:34) is the
son of Ahithophel, David's counselor (cf. 15:12). On Ira the
Ithrite (23:38), see above on 20:26. Uriah the Hittite (23:39;
cf. 11:3) is given a special place, last in the list.

DAVIDIC ORIGIN OF THE JERUSALEM CULT
(24:1-25)

The last account in the books of Samuel returns once again to
the central theme of the Davidic origin of the Jerusalem cult, with
which chs. 6–7 have already dealt. It is placed at this point
probably as a preparation for the account of the construction of
the temple by Solomon in 1 Kgs. 6–8. Though the temple was
built by Solomon, the author is keen to stress that the origin of
the Jerusalem cult goes back to David, the ideal king of Israel.
Here we are told about the purchase of ground for the future
temple and the founding of the cult. Because this is an important
theme in Israelite tradition, the account could have undergone
changes in the course of Israelite history. Such becomes evident
even from a cursory comparison of this account with the Chronicler's version in 1 Chr. 21.

Perhaps behind this narrative lies an ancient saga associated
with a Jebusite altar at the threshing floor of Arauna. According
to the Chronicler's version, it was Arauna who first saw the angel
of the LORD (1 Chr. 21:20, "Ornan"), a detail that probably
belonged to the original version of the saga. It is possible that in
Samuel we have a shortened form of the saga. On seeing the angel
over his threshing floor, Arauna could have immediately realized
the sanctity of the place and built an altar there, offering his oxen
as sacrifice. Such heavenly visions were behind the origin of most
cultic centers in Israel (cf. Gen. 28:10ff.). In the course of its
adaptation by the Israelites, the saga seems to have undergone
changes; David becomes the founder of the cult having acquired
Arauna's property legally.

Yahweh Incites David (24:1-9)

Yahweh is angry with Israel for some inscrutable reason. He incites David to sin by numbering Israel and Judah, so that Yahweh may have a justification for punishing Israel. The Priestly tradition in the OT looks positively at numbering people. The negative attitude towards numbering probably goes back to the prophetic tradition. Why is this act sinful? Here it appears to be done primarily for military purposes, as is evident from 2 Sam. 24:9, according to which only "valiant men who drew the sword" were numbered and women and children were not included. Thus numbering people could have been seen by the prophets as reliance on human might and lack of trust in Yahweh, whom "nothing can hinder . . . from saving by many or by few" (1 Sam. 14:6).

We have here a primitive understanding of the moral nature of God — that God incites people to sin. That later generations saw this to be incompatible with their understanding of the nature of God is evident from the fact that in the Chronicler's account it is no longer God but Satan who incites David to sin. Such accounts of primitive beliefs "are preserved in the Bible by divine Providence for our instruction of a primitive and imperfect interpretation of the ways of God" (W. H. Bennett).

The word "again" in 2 Sam. 24:1 might indicate that in its original context this account was preceded by similar incident which kindled the anger of Yahweh. We have no way of knowing what that incident was. Joab tries to dissuade David from the act but to no avail, because the motivating force behind it was Yahweh. David was only an instrument in the hands of God, and he had no choice in the decision. Underlying David's conduct is the prophetic motif of "the hardening of the heart," as seen in the Plague narratives in Exod. 7ff. It was later developed in Isaiah (Isa. 6:9ff.).

Following David's command (2 Sam. 24:2), Joab and the commanders of the army number the people from Dan in the north to Beersheba in the south. The task takes "nine months and twenty days" (v. 8), after which they bring the result to David in Jerusalem.

Repentance and Punishment (24:10-15)

As the numbering is completed, David realizes his mistake (v. 10). How he came to this realization is not told. That David was incited by God and that he was not directly responsible for the act are not taken into account. Now the only solution is repentance and forgiveness. "David's heart smote him." In Hebrew psychology the heart is conceived as the seat of thinking, the center of conscience. In modern language it means that David's conscience pricked him. David repents and prays for forgiveness.

God's answer comes through his prophet Gad (vv. 11-12). Gad was David's "seer" (on "seer," see above on 1 Sam. 9:9; on Gad, see 22:5). Through Gad Yahweh places three evils before David, the three divine punishments which in later prophecy came to be known as "the sword, famine, and pestilence" (cf. Jer. 14:12; 15:2; 16:4; Ezek. 5:12; 6:12). The first evil, "the sword," comes from the enemy. Though the second, famine, is caused by God, one can survive it only by depending on the mercy of other people (cf. Gen. 42–43). The third evil, pestilence, comes directly from God, and survival depends totally on the mercy of God. Thus David resolves to "fall into the hand of the LORD" (2 Sam. 24:14) by opting for the third evil. Accordingly God sends the pestilence, and seventy thousand men die. Again there is no mention of women and children. Because men alone were counted, men alone are punished. For the sin committed by the king, the people are punished. The king as leader of the community becomes the source of blessing or curse for the people. A righteous king ensures justice and peace for the people, but an unrighteous king brings adversities upon the people.

The Founding of the Cult (24:16-25)

The angel who was spreading the pestilence "stretched forth his hand toward Jerusalem to destroy it" (v. 16). At this moment Yahweh "repented of the evil," which means that Yahweh changes his plans in the light of the new circumstances. He commands the angel to halt the destruction. This divine intervention precedes David's plea to stop the punishment of innocent people for his sin (v. 17), and it vindicates David's confidence in Yahweh's mercy (v. 14). According to this tradition, God's mercy is not dependent on the cultic act of mankind. However, mankind's cultic act is their response to God's act of mercy.

In this second confession of David (v. 17) lies a further corrective to the earlier understanding of human responsibility for sin. David complains here that for the sin which he committed, innocent people — described as "these sheep" — are punished. David prays that he and his house alone be punished and not the people: "Let thy hand. . . . be against me and against my father's house." Individual responsibility for one's own act emerges here. This concept is further developed during the exile (cf. Jer. 31:29-30; Ezek. 18:2-4).

2 Samuel 24:18-25 returns to the theme of the founding of the cult. At the instruction of the prophet Gad (v. 18), David builds an altar on the threshing floor of Arauna. Only then, it is said, the LORD "heeded supplications for the land, and the plague was averted from Israel" (v. 25). Neither the three-day time limit nor Yahweh's earlier decision to stop the evil brings the pestilence to an end. Only the sacrifice offered on the altar in the new cultic site averts the evil. This information is aimed at highlighting the efficacy of the Jerusalemite cult. The institution of sacrifice further indicates that, according to OT belief, forgiveness is costly and needs the shedding of blood. Jesus Christ, by shedding his blood on our behalf, has acquired forgiveness for us, and those who live in him receive forgiveness by grace.

Verses 19-24 deal with the purchase of the threshing floor. Arauna hands over the ownership right to David for a price of "fifty shekels of silver." David will not receive the ground and the oxen for sacrifice as gifts from Arauna; he will buy them legally. A similar motif is found in Gen. 23. The point here is that a sacrifice must cost the devotee some price, in order that the sacrifice may become effective (2 Sam. 24:24). Thus David buys the threshing floor and the oxen. He then builds an altar on the threshing floor and offers the oxen as sacrifice to the LORD. This cultic performance proves its effectiveness immediately by bringing the pestilence to an end. This altar where David offered the sacrifice is believed to be the same rock as that on which the modern el-Aqsa Mosque stands in modern Jerusalem, thereby giving the Muslims a foothold in the Holy City.

The Jerusalem cult is thus established, and David becomes the head of the cult like all the oriental kings. Here again the people's desire to be "like all the nations" is accomplished. The cult is seen here as the mediator of divine grace, and in this respect it becomes a pointer to the revelation in the NT. Jesus Christ supersedes the cult and offers himself in its place as the only mediator of divine grace (cf. Matt. 12:6; John 2:19-21). Christ himself becomes the center of worship for all people. Worship is no more confined to any particular earthly locality. It becomes a matter of the Spirit, and it becomes accessible to all people. Thus Jesus says to the Samaritan woman, "the hour is coming when neither on this mountain nor in Jerusalem will you worship the Father. . . . But the hour is coming, and now is, when the true worshipers will worship the Father in spirit and truth" (John 4:21-23). Jesus replaces the earthly temple by himself becoming a spiritual temple, a temple with no wall, "a house of prayer for all the nations" (Mark 11:17).

The NT itself recognizes David to be God's choice of the ideal king, the significance of whose kingdom is made plain in that of his "son" Jesus, through the completely unchanging reliability of God's "covenant love." Therefore we may legitimately conclude this commentary by affirming that the kingship, which the Israelites originally took up in their desire to "be like all the nations," became in the hand of God an effective means of God's salvation for all nations. Jesus, the son of David, the Anointed One of the LORD, becomes the source of salvation for all nations. The history of kingship in Israel thus bears witness to the mysterious working of God's saving grace in and through human history.

SELECTED BIBLIOGRAPHY

Commentaries

Ackroyd, Peter R. *The First Book of Samuel.* Cambridge Bible Commentary (Cambridge and New York: Cambridge University Press, 1971).

————. *The Second Book of Samuel.* Cambridge Bible Commentary (Cambridge and New York: Cambridge University Press, 1977).

Bennett, W. H. "I and II Samuel," in *A Commentary on the Bible,* ed. Arthur S. Peake (London: Thomas Nelson, 1919, and New York: Thomas Nelson, 1920).

Budde, Karl. *The Books of Samuel.* The Sacred Books of the Old Testament 8 (Leipzig: J. C. Hinrichs and Baltimore: Johns Hopkins University Press, 1894).

Caird, George B. "The First and Second Books of Samuel: Introduction and Exegesis," in *The Interpreter's Bible,* ed. George Arthur Buttrick (New York: Abingdon, 1953), 2:855-1176.

Goldman, Solomon. *Samuel.* Soncino Books of the Bible (Bournemouth: Soncino, 1951).

Hertzberg, Hans Wilhelm. *I and II Samuel.* Old Testament Library (Philadelphia: Westminster and London: SCM, 1964).

Kennedy, Archibald R. S. *Samuel.* Century Bible (Edinburgh: T. C. and E. C. Jack and New York: Oxford University Press, 1905).

McKane, William. *I and II Samuel.* Torch Bible Commentaries (London: SCM, 1963).

Smith, Henry Preserved. *A Critical and Exegetical Commentary on the Books of Samuel,* 4th ed. International Critical Commentary (Edinburgh: T. & T. Clark and New York: Scribner's, 1951).

Stolz, Fritz. *Das erste und zweite Buch Samuel.* Zürcher Bibelkommentare 9 (Zurich: Theologischer Verlag, 1981).

Articles

Dus, Jan. "Der Brauch der Ladewanderung im alten Israel," *Theologische Zeitschrift* 17 (1961): 1-16.

———. "Die Erzählung über den Verlust der Lade 1 Sam. IV," *Vetus Testamentum* 13 (1963): 333-37.

———. "Noch zum Brauch der 'Ladewanderung,'" *Vetus Testamentum* 13 (1963): 126-132.

Knight, George A. F. "Is 'Righteous' Right?" *Scottish Journal of Theology* 41 (1988): 1-10.

Koch, Klaus. "Der Spruch 'Sein Blut bleibe auf seinem Haupt' und die israelitische Auffassung vom vergossenen Blut," *Vetus Testamentum* 12 (1962): 396-416.

Noth, Martin. "Samuel und Silo," *Vetus Testamentum* 13 (1963): 390-400.

Robinson, Gnana. "The Idea of Rest in the Old Testament and the Search for the Basic Character of Sabbath," *Zeitschrift für die alttestamentliche Wissenschaft* 92 (1980): 32-42.

———. "A New Economic Order: The Challenge of the Biblical Jubilee," in *A Vision for Man: Essays on Faith, Theology and Society,* ed. Samuel Amirtham (Madras: Christian Literature Society, 1978), 363-379.

Thomas, David Winton. "*Kelebh* 'dog': its origin and some usages of it in the Old Testament," *Vetus Testamentum* 10 (1960): 410-427.

General Works

Albright, William Foxwell. *Archaeology and the Religion of Israel,* 5th ed. (Garden City: Doubleday, 1968).

Bright, John. *A History of Israel,* 3rd ed. (Philadelphia: Westminster and London: SCM, 1981).

Noth, Martin. *Die israelitischen Personennamen im Rahmen der gemeinsemitischen Namengebung.* Beiträge zur Wissenschaft vom Alten und Neuen Testament 10 (1928; repr. Hildesheim: Georg Olms, 1980).

de Vaux, Roland. *Ancient Israel: Its Life and Institutions* (New York: McGraw-Hill and London: Darton, Longman & Todd, 1961; repr. in 2 vols., 1965).

Wright, George Ernest. *Biblical Archaeology,* rev. ed. (Philadelphia: Westminster, 1962).